Performers and Performances

Introduction by **Joseph Bensman**

PERFORMERS & PERFORMANCES

The Social Organization of Artistic Work

JACK B. KAMERMAN / ROSANNE MARTORELLA

AND CONTRIBUTORS

PRAEGER SPECIAL STUDIES • PRAEGER SCIENTIFIC
J.F. BERGIN PUBLISHERS

Library of Congress Cataloging in Publication Data
Main entry under title:

Performers and performances.

Bibliography: p. 293.
Includes index.
1. Performing arts—Addresses, essays, lectures. 2. Creation (Literary, artistic, etc.)—Addresses, essays, lectures. 3. Arts and society—Addresses, essays, lectures. I. Kamerman, Jack B. II. Martorella, Rosanne. PN1584.P46 1982   306′.484   82-12812 ISBN 0-03-059743-9

PN
1584
K26
1983

Published in 1983 by Praeger Publishers
CBS Educational and Professional Publishing
A Division of CBS, Inc.
521 Fifth Avenue, New York, New York 10175 U.S.A.

0123456789   056   987654321

Printed in the United States of America

To Connie and Louis,
for listening and understanding

Contents

List of Tables

List of Illustrations

"The Rehearsal on the Stage" by Degas. Reproduction courtesy of the Metropolitan Museum of Art, The H. O. Havemeyer Collection. Bequest of Mrs. H. O. Havemeyer, 1929 (29.100.39). (*Frontispiece*)

"String Quartette" by Jack Levine. Reproduction courtesy of the Metropolitan Museum of Art, Arthur H. Hearn Fund. (*Facing p. 1*)

Edward Villella in "The Prodigal Son." Photograph courtesy of Martha Swope. (*38*)

Giulio Gatti-Casazza, Arturo Toscanini and Geraldine Farrar. Photograph courtesy of the Metropolitan Opera Archives. (*90*)

Arturo Toscanini in concert. Photograph courtesy of the New York Philharmonic Archives. (*130*)

Audiences express their power by their willingness to purchase tickets. Lincoln Center, New York City. Photograph courtesy of Louis Melancon and the Metropolitan Opera Archives. (*194*)

Commemorative plaque, Lincoln Center, New York City. Photograph courtesy of Susanne Faulkner Stevens and the Public Information Office, Lincoln Center. (*246*)

Foreword

The performing arts differ from all the other arts, as Joseph Bensman remarks in his introductory chapter in this volume, in that live performance involves the immediate participation of audiences as well as of the professionals who create the art. Since audience members are present as the work is being created, the artists have no chance to hide or cover over their mistakes. They cannot rewrite a bad section, cannot edit out a slip or replace it with another bit recorded at another time. If mistakes happen, if a performance is amateurish or uninspired, the audience is there to know it and there is no way to avoid either the embarrassment of the moment or the serious consequences for reputations and careers that may follow.

Because every aspect of a performance may be fateful, live performance makes possible some wonderful excitements, when everyone involved, artists and audience alike, is caught up in the moment of creation. The tension of possibly being wrong makes being right that much better, just as the possibility that a physician may kill a patient makes saving the patient's life that much more praiseworthy. Everyone involved likes the excitement, but no one cares much for the failures that are its necessary price.

That being the case, performing artists take as much care as they can to avoid such failures. Their preparations include all the organizational matters to which so much of this book is devoted. They build permanent organizations which attract audiences prepared to appreciate what they will see and hear. They train carefully and rehearse and practice until the chance of errors and uninspired performance is as minimal as it can be. They organize careers so that professionals, who can be counted on to deliver competent performances, dominate situations of live performance.

All the people who cooperate in the production of live performances—the creators of works, the performers themselves, critics, administrators and financial personnel, audiences, unions, distributors—can be thought of as aiming their efforts at the production of perfect, inspired performances. That is not completely true, of course. People have more private or segmentalized motives as well. A symphony player or actor may not care much how a performance goes overall, if their part sounds and looks good and improves their reputation where it will matter.

A fine dialectic is at work, then, in the performing arts. The dangers that give live performance its special excitement lead people to do what they can to take that excitement out of things by careful preparation and control. Yet the desire to perform in an exceptional and unique way pushes performers to go beyond what they can do well without danger. Since professionalism is so much the norm, as many of the chapters in this book make clear, we usually enjoy competent performances that are interesting, informative, and worth what we have invested of our time, money and effort. We seldom hear or see those rare occasions on which people try for something more and succeed. But that is what everyone is there for, on both sides of the foot-lights. These chapters explore the organizations and processes involved subtly and comprehensively.

Howard S. Becker
Northwestern University

Preface

This book grew from our love and commitment, as consumers, to the arts. We have both stood on many long ticket lines. As sociologists, however, we here attempt to analyze the role of performers, and their socialization and recruitment into the occupations of dance, symphonic music, theater, and opera. Their creative work must be seen as part of a process involving the interdependence of individuals in interaction, and of the institutional settings in which perfomances are made, including the producers and organizations that hire performers, and the managers, patrons, critics, and audiences that support them. Although we cannot lose sight of the performing arts as individual creative expressions, our questions must address the cultural and social factors that influence the aesthetic content, form, and style of the performing arts. Consequently, the not-for-profit arts organizations and companies that produce the classical performing arts will be analyzed by focusing on structures, roles within the organizations, and the marketplace within which they function.

The book is divided into six sections, each highlighted by a particular question crucial to a sociological analysis of the performing arts. The introductory essay by Joseph Bensman of the City University of New York is a remarkable attempt to develop a social theory of performance. In comparing each of the performing arts, Bensman finds similarities among them in content, form, and style, and evolves a sociological theory based on performance as an act of social communication. His analysis incorporates the institutional setting of the arts by discussing their increasing professionalization and rationalization in modern society.

Section Two, "The Performing Arts as Occupations," focuses on the performer. Using the performer as a basis for analysis, it allows us to ask questions about the nature of the role as an occupation, socialization and mobility in a performer's career, and development of a professional identity. This section develops the theme that the performing arts are influenced by factors beyond individual expression. Thus, the notion of "social organization" takes on a twofold dimension. It addresses, on a micro-level, the influence of a group of performers on one another as they work.

On a macro-level of analysis, in Section Three we discuss "management" of the arts as an increasingly significant element in the changing institutional setting of the arts.

Section Four, "The Social Determinants of Performing Styles," examines factors influencing the development of style, such as the organizational setting, market demands, and political forces within society.

Audiences and critics are studied in Section Five, with particular emphasis on the impact of box-office demands and the development of "taste cultures."

The final section, "Support Systems," traces the role of the patron throughout history, and the influence different forms of patronage have had on artists' lives and on the development of performing styles. The issue of cultural policy is also examined.

We wish to express our appreciation to the contributing authors whose work embodies their respect for the performers they observed, interviewed, and researched. Special thanks to the artists who shared their ideas with us, and especially to those interviewed for this book. We are also grateful to the following people and organizations for assisting us in our search for representative illustrations: the Metropolitan Museum Photography Library, the Lyric Opera of Chicago, the Metropolitan Opera Archives, Robert Resnikoff and Toni Gerette Bilotti of the New York Philharmonic Archives, Mary Frances Duffy of the Public Information Office of Lincoln Center for the Performing Arts, Jack Levine, and Martha Swope. We also wish to thank W. W. Norton for permission to quote excerpts from Paul Henry Lang's *Music in Western Civilization*. We are grateful to Constance Munro and Jeanne Ray Juster for editorial and design assistance respectively, and to Donna Kecher for typing sections of the manuscript. Finally, our thanks to Jenna Schulman of J. F. Bergin for being helpful, patient, and tough in the proper proportions and to Jim Bergin, our publisher, for sharing our commitment to this project.

Jack B. Kamerman and Rosanne Martorella
New York

SECTION ONE

INTRODUCTION:
THE PHENOMENOLOGY
AND SOCIOLOGY
OF THE PERFORMING ARTS

Joseph Bensman

In this introduction, I will attempt to state and develop a phenomenological and sociological theory of the performing arts. Although a great deal of theoretical work has been done on the individual performing arts—opera, symphony and other instrumental music, the theater, the dance, and choral and other vocal music—little has been done on the common generic character of these arts as a whole. This is perhaps understandable, since each individual art form has its unique techniques, dynamics, and history, despite the fact that some arts (e.g., opera) are essentially mixed media; and others (e.g., dance, symphony, and Lieder) may base their programs or librettos on either the drama or on a non-performing literary art. Dance, of course, can be based upon pure as well as upon programmatic music.

In focusing upon the performing arts, I will stress not only their commonalities and, to a lesser extent, their differences—these are likely to be obvious—but I will also stress, and use as a point of departure and comparison, the non-performing arts, primarily literature, painting, and sculpture. In making this contrast, I recognize that some non-performing arts, poetry, for instance, may be best appreciated when read aloud or performed before an audience, whereas the play can be enjoyed and, in some cases, make more sense read than performed. The literary value of a play may be at the expense of its performance values, thus accentuating the differences in the criteria for evaluating the performing arts as opposed to other art forms.

I will focus upon the performing arts as practiced by professionals and not by amateurs performing for recreational or training purposes. However, myth and folk themes abound in the dance, the opera, poetry, and drama; and folk dance forms—the sarabande, mazurka, musette, czardas, and gigue, among others—have been incorporated as the basic forms for classical music and dance.

Implied in these distinctions between the professional performing arts and the folk arts is a parallel distinction between the serious ("classical") arts and the popular (commercial) arts. Those making this distinction are often charged with snobbery and elitism. And the charge may be true in the sense that those who advocate and defend the serious arts believe in their superiority, even when they, as individuals, enjoy and participate in folk and popular arts. Conversely, those who attack the snobbery and elitism of the serious arts maintain the distinction even in their defense of the popular arts. Yet, regardless of value position, the distinction between classical and popular arts is a traditional and conventional one. The arts, as we have already implied, eschew neat distinctions. Thus musical theater, operetta, professional folk-dance companies, classical jazz, and sitar–violin duos straddle the two conventional areas and produce conflict: is musical theater, for instance, a serious art form? The advocates and decriers of the "popular arts" from time to time engage in heightened polemics, which often result in either the acceptance of new forms of serious art, new styles, new techniques, or, at other times, the rejection of individual works, styles, and forms, as vulgar, amateurish, and frivolous. The history of the serious arts does suggest that some folk and popular arts and artists do eventually break through and contribute to the serious arts, while others do not.

Finally, I will emphasize live performance: film and records will, at most, be considered as outer boundaries of our discussion. This stipulation is in some sense conventional. By now, records and radio are major media for the diffusion of music. Radio, film, and television have been major media for the broadcasting of serious drama and opera, while television provides the dance with audiences of millions. Indeed, one highly promoted live performance of a popular ballet on prime time, especially on a holiday, may be viewed by a larger audience than the total audiences for all live performances for that ballet not performed on the mass media.

The mass media not only enlarge the audiences and contribute to the popularization of the performing arts, but also provide a substantial part of costs of their production; but this financial support is usually supplementary to box-office income, philanthropic contributions, and government support. In some cases, radio and television may support a symphonic orchestra, as have NBC and the BBC; and on some occasions a television network has supported an entire opera season, as well as individual performances by companies that exist primarily to provide live performances.

The use of electronic media, or course, involves new techniques of camera work, sound production, choreography, and preparation of works for performances. The use of film and tape, multiple camera and microphone placement and camera shots, together with sound and film editing, allows for a final presentation that is different from that prepared for live performances. In some cases, edited performances are more perfect than those of live performances. Mistakes and imbalances in performance are corrected, entries are redone to make them more clean-cut, and, to some, the performances are cold and sterile: they lack the spontaneity of live performances.

In the cases of opera and the dance, the choreography and direction can, in anticipation of broadcasting or film, be directed at the camera. The camera and microphone act as the eyes and ears of the audience, and the audience sees what the director, choreographer, camera man, and editor want seen. The television or movie audiences then no longer have the freedom to focus their attention on aspects of the total production that may interest them at any given moment of a recorded performance. Yet the use of the close-up—especially in the case of the dance—may draw attention to fine details of performance that are not noticeable in the rear seats or balcony.

Because live performances provide the basic paradigms for the performing arts, my focus will be on them. The mass media and the production and reproduction and diffusion of live performances will, in this Introduction, constitute a set of limits and a framework of comparison for the analysis of the live performing arts, just as these performances constitute a set of comparisons for the mass media arts.

The Essential Characteristics of the Professional Performing Arts

To summarize the discussion so far, our analysis of the performing arts will be based on a set of five separate distinctions and polarities between the live professional performing arts and all other performing and non-performing arts. They are presented in Table 1.

As we have indicated, and as we shall further see, these five defining characteristics set the bases for a set of logical and comparative polarities. Some of the defining characteristics are most evident in the comparative characteristics and vice versa. Together they present only the framework for a more detailed discussion, which will not only expand our initial discussion, but will present a variety of additional characteristics and will, hopefully, present the basis for an integrated theory of the professional performing arts.

Table 1. Defining Characteristics of Performing and Non-Performing Arts

Dimension	Performing Arts	Non-Performing Arts
Final product	Is performed, a performance	An object: book, poem, painting, sculpture, film or recording
Executors	Professionals, whose work, in principle, constitutes a full-time career and livelihood	Amateurs and "folk," whose activities are recreational, ceremonial, unpaid, and who, in principle, are occasional and part-time workers
Training	For a career; intensive, continuous, self-conscious	Traditional, occasional, or unsystematic
Methodologies	Explicit, planned, worked out, systematic, formalized, and "rational"	Traditional or occasional, less systematic and intensive
Performance	Live	Recorded; broadcast, mediated by tape, film, microphones, and by simultaneous or post-production editing

Performances

The central defining characteristic of the performing arts is, of course, live performance before an audience; and this has many implications for all the performing arts taken as a totality.

The fact that the final product is a live performance distinguishes the performing arts from all other arts: for in them, the final product is revealed only in the act of execution and within the very duration of execution. The art product appears, ideally, to be spontaneous, a matter of the moment, with a rhythm, flow, and dramatic rise and fall achieved within the duration of performance. Part of the satisfaction of the audience is that the rise and fall, ebb and flow of time, produces a tension and release that may correspond to a satisfactory tension and release, problem and resolution, of the audience member's own psychic rhythms and *durée*, his or her own experience of the passage of time. But the flow of time within the performing arts is controlled by scenario, a score, choreography, acts and scenes, and by the skill of performers, actors, and directors in managing the flow of time during the course of performance.

But, in performance, the flow of time has a quality of finality. Moments of performance occur and, once performed and experienced, are forever lost. This makes the performing arts entirely different from the non-performing arts. The writer can plan his production, do a draft, study it, revise, rewrite, and edit, or even do it entirely over. He or she finally selects a version that constitutes the final product. The reader need only see the final product and can see or hear it as an entirety. In the case of a painting, and in all of the literary and plastic arts, the artist can control the time of his participation. He can stop, put the work aside—sometimes for years—and return to it at will. The viewer of a painting can, first, study the painting as a whole, observe a detail, contemplate the meaning of a part before again contemplating the work as a whole. The continuous, uninterrupted passage of time is thus not an intrinsic characteristic of the non-performing arts, although it may become a desideratum of those arts. Thus the novelist or short-story writer, and even the essayist, may attempt by stylistic devices to present a flow of action or a sinuosity of style such that the reader cannot put down the written work.

The painter may attempt to transcend the essential characteristic of his medium by portraying the flow of time; Duchamp's *Nude Descending* may be viewed as such an attempt; and Franz Kline's action painting may be an attempt to portray, in the work itself, the spontaneous flow of work in the very act of painting. Tempera and water-colors compress time because they require special virtuosity in that they allow for little reworking and revision. Wassily Kandinsky even attempted "spontaneous" oil painting by allowing the final execution of his art to be free and uncontrolled; but he made numerous preliminary drawings and worked out and drew upon the canvas the outlines of the final composition of his ultimate work before he spontaneously deviated from plan. In this respect, the spontaneity in the artist's use of time resembles the improvisation of the jazz musician or the great piano virtuosos of the eighteenth and nineteenth centuries who could improvise within the framework of themes, techniques, and paradigms that had been worked out over countless prior performances.

The sculptor working in clay can "edit" and improvise, prior to final execution, but he ultimately ends up with an art object that is fixed in its shape and form; and when he works in wood, stone, or metal, the objectivity of his art work is even more frozen in time than is a novel or short story. The work itself sums up, in one moment, all the processes and time in the production in one culminating object. To escape this limitation, sculptors have created mobile art, self-destructing art, and kaleidoscopic, motorized, and multi-media art, and even art where random activities of wind, the viewer, motors, lights, and switches alter the appearance of the object after it has been given its essential character by the sculptor. Minimal and conceptual art have attempted to devalue the "objective" character of art, but only occasionally in order to emphasize the time dimension in the perspective of the viewer.

Of course, all art is subject to the vicissitudes of time in the sense that the viewers interpret an art object from the standpoint of the cultural era in which they live. Yet this sense of historic time, apart from the dramatic and psychological time within the performance, is characteristic of all the arts and culture and is not peculiar to the performing arts. Only the control of time within the framework of the performance, the exceptions noted, is unique to the performing arts.

The finality of performance, the rendering of the art product into a series of controlled passages of continuous time, makes the performing arts similar to sports and to some professions where the instantaneous exercise of highly developed skills is tested in a series or crucial chain of spontaneous actions and responses under the pressure of compressed time. Thus the quarterback in football, who, after having practiced a good part of his life, worked with his coaches on a game plan, reviewed scouting reports of the opposition, and worked out the techniques for overcoming the opposition, must act and respond in a series of controlled yet spontaneous movements to produce a series of momentarily irreversible events. He cannot edit or revise the action of each moment after he has executed it. Each action is final, though he may attempt to counteract mistakes and unforeseen contingencies in other, subsequent but discrete events up until the final outcome, victory or defeat. The courtroom lawyer and the surgeon also face the finality of performance; they make momentary, irreversible decisions even after a great deal of detailed planning has been undertaken.

The control of time and the finality of performance also underline the differences between live performance and the edited versions of live performance on film, tape, and recordings.

The fact that the live performances are based upon the finality of performance means that preparation prior to performance is, in principle, stressed rather than the editing of completed performances. Since mistakes before an audience are not easily correctible within the duration of the performance, rehearsal, preplanning, and preperformance trial and error are mandatory, as are rehearsal and correction between performances. Because of this, the development of the performing arts favors professionals, who by their previous training and practice are likely to minimize mistakes and who can devote full time to rehearsal, preparation, and performance unhampered by any other full-time occupational commitments. They also require less rehearsal to achieve a finished performance. Rehearsal, of course, facilitates the development of the internal rhythm, timing, flow, and build-up and release of tension within the presentation of the work, as well as the achievement of "intonation" and balance of the component elements in the work itself. Rehearsal is thus a form of pre-editing. Of course, the finality of performance makes demands upon performers other than the full preparation of the work. A fully prepared and rehearsed performance, if executed totally to plan, can sound or appear to be mechanical and lifeless. The finality of performance includes, at least, the appearance of spontaneity, a sense of excitement, and rhythms that evoke the immediate emotional participation of the audience. In part, this appearance of spontaneity is accomplished by rehearsal, direction, conducting, and choreography. In part, the finality of performance may evoke an extra intensity, a sense of the immediacy of the work performed, that transcends the written score, planned choreography, libretto, or text. And finally, the personal quality of the performers, their sense of dramatic presence, stage presence, star quality, or "charisma," may transcend training, technique, rehearsal, and direction. The "star" is able to project himself, his performance, and, ideally, the work directly to an audience, at best bringing the prewritten, planned, rehearsed, and prepared score directly and immediately to life and to the audience. The quality of immediacy of performance thus embodies the directness of communication that is the unique ideal and goal of the performing arts.

The Social Character of the Performing Arts

By communicating directly to an audience in performance, the performing arts are the most directly social of all the arts, even though all of the arts are means of communication and are based upon social experience. Thus literature, painting, and sculpture are means of communication that may be accomplished across centuries in which the author's intentions may be entirely different from those understood or perceived by the audience. The meaning of the work derived by readers or viewers may continuously change or, in fact, reverse itself over the course of centuries; but the fact that a great work of art continues to evoke emotional response and meaning attests to the social and communicative character of all the arts. But the performing arts, in the finality of performance and in the interpretative mediation of the performer, conductor, director, or choreographer, not only provide directness and immediateness of meaning, but they also add increments of meaning by the very act of performance. Thus it is argued that the performer is more than an interpreter: he or she is a creator who supplements the composer, dramatist, or original choreographer. It is also possible, of course, that a performer or director, driven to express his own creative role, may significantly alter the manifest meanings and intentions of the original work. Thus vast historical battles have been fought—and continue to be fought—between advocates of romantic virtuoso revisions of original works and those who would remain faithful to the original score, scenario, choreography, instrumentation, language, and setting, even if such fidelity involves research and reproduction of original instruments, performance styles, scenery, etc.

The immediacy and finality of performance, which places premiums upon the presence, projective ability, or star quality of the performer—whether diva, instrumentalist, actor, conductor, or prima ballerina assoluta—results in another unique quality of the performing arts, the emphasis on personality, individuality, in what are otherwise essentially collective and socially prescribed performances. This, we have noted, involves both mastery of technique and that indefinable quality of "presence," a term that implies immediacy of affect and communication. But personality and individuality are especially important in the performing arts, because the artist's body, his posture, musculature, physical expression, limbs, and features are essential instruments of performance.

For the writer, the final product is words on paper, not even in his own handwriting. The painter, of course, uses his eyes and arms to paint. Yet it little matters what he looks like; what matters is what his work looks like. This is true despite the fact that some painters may portray their own features in their portraits of others. Sculptors in stone and wood may need strength, and all need a steady hand; but, once the art object leaves their hands, it matters little what the sculptor was like.

The actor, on the other hand, must be able to control every aspect of his body, the expression of his face, his voice, tears, posture, movement, and even his repose; and, in his control, he must concentrate, without making that control appear to violate the spontaneity of performance. The acquisition and maintenance of the various aspects of expressive control is a lifelong task, as is, especially as one ages, the ability to maintain concentration.

For the singer, control of the body is centered in the mouth, the vocal chords, the chest, and the diaphragm. The body itself is a musical instrument; and all the subtleties of instrumental performance, including sonority, are to be achieved by bodily control. The body is, in the case of vocal music, a delicate instrument, subject to abuse and damage by overuse, misuse or incorrect practice, teaching, or casting. It is subject to the vicissitudes of weather, of nonmusical regimens, diet, and physical activity. Despite these dangers to the instrument, the singer must continuously vocalize, practice, and study to increase his range, subtlety, and interpretative skill, all in addition to the mastery of specific vocal, dramatic, and linguistic roles in specific vocal works. The singer, like all other performing artists, must maintain these forms of bodily control against the erosion of time: age is the greatest enemy.

The dancer, perhaps, requires even greater physical skills, though, in this case, the control is over the legs, arms, torso, ankles, feet, and hands. Yet such a description is simplistic, for the control extends to virtually every muscle in the body, so that each muscle should ideally respond instantaneously to the dancer's and the choreographer's intentions. This entails the mastery of hundreds of positions, steps, leaps, turns, extensions, and gestures, each of which must be mastered, reduced to instantaneous control, and then maintained by constant practice. The control entails not only strength, but grace, ease of movement, fluidity between movements, line, and dramatic intensity. All of this is to be achieved within the limits of a subservience to music and, in final performance, to a central choreographic and dramatic plan. It is no wonder that the dancer, whether ballet or modern, must begin early and practice eternally, even after he or she has initially mastered the basic repertoire of the dance movements that lie within the specialty. The loss of even a day's practice causes some loss of body tone. Thus the dancer is a slave of practice. He or she must maintain muscle tone, ease, and fluidity, strength, and suppleness, as well as mastery of specific movements and the continuous demands of specific roles. He or she is also subject to the continuous abuse of body, especially since dancing, like sports, presents the continuous risk of broken bones and muscle strains. In addition, as in the case of the singer, the premature acquisition of techniques may permanently damage essential parts of the body.

The instrumental musician has an advantage over the dancer, actor, or vocalist in that he uses an external instrument. Yet he too must spend large parts of his life acquiring, mastering, and maintaining control over his body in the interest of his ears and musical intelligence. Depending on the instrument, the control may be over breathing, embouchure, teeth, fingers, wrist, and arms. While less of his body may be involved, the absolute control of the body parts involved may be as great. Thus pianists have described sixty-four different kinds of touch; and the free and independent use of each finger must be developed, each having equal strength. Speed, of course, in use of fingers, lips, and arms is indispensable, as are nuances in touch and in coordination between fingers, arm, and mouth, and in separation and combination in sound production. The control of sonority, intonation, phrasing, tempo, and dynamics are all acquired crafts, though phrasing may go beyond teaching. The acquisition and mastery of all of these techniques, of course, requires years of intensive practice, which must be maintained after mastery by less continuous practice. But if the musician is to develop a repertoire, he must continue his preparation and practice to do so and to maintain it. As part of a performing company, he is also required to rehearse and minimally—depending on the size of the company—coordinate his playing with that of other musicians and, if present, the conductor.

The musician, too, is subject to the limits and liabilities of using his body as an extension of his instrument. Physical injury, mispractice, arthritis, age, failing eyesight, hearing, and dental problems can interrupt a career.

This recitation of the use of the body as an instrument or extension of the body as a special characteristic of the performing arts perhaps overstates the importance of the performing technique. While it stresses the necessity of a mastery of objective techniques that require intensive long-term education, practice, preparation, and rehearsal, and a concern with self, by itself it understates the central talent, musicality, rhythmic predisposition, intonation, i.e., the "ear," the sense of phrasing, the musculature, and the special perception and intelligence that are appropriate to each respective performing art. Yet such perception and intelligence may not go beyond that which is necessary for one's performance role. The performing musician may not be interested in or adept at musical theory, composition, or music for other than his own instrument. And a dancer may place himself entirely in the hands of a choreographer, yet dance beautifully. An actor may be only dimly aware of literary, political, or psychological themes underlying his role in relation to the total performance and still do an excellent job, especially if he or she has a great director. Moreover, the performer may with great success emphasize the virtuoso elements in the work, excelling in celebrating technique per se. Yet minimally the objectivity of his art form, the "score" or the entire performance, may impose upon him an additional discipline to that of pure technique.

The great performers master, then transcend, technique; they divine and present with immediacy the underlying intention of the score, the scenario, the choreographic plan. They may in addition project and present their own personality. But even not so great performing artists, "professionals"—the corps de ballet, the symphonic musician, the choir—all, ideally, acquire high levels of technique and exercise their craft with high levels of competence, discipline, and concentration.

The Conductor: Backstage and Onstage

The conductor represents an interesting example of the performing artist. He is both an onstage performer who uses his own body and a person who uses the performance of others as his instrument. He interprets the score and, in that sense, mediates both between the performers and the composer and between the performers and the audience. As conductor he plays no instrument other than the orchestra as a whole; yet he provides the tempo, balance, overall intonation, color, and rhythms, and guides the entries, dynamics, and sonorities after he has rehearsed the orchestra in these same aspects of performance. He is the only performer who, in principle, interprets the work; but the various instrumentalists must necessarily interpret their respective parts under his direction. This, of course, may lead to conflict, since the individual performers are themselves likely to be near virtuosos in their respective instruments and may feel superior to the conductor. At the same time, they have also been trained as interpreters and may have their own understanding or misunderstandings of and ideas about the totality of the work being performed.

Soloists working with an orchestra, and opera stars, especially, have a vested interest in interpretation that devolves not only on the score itself but also on their self-images as stars, virtuosi, and individual performers. The conflict between soloist and conductor is one of the classic themes in music, as is the conflict between the superstar and the director in the theater and dance. But in music, especially in the symphony orchestra, the conductor has become a star in his own right. Not only has he become a performer, with torso, arms, hands, and tonsure, and a "dancer"; but he also has become a "charismatic" hero, a personality, the subject of both myth and public relations. He may have based his powers on his arbitrariness and terrorism over the orchestra, his virtuoso-like revisions of the score, or his absolute accuracy and precision in researching, interpreting, and performing the composers' intentions. This includes not only precision in entries, intonation, and tempi, but orchestra composition, placement and balance. All of these changes in the status of the conductor that have made him into a star began near the end of the nineteenth century. A hundred years earlier, the conductor merely beat time with a gavel or conducted from the harpsichord or from his position as concertmaster.

The position of conductor thus suggests the social complexity of the performing arts. It indicates not only the complexity, but the high degree of specialization, the competitiveness and necessity for integration within complex performances. Moreover, it indicates the relationship between onstage and backstage behavior. In the dance, the choreographer works at the backstage level, though his work is revealed onstage; the stage director in the drama and opera also works backstage, and both the choreographer and the director work primarily in preperformance planning, directing, and rehearsing. They stand as surrogates for a whole host of backstage personnel—stage managers, rehearsal conductors, lighting designers and technicians, costume makers, etc.—whose work is present on stage but who themselves are not. The conductor bridges the gap; he is at the interface of onstage and backstage performance. He is responsible for much of the actualization of backstage planning, preparation, and rehearsal at the same time that he is himself a performer.

The producer, impresario, and a host of other business management personnel, including financial officers, public relations officers, and technical administrators, may be less directly concerned with the immediacy of production; but they as a whole, and especially the general manager, producer, and impresario, are primarily concerned with the overall relationship between the performance and the performing company and with the audience—actual and potential—and other external publics to the performance, i.e., government, contributors, elites, and foundations. They are also concerned with the selection of repertoire, artists, and other onstage and offstage personnel, and with funding arrangements. In these aspects of their work they may directly contribute and control the onstage offering of the performing arts.

Thus, while the unique, defining characteristics of the performing arts are those related to the finality of performance and the immediate interaction between performer and audience, the performing arts, as an institution, are based upon much more than these defining characteristics. It is thus necessary to consider the various performing arts as social institutions and as social organizations.

The Performing Arts as Social Communication

We have indicated that the performing arts are a means of social communication. That communication takes place directly and immediately within the act of performance. But these arts are also the means of communication between the playwright, the composer, the librettist, the choreographer—whether these be live or dead—and the audience. These creators, while major contributors to the performing arts, are not themselves necessarily performers; but, to be effective, they usually must have had performing experience. At another level, they represent the interface between non-performing and performing arts. Since all arts entail the communication of meaning and emotion, as well as the pure form of their respective media, the performing arts add a separate dimension of meaning to the non-performance meanings provided by or realized in the score, libretto, scenario, or choreography. We have indicated that these meanings may be directly present in dramatic tension, rhythm, concrete personification, emotional expression, and in directness and immediacy of presentation. But, to the extent that there is a literary or programmatic character to a basic "scenario," the performing arts necessarily communicate non-performance themes. This means that literary, cultural, philosophic, and aesthetic values, themes, philosophies, and ideas can become imbedded in the performing arts. The composer–choreographer in these cases faces the task of translating non-performing themes into the particular idiom and technique of a performing art; and the producer–director, on the other hand, faces the task of embellishing the performance with the products of the non-performing crafts, such as painting and art in stage design and scenery, costumes, and lighting. These transformations, at least in the twentieth century, are subject to continuous conflict among the various contributing arts. As we shall see, each specialist emphasizes his contributions to the entire ensemble.

On the other hand, attempts have been made to produce pure music, pure dance, even pure vocalization, in which all literary, intellectual, or psychological programs, values, and non-performing embellishments are absent from the performance in a quest for the essential form of the art itself. Yet, we have indicated that in the control of time through the accumulation and release of tension, the performing arts may play with and construct parallels to embroider upon basic psychological and emotional rhythms of the human psyche and soma. Moreover, in the logic of "theme and variation," the performing arts may present totally formal and abstract play upon the logical and intellectual capacities of the human intellect or mind. They may attempt to present and exhaust all the logical alternatives to a given theme within the rules of an aesthetic paradigm, yet they do so in a smooth, pleasing flow. The particular technique and craft of a performing art may then represent only a particular vehicle in which the quality of pure intellectual and logical play can be worked out. To the extent that this is the case, the formal, rational, and intellectual character of an art may be so developed that literary, psychological, and dramatic values are deemphasized, though—in the case of the dance—formality in patterning may embody visual values, i.e., the pure beauty of the interplay of complex patterns of mass, shape, line, and movement.

Generally, however, abstract formality in the performing arts requires, minimally, a highly educated and sophisticated audience if it attracts audiences at all. Yet when performances attract audiences, they necessarily com-

municate, even if that which is communicated is pure form; formal perfection
has an aesthetic appeal to audiences. All the arts, including the performing
arts, thus have a formal dimension to the extent that they can be labeled as
arts: they are both artificial and have significant form to the extent that they
are well composed and executed.

Moreover, form, the objectivity of technique, style, rules, and paradigms,
the web and woof of the respective media themselves, are social, the product
of the collective, cumulative work of authors, composers, and creators in
response to the past, and to each other, performers, audiences, and other
significant publics. The cumulative historical development of their respective
forms represents a significant social dimension to the performing arts, as it
does to all the arts.

The communication of non-performance content, literary, normative,
programmatic, and psychological, represents special problems for the performing arts, even beyond those of the translation of non-performance
themes, ideas, and conventions into the significant form and media of the
performing arts. At this less formal level, the performing arts have, to repeat,
been involved in every cultural, social, philosophic and religious movement
of their times. In Western history, they have been dominated by classicism
or romanticism, "artificiality" or naturalism, realism or impressionism,
expressionism or symbolism. They have been nationalistic, patriotic and
militaristic, or internationalist and pacifist. They have supported the establishment, or a given class or elite, or have been "reactionary," anti-estab-
lishment, or revolutionary, or have supported a rising or oppressed class.
They have supported sacred or profane values, as these have been defined
by particular proponents of each, within or without the arts; they have been
traditionalistic or modernistic, conventional or experimental. There is, in
fact, no end to the categories of *non-performing* themes which the performing
arts have incorporated into themselves and to whose criteria they have become
subject.

These facts have two consequences. At any one time, each performing art
is likely to be subject to internal conflict on grounds of both its formal,
technical development and its non-performance content. Moreover, significant external publics, including audiences, make demands upon the performing arts, as they do upon all the arts, on the basis of nonartistic criteria.
Even the emphasis on pure form, that is, the rejection of all values other
than technical, aesthetic, and performance values, is seen as a rejection of
the nonformal and nonaesthetic values that external groups (and some internal
groups) place upon the arts. Thus "formalism" is a pejorative label placed
upon the arts by both "reactionaries" and revolutionists, the church, com-
munist regimes, Nazis, and democratic "philistines." Yet such critics are
likely to be arguing not only in defense of "content," but from the standpoint
of a particular content, that is, from a theory of the arts that embraces non-

artistic doctrines, whether political, social, economic, or religious. Thus the arts are inevitably social and political, and intrinsically involved in the very fabric of society.

In this context, even the total formalism of the arts, "art for art's sake," is a political statement: it is a rejection of the values and themes that outsiders would impose upon them. In some cases, formalism is merely the attempt to emphasize the intrinsic medium or form of an art to the exclusion of nonartistic values; in other cases, it is a conscious act of defiance against would-be controllers. Where certain themes, styles, repertoire, and manners of execution are proscribed, the conscious selection of proscribed practices is a means by which the artist expresses his defiance of the "philistines." Satire, allegory, or humor either in form or content may express the rejection of prescribed form and content. Subtlety in execution is analogous to allegory in its commentary upon a rejected present. It both expresses and conceals its intention.

In all of these cases, the performing arts are means of communication that embody societal, cultural, and political values that are also present in the non-performing arts as well as in religion, philosophy, politics, and public opinion; but they also embody the special values and assertion of values of art as an activity itself and those of each respective performing art. These include both the special ability to transform nonartistic values into the media of an art form and the emphasis on pure form, the attempt to present a work in which only the values, aesthetics, craft, and technique of an art are present in the performance. Each art and work of art may communicate in all of these ways; but the extent to which a performance communicates depends on the accessibility of its underlying message to an audience, on the universality or particular salience of its underlying theme, on the "artistry" of its execution, as well as on the existence and sophistication of an audience for the specialized craft, technique, and style of the art form. In the latter case, as an art develops in "formality," abstractness, or specialized complexity, it may leave its traditional audiences far behind. Only by repeated exposure to increasingly sophisticated audiences can one establish whether a work, style, or paradigm communicates to its audiences. In this sense, the individual work or style creates or fails to create its own audiences.

Yet these ultimately are macroscopic aspects of social communication, the communication between the artistic creator as receiver of social, cultural, and artistic tradition, and as creator, modifier, and presenter of these traditions to audiences in either the immediate present or distant future. The performing arts can also be analyzed as much simpler, more direct forms of communication.

When the unaccompanied instrumental soloist, singer, reciter of poetry, or dancer in performance directly presents a work to a live audience, he directly embodies the macroscopic elements of the communication of arts in his performance. He also embodies those "backstage" elements of social machinery of his art, artistic management, publicity, reputation, advertising, and all the organizational machinery of the arts that make a given artist and repertoire salient to an audience at a given time, place, and price. But even when two artists perform together, new, additional forms of communication are essential between the performers. This intra-artistic communication is unique to the performing arts. The novelist, painter, sculptor, and other non-performing artists, of course, learn their craft, its techniques, styles, and traditions from others, including peers; but they then create a physical product by what is essentially a solitary act. In the performing arts, apart from the solo performance and other exceptions to be noted, the act of performance is necessarily a social, collective one. Thus, we have noted, the conductor is a controller, a coordinator of the action of other performers, guaranteeing not only the rhythm, balance, and flow of action and theme, mood, color, and ideas embodied in the score, but also that of the actions of up to hundreds of performers who respond both to him and to the score. Intonation, balance, color, rhythm, and tempo thus are social as well as aesthetic attributes of a performance. This is most easily understood with respect to the conductor and orchestra members; and their struggles quite often appear to transcend submission to the score. They may be "psychological" struggles, personality conflicts, conflicts over style, repertoire, and professional competence. They may, of course, include conflicts over prestige, i.e., headline grabbing, jealousies over headline grabbing, and jealousies over the rewards of successful performance. The same types of conflicts, as we have indicated, are likely to occur between soloists and conductors, stars, soloists and principal singers in the symphony and opera, and principal dancers and choreographers in the dance. In these latter cases, differing conceptions of style and interpretation may be additional and important sources of conflict.

Yet conflict is only one aspect of internal communication within the performing arts. Cooperation in communication is even more intrinsic to performance. This aspect of communication is perhaps best illustrated in chamber music, particularly in the string quartet. Here, there is no conductor or director. The players are relatively equal in importance to the whole work, and lack of coordination in all aspects of performance is usually noticeable instantly in performance, even as that performance requires a continuous, coordinated flow of simultaneous individual performances. To the extent that the artists are professional, they can prepare for their performance in advance of joint rehearsal by individually preparing and practicing their parts. Yet, even after individual preparation, they may have differences in familiarity with a given work, differences in training, stylistic preferences, interpretation, and ingrained personal and performance styles. That is, some chamber groups and individual performers may prefer or will concentrate on the lyrical values in a piece, others on dramatic values, while still others may emphasize tempo and rhythmic thrust, inner voices, or historical accuracy.

Differences in interpretation, so defined, may be resolved by example, by the performance of alternative interpretations of a section of a work, by discussion and debate, by vote, or by the acceptance of one performer as authoritative arbiter, depending on his knowledge or total philosophy of interpretation of a work. Yet such explicit methods of decision making only scratch the surface. In performance, especially in final performance before an audience, the artists manage by extreme concentration to see and to hear themselves and each other in the succession of microseconds of their joint performance. Ideally, they can adjust their rhythm, pitch, phrasing, and sonorities to one another instantaneously, with no communication other than the act of seeing, listening, and responding to the others and the score. When this is achieved, the total performance may acquire such an intensity that electricity is communicated to the audience as well as by each performer to the others. This sense of unity with the score and with one another is perhaps the supreme value of chamber music to its performers; and it accounts for much of the attraction of the genre to virtuoso and orchestra players. Yet the silent communication and unity to be found in the performance of chamber music represents the sublime value and goal of all music.

Although absolute communication finds its ultimate goal in the internal communication between performers of chamber music, it is the sine qua non of excellence in all the performing arts.

The very dramatic nature of the character of the theater implies communication. Actors who have mastered all the necessary physical, facial, vocal, and bodily gestures and expressions must still appear to be relating to one another as well as to the dramatic themes and action of the play as interpreted to them by the director. Virtuosity in individual performances can, however, be achieved at the expense of the total performance of the play, a not infrequent occurrence. And the failure of actors to appear to be talking to, listening to, or hearing one another is generally attributed to poor direction, given a professionally qualified company. Thus in the theater, as in other performing arts, ensemble acting and performance compete as principles with virtuoso performance.

In the opera, these conflicts are more intense, for, in that art, orchestral music and the conductor may compete with choral music, with the individual and ensemble singing of the principals, as well as with lighting, stage design, and costumes, i.e., with production and dramatic values. Each of the various elements in opera is so highly specialized and differentiated that the achievement of total integration is extremely hard to define and achieve. In fact, the history of the opera may be written from the standpoint of successive attempts to shift the central emphasis of the total performance from one element to another: from libretto to simple musical line, then to complex ensemble singing, to orchestral and choral dominance, and to "total," integrated performances. The focal element has then become the diva, the tenor, and the star conductor, and—finally—stage design, scenery, lighting, and the stage director's recreation of the libretto and score.

In performance, a great singer may so excel in his or her primary sphere of specialization that he or she may achieve the highest level of stardom with little ability or development of his or her dramatic abilities, physical appearance, resemblance to a role, or attention to stage movement. The conductor, stage manager, and designer may attempt to achieve integration of the total performance by preperformance; but onstage communication becomes a special tour de force, because of the very complexity and differentiation of the various constituents of the total performance.

In the dance, communication through the use of the body is the essence of the art form. All of the complexities of practice, training, and rehearsals are mere preliminaries—the vocabulary of the dance—which are exercised in communication by movement through space, usually accompanied by music. As in the chamber group, simultaneous performance among relatively equal principals emphasizes the unity to be achieved within differences in movement. In larger works, the maintenance of "balance," "color," and "mass" resembles the attempt to achieve the complex thematic unity of the symphony orchestra. But since the dance achieves its internal dramatic and communicative unity by the movement of bodies through space, the total effect is visual. Unity in tone, gesture, flow, and effect transcends, ideally, the virtuosity of the individual performer. The achievement of these unities is, of course, the task of the choreographer, an offstage director. Yet when fully achieved on stage, in the exact moment of execution, an intense, vibrant quality is achieved among performers and audiences that transcends the virtuosity of individual performers. As in the magnificent chamber music performance, the dance can achieve a sense of total internal communication and unity that transcends technique and individual performance.

The ideal of the achievement of absolute internal communication in performance raises again the problem of the relationship between the onstage performer and the offstage creator of the performing arts in the act of communication. The playwright, composer, librettist, or choreographer, as we have noted, provides macroscopic, programmatic, literal, psychological, and cultural themes and values to the work performed. The "score" is also a set of instructions to performers. But since the act of composition is separate from that of execution, the work as composed or written is necessarily distinct from the one performed. The composer of solo music, to the extent that he is a virtuoso performer, can, within a relatively short time interval, capture the sense of his production as it will sound in execution. A community of professional performers may provide the composer with opportunities to hear his larger works realized. The existence of an electronic synthesizer may reduce the time gap between composition and realization to virtually nothing; and this is a major advantage to these electronic instruments. In fact, no other performer or audience is necessary. But in all other cases, the composer is dependent upon the performer to achieve the aural sense of his work. And as the scale of composition increases, the necessity for performance entails a live, paying audience: the rehearsal and printing costs that allow the composer to hear the work are so great that he or she can only hear it if a paying audience also hears it. "Reflexivity," the feedback derived from being able to hear one's work, and the self-criticism that can be as valuable as that of audience response, is in large part a product of the social, economic, and collective organizational systems of the performing arts. This dependency on external support, on orchestras, foundations, and special grants that subsidize the rehearsal and performance of new works, is far greater in the performing arts than in the non-performing arts. It is no wonder that modern composers increasingly prefer small-scale works, or are dependent upon semiprofessional orchestras at universities. For the same and other reasons, it is not surprising that great composers of the past have left a heritage of unperformed and unheard works.

The playwright is in a similar position. In writing, he must imagine the dramatic flow of his work in performance, the tempi of dialogue and movement. He can confront his work as a finished product only in the late stages of rehearsal by a professional company. He may be called into rehearsals to rewrite, tighten up, and correct deficiencies that can be experienced only in performance. At that time, he is subject to the performance demands of the director or producer, who may have different intentions and give different meaning to his work from those he intended. Yet, again, the opportunity to judge, evaluate, revise, and correct one's work depends on its acceptance for performance and upon subsequent preparation and rehearsal for staging. The unperformed playwright lacks an essential element of the writing experience that makes his work worthy of performance.

The choreographer is in an even more precarious position, for the very act of composition is that of performance. For the choreographer, once having selected his music, his overall "plot line," and having visualized the overall flow of work in his imagination, cannot translate it into actual dancing without the direct and immediate participation of the dancers necessary to perform his work. He is dependent on a company or on a school of dance. If he is fortunate, the successful dancer who wishes to may be allowed to choreograph, may be given permission by the directors of a company or school to attempt choreography; but he cannot do so by himself. Even when he or she receives a philanthropic grant to choreograph a work, the grant is necessarily tied to a performing company or workshop. He may have to organize his or her own company or school in order to do his or her own work. In this sense, creativity is more closely tied to performance in the dance than it is in any other performing art.

Professionalism

In the entire discussion up till this point, professionalism has been virtually taken for granted as a necessary ingredient in defining the performing arts. Professionalism in the performing arts generally means the possession of high levels of technical skill by performing artists who are oriented toward a full-time career in an art. It includes the acquisition of levels of training, experience, practice, and commitment. In most cases, the routes by which such training and experience are acquired are not rigidly prescribed, but the value of one's training and experience can be judged by performance. In some countries, licenses and certificates to teach a performing art are granted only after prescribed courses of training and examinations. In general, however, the performing arts are unlike other professions in that they are more based on talent, are less based on prescribed courses of training, and are less likely to be based on certificates or licenses (though winning a contest or study in a prestigious school or company may be helpful). They do not have a formal ethical code, nor are they likely to have a professional association, although musicians and dancers may belong to unions, composers to ASCAP, and so forth. But none of these organizations has succeeded in coalescing such all-embracing professional power as the American Medical Association or the American Bar Association.

Even though we understand professionalism in the performing arts merely as the achievement of high levels of competence oriented toward a career, we are still required to understand the institutional sources and consequences of professionalism.

Professionalization in the arts is rooted in full-time training, systematic instruction, practice and rehearsal, and guided entry into performance.

One of the earliest sources of such training was the church, which trained organists, instrumentalists, choirs, and soloists for performance of the mass and for other church services. Christian churches, with very few exceptions, rejected the dance for religious rites, since the dance was deemed to be orgiastic in character. In more ways than one, the church can be called the mother of the performing arts, especially of music. Church schools trained youths and employed castrati, other singers, organists, instrumentalists, and composers. It would not be possible to imagine the emergence of Western music without the training and employment provided by the church, including Protestant churches, from the fourteenth to the nineteenth century. Just to name a few great composers, Bach, Haydn, Palestrina, Monteverdi, Mozart, and the Scarlattis were among the thousands either trained or employed by the church or churches.

Yet this powerful nurturing force created limits to the development of music. Musical education and careers were often prescribed by the necessity of furnishing accompaniment to church services; and the autonomous development of music was limited by the necessity of complying with religiously defined themes and programs. Great composers found that often their work was condemned for being too secular, profane, sensuous, or otherwise irreligious; and they were often driven to seek alternative forms of employment. In addition, they were often subject to the arbitrary personal demands of clerical and lay officials over repertoire, rank and privilege, pay, patronage, and the amount of outside performance they could do.

In these respects, the conditions of employment were not much different under the secular patronage of princes, aristocrats, kings, and patricians who during the Renaissance installed professional musicians as parts of their courts and salons. Yet even without the routine of masses and religious ceremony, professionals served to celebrate weddings, birthdays, and coronations of their masters and to provide music for concerts, balls, masques, and other entertainment. They displayed their virtuosity in composition, improvisation, and performance before their patrons, and they taught aristocratic and patrician amateurs and composed works appropriate to the taste and performance skills of their masters. While the range of performance and composition was extended under courtly, secular patronage, the composer–performer was still subject to the arbitrary tastes and whims of his patron. Musician–composers attempted to enlarge their areas of freedom by moving from court to court, seeking better conditions of pay, work, and artistic freedom, especially when their past successes produced rising reputations; but they were always subject to the vicissitudes of musical preference, including the loss of patronage due to the death and succession of patrons. They sought, achieved, and lost financial support from aristocrats, based on the prestige accorded those who supported great composer–performers, hired them for concerts, and commissioned them to do specific works.

Composers, in addition, organized their own "academies" in which they performed together, provided competitions in performance and composition, and elected aspiring composers to membership, which certified their professional excellence.

From the sixteenth through the eighteenth centuries, the prestige competition among princes and aristocrats often entailed support of arts, including the performing arts; and the employment of artists embraced the creation of and support of performing companies. This included not only the creation of orchestras and the employment of musical directors and composers, but also the training of musicians, the standardization of performance styles and instruments, and the recognition that the musician was a professional.

The same process occurred to a greater or lesser degree with respect to the dance, the opera, and the theater. The dance originated in masque, the courtly entertainments of aristocrats who were themselves the dancers. The ballet master was the teacher of aristocrats and the choreographer of balls in the seventeenth century. Professional dancing became a vogue only in the nineteenth century, but training in dance was largely conducted in companies attached to the courts of tsars, kings, and princes.

While the opera was often supported by courts as early as in the seventeenth century, a tradition of the independent entrepreneur emerged much earlier in the Italian *commedia del arte* and *opera buffa* in the sixteenth and seventeenth centuries. These were essentially different from the community opera and drama of Northern Europe, especially Germany, and the medieval morality plays, which were primarily composed by amateurs sponsored by guilds or by the community as a whole.

Traveling opera companies provided their own training and support, but were willing to accept the support of the courts, princes, and the public. In this they were no different from theatrical companies, who, by the sixteenth and seventeenth centuries, were highly developed. In some cases the independent entrepreneurs—who organized performing companies, composed the plays, opera, and oratorios, and engaged the performers—became incorporated in nationally sponsored organizations. Molière was one such impresario. At other times, they depended primarily on subscriptions, i.e., ticket sales, and less upon subscriptions. Shakespeare and, later, Handel are examples of the latter.

The emergence of the subscription concert in the eighteenth century freed some musicians from individual and courtly patronage, but the use of subscriptions or ticket sales was present much earlier in the opera and theater. By the seventeenth century, nationally sponsored orchestras, dance, and theater coexisted with those operated by individual impresarios. By the middle of the nineteenth century the "liberation" of the artist from the specific patron was virtually complete.

All of these changes were due, ultimately, to the rise of middle-class audiences. They were the result of the increasing numbers and affluence of the bourgeoisie, and to their desire to celebrate their ascent by participating in high culture both as performers and as audiences. These aspirations were of course facilitated by the decreasing costs of instruments, especially of pianos, by the new availability of printed music, and by the possibility of becoming a part of the large audiences due to developments in architecture and the construction that made large auditoriums possible.

All these "external" changes were accompanied by a simplification of music, a new emphasis on melody and tunes, and a stress on popular and emotional themes in the arts. Overall, the new music was easier to whistle, to listen to, and to comprehend by amateurs who could not devote a major part of their working or intellectual life to the arts. The same simplification and romanticism increasingly pervaded all of the arts during the nineteenth century.

As a result of these changes, education in the arts, after initially being dominated by the church, became dominated by state-sponsored conservatories and dance schools, by individual teachers, and by the performing companies of impresarios. In the latter case, it was unsystematic. Recruitment was on a catch-as-catch-can basis, and training was largely a matter of on-the-job training. The development of the state-sponsored conservatory had several results: (1) systematic training; (2) the breakdown of the arts, especially music and dance, into more finely developed specialties; (3) the systematic and early recruitment of talented youngsters; and (4) specified regimes of training, all leading to entrance into performance positions in state-sponsored companies. The ultimate direction and control was oriented to serving the performing company. Teachers in the conservatory were often composers as well as teachers of performance.

Self-education and private instruction, of course, emerged in the era of transition between churchly sponsorship, the rise of secular courts, and the subscription performance, and the conservatory. Thus, Handel would travel to hear Buxtehude; Beethoven would take lessons from Albrechtsberger, and a few from Haydn; and Mozart would both learn from, and teach, the older Haydn. Thus, by the beginning of the nineteenth century, a variety of modes of becoming a professional had come into being. The overall trend, however, was a shift away from the predominance of the church and toward greater variety in the means of becoming a professional. The development of secular training based upon the performing company was giving way to a separation into conservatories and performing companies, with the former providing systematic, specialized training. All of this was accompanied by an increase in nonsponsored, private instruction of not only professionals but middle-class amateurs.

The nineteenth century saw the rise of mass audience, the growth of the importance of the impresario, and the development of secular, nonstate, nonsponsored education. The independent conservatory began to emerge, as did private schools of music and dance. Opera and drama lagged in these developments, depending more upon either the company or the state.

In the twentieth century, the university began to enter the scene, with the emergence of the music school, the drama school, the dance department. This reflected a general tendency for universities to embrace all the arts and professions. But the cooptation of the performing arts by the universities is not even yet complete. Relatively few universities now provide instruction in all aspects of the performing arts; and the performing arts, as yet, are not dependent on the training and personnel provided by the universities. Conservatories still predominate in music, and separate ad-hoc schools still give instruction and practice in the drama, as do schools attached to performing companies in the dance. At the same time, conservatories are increasingly converting themselves into academic institutions by granting degrees, making their curricula more systematic, and providing academic courses to their students. They attempt to provide professional certification.

Yet the "invasion" of the university into the performing arts expresses a major secular trend in the arts in that, as they standardize and make explicit and self-conscious the techniques of their arts, they begin to subdivide and specialize the respective arts.

One result is that the level of performance in some of the performing arts, especially music and the dance, appears to have risen. This is undoubtedly due to the increasing importance and systematization of training in the conservatory and in dance schools. Thus, performance standards in music and dance have risen to such an extent since the end of the nineteenth century that music previously thought to be unplayable and feats of unique virtuosity in the dance appear to be commonplace in performance among relatively large numbers of highly trained virtuosos. As a result, the average level of professional performance, in the symphony and the corps de ballet, appears to have risen far above nineteenth century standards.

Whether this is true of choreography, composing, and playwriting is subject to debate. Perhaps training in performance can be subject to more objective standards; its elements can be broken down, studied, and researched, and then reconstituted under the discipline of supervised practice. In the "creative" aspect of the performing arts, such "objectivity" may not be as successful; or, perhaps, concentration on pure technique may be less fruitful. Certainly, the "academization" of the arts in conservatories and universities has led to a separation of the various aspects of the arts. Each aspect becomes the subject of separate disciplines, courses, and instruction. Thus, in music, conducting has become a specialized field, as has composing, individual performance, instrument, and literature; and each of these is further subdivided. In the theater, writing, acting, stage management, directing, scenery construction, literature, and lighting are separated. And all of these internal, technical operations are separated from the business of management: finance, sales, public relations, etc. Each aspect requires a separate curriculum, and "survey" courses attempt to bridge the gap caused by specialization. In the older tradition, mastery of these specialized functions was part of the total experience and career of the performing artist.

It would, however, be inaccurate to attribute all these changes toward specialization and professionalization to the academization of training provided by the conservatory and university. Similar changes have occurred in all aspects of society. One can speculate that the greater size, scale, and scope of the performing arts requires greater professional specialization. Further, the quest for organization and technical and aesthetic rationality—i.e., for systematization—causes greater demand for technical proficiency, which, in turn, causes greater specialization. But once professionalization occurs, demands for greater integration of an art as a whole must occur in the face of the fact that all specialists develop loyalties and the trained incapacity and occupational blinders of their own field. This includes the "occupational psychoses" of specialized administrators, organizers, and integrators. Thus the "integration of complex functions," administration, becomes a specialized feature of the arts that may supercede the programmatic integration of the scenario, score, or choreographic plan.

A second consequence of the academization of the arts is the rise of specialized professional teachers, who, by virtue of their teaching positions, become separated from the problems of live professional performance before a paying audience. To them, the work of art becomes a theoretical problem to be solved in an academic journal, in the classroom, or as a training exercise. The performance is not seen as a totality; rather, separate critical and intellectual strands in a work, style, or tradition are analyzed; and the elucidation on each strand constitutes the solution of a particular performance or creative problem.

External Control over the Performing Arts

Our brief and hasty overview of professional training and sponsorship points to a shifting but underlying pattern of sponsorship and, in the final analysis, control over the performing arts. In sum, this historical pattern entails patronage and control by the church, by secular aristocrats and their courts, by the emerging national state, and finally by the bourgeoisie—as sponsors of municipal music and theater, as ticket purchasers, and as philanthropic supporters of the arts. In the present, such sponsorship and control have devolved upon the mature national welfare state, the universities, and local and regional art councils. By and large, then, the dominant patterns of sponsorship and support for the arts follow the overall pattern of the dominance of classes, elites, and other social and economic institutions over society. In the midst of this shifting pattern of support and control, the arts have attempted to assert their own autonomy, their own technical, aesthetic, and cultural stan dards as well as the standards they have internalized or been forced to accept from the outside society.

The rise of the dynastic and national state resulted in the use of arts to support imperial pomp and splendor and, later, nationalism. And, by this very attempt to control the direction of the arts, counternational revolutionary arts of both bourgeois and "proletarian" character came into existence. But as the power of the bourgeoisie rose, the bourgeois attempted to use the arts both to achieve the prestige of the aristocracy and to celebrate the triumph of the bourgeoisie over society. This resulted not only in the incorporation of bourgeois themes in the arts—nationalism, simplification, technical virtuosity, emotionality, romanticism, etc.—but in the sponsorship and support of the arts, especially the performing arts, by both mass audiences and bourgeois Maecenases.

The rise of mass patronage, especially through the subscription or ticket, allowed performing artists to escape from the demands of the particular patron so long as they could support themselves by playing before a large audience. This meant, of course, that the artist—to support himself from ticket sales— had to appeal to the emerging tastes of these new audiences. This resulted originally, during the nineteenth century, in simplification of styles, emotionalism, and virtuosity in technique and performance, as well as an artistic content that was immediately accessible to an audience.

The liberation of the arts from the immediate demands of particular patrons and audiences, whether aristocratic or bourgeois, allowed artists to pursue paths that were not dependent on either the patron or the audience. These included the purely technical development of the artistic media, beyond the virtuosity in technique that attracts audiences. It included purely abstract, formalistic development of the media, ideas of "art for art's sake," and antibourgeois art. Experimental arts were aimed primarily at solving purely aesthetic or technical problems or the problems of working out or fulfilling the rational principles underlying a style or set of aesthetic assumptions. In working out these purely internal dynamics of the arts, the artist could then ignore audiences and pursue intellectual, technical, and aesthetic goals that were meaningful only to other artists or to those amateurs who virtually made themselves into specialists in the art. Included in the new audiences were those who were attached to "modernism," regardless of its content. These were the antibourgeois bourgeoisie, who would follow modernism wherever it went, because the prestige of the arts, by the nineteenth century, was autonomous.

An overall result of all this has been the development of at least two forms of repertoire in the serious arts. One form looks back to performance of great classical and romantic art of the late eighteenth and the nineteenth centuries; the other form is modernistic, abstract, and formalistic. By and large, the two repertoires do not intermingle. The great performing companies in the symphony and opera and the great popular masters of performance in smaller groups perform the nineteenth-century repertoire, whereas newer works are slow to gain entry into that repertoire. This is somewhat less true of the dance, since modern dance entered the scene in the twentieth century, and—in ballet—a few great choreographers, primarily under the influence of Balanchine, have introduced abstract and formal elements into the dance.

The second tradition of performing arts, the tradition of modernism, has largely become centered in the universities. Here, academic self-consciousness and the freedom from the demands of an adult bourgeois audience have allowed academic impresarios and staff to explore a wide range of current creation as well as to perform older interesting and prestigious works that do not command audiences large enough to make them sufficiently profitable to justify commercial production.

Thus, underlying current production and performance are the familiar devils of economics. But this has always been the case. The church subsidized the arts for religious purposes, the aristocracy for political and prestige purposes, the dynastic and national states for national purposes. The nineteenth-century boom of the performing arts was supported not only by mass audiences, but by Maecenases and the state and municipalities. In the last half of the twentieth century, the performing arts have increasingly been supported by the welfare state to such an extent that the threat of withdrawal of state support is adjudged to be a crisis in the arts.

Underlying all of this is another set of economics: the live performing arts rest on the real-estate business. Performance before live audiences rests primarily upon the construction of expensive auditoriums and theaters, usually on valuable, accessible plots in high-traffic urban areas. As the size of the auditorium increases, real estate and construction costs also increase; no substantial cost reduction is achieved by creating smaller auditoriums. Costs per seat are high. Unit cost reductions can be achieved only by having a full house at each performance, having performances on as many days a year as possible, and having as many performances a day as possible. The necessity of continuously attracting full houses is a challenge to the individual impresario; some are successful. But this means that the performing arts as a whole depend upon such very high levels of audience support that very few are self-sustaining. Most large theaters, auditoriums, and performing companies must depend on state and philanthropic contributions, the latter being, in the United States, partly underwritten as tax exemptions.

Small performing groups and soloists and stars can, of course, make highly profitable careers, either because their costs are low or because they can fill seats. Individual productions of the commercial theater can also be profitable, usually at the expense of countless failures. The failures may be pleasing to audiences, but do not fill a sufficient number of seats to permit the prospect of overcoming high initial costs. Off-Broadway and off-off-Broadway performances overcome high real-estate costs by playing in the low rent districts, in abandoned commercial theaters, or in improvised theaters. Works are performed by semi-professional performers, by hopefuls, and by "at liberty" professionals. The audiences are thus subsidized by performers working at less than professional scales.

For the rest, subsidies are the way of the arts. The universities subsidize the dance, the theater, and music as an intrinsic part of their subsidized existence, with the justifications of raising the cultural and intellectual level of future audiences and of providing professional training to hopeful professional performers.

Regional theaters are usually subsidized by local Maecenases as well as by local, state, and national art councils and endowments. Municipal, regional, and even national art centers and performing groups are justified as contributions to the tourist industry, to the achievement of national and local pride, and to the edification of the masses or the classes.

The economics of nondecreasing costs is exacerbated in the twentieth century by the discovery among professionals at all levels in the performing arts that they are entitled to a living wage. Not only do they (and production staffs) unionize and demand annual contracts whose minimums would support a lower-middle-class style of life, but they also demand employment throughout the year, standby payments, overtime payment for extra rehearsals, control over hiring and firing, and all the other benefits of unionism. In this, they not only raise fixed costs, but they alienate and restrict the established rights of directors, impresarios, conductors, managers, and governing boards, the latter usually being benefactors of the arts.

The costs of the arts are further raised by a star system that causes major performing companies to compete at fantastic salaries for a handful of stars. The very same competition results in the overproduction of a limited number of works that have known appeal among established audiences and benefactors. In these productions, the competitive advantages of performing a prestigious work, even at great expense, may result in financial losses that are compensated for by the prestige accruing to the performing company for so doing. Thus subsidies are necessary.

But, to repeat, this has always been the case; the church, the aristocracy, the state, the upper bourgeoisie have always subsidized the arts—for their own purposes—as do the welfare state and the universities at present.

One can argue that the arts are intrinsically valuable and require subsidies, including tax exemptions to contributors to the arts; or one can argue, as Herbert Gans has done, that no such support to the "class" arts is desirable:

let the market determine the desire for and value of the arts; support of the arts by the government is a subsidy to the upper-middle and upper classes, who are the primary consumers of the serious performing arts. Such an argument would, of course, logically entail the elimination of all tax exemptions for contributions to the arts, for these exemptions are, in fact, subsidies by government for decisions that are made by the affluent.

It is undoubtedly true that, if all government subsidies were eliminated, the arts would shrivel. Moreover, they would become more narrowly based: they would become more vulgar, on the one hand, and more elitist and sectarian, on the other. They would, however, survive. Yet the current clamor for retaining government subsidies indicates how dependent the performing arts are on government support and, more generally, how vulnerable they are.

Whatever the outcome of conflicts over the amount and distribution of public support for the performing arts, the conflict demonstrates anew that the arts are profoundly social and political and therefore that artists cannot avoid politics.

The Forms of Rationalization of the Arts

Max Weber, in his *Rational Foundations of Music*, sought to apply his overall theories of rationalization to music. He pointed to the attempts of modern Western composers to make the composition of music increasingly subject to systematic, formal, logical rules "with nothing left over," i.e., without gaps, inconsistencies, or exceptions from rule. He indicated, however, that this attempt, the product of centuries of work, took place in the face of the fact that music is subject to an ultimate irrationality: something is always left over. The octave cannot be subdivided, tempered into exactly equal intervals, so that all scales can be performed on keyed instruments with equal intervals going up and down the scale. And this "lack of temperament" was the driving force in the rationalization of music. Weber also noted in considerable detail the rationalization that occurred in the construction of instruments. Since the seventeenth century, a consistent trend has been to standardize and systematize the construction of instruments, so that they could all be subject to common, systematic modes of instruction, composition, and performance.

Weber's essay on music was only a footnote in a larger scheme that entailed the "rationalization" of religion, the economy, the state and law, bureaucracy, the various forms of knowledge, and even "personality" itself. It is important to note that Weber meant by rationalization only the subjection of these areas of activity to rational, systematic, methodological, and calculable rules and practices. He did not imply that the process of rationalization meant the achievement of some higher, metaphysical state of reason that lay beyond or below the individual or the collective activities of people in their own time and place. There was no ultimate goal to this process beyond its consequences for the action of people in their own history. Thus the quest for rationality, so defined, could lead to higher forms of irrationality based on the rejection of the opacity of meaning that a purely formal rationality entailed. This included "the disenchantment of the world," the death of poetry, of myth, and of common humanity. Moreover, the rationalization of politics, law, the state, and the economy brought about the creation of formal structures, especially bureaucracy, that not only disenchanted the world, but made it subject to both rational and irrational controls, authority, and inhumanity.

Weber subdivided the process of rationalization into three basic forms: (1) intellectual rationalization; (2) formal rationalization; and (3) the rationalization of everyday life.

Intellectual rationalization deals with the attempt to treat all forms of knowledge, religion, philosophy, science, and culture as if they were systematically and methodologically derivable from a set of logical, self-consistent propositions that located all the derived knowledge and theory in a logically closed system; that is, nothing is left out or left over.

Formal rationalization consists of the attempt to render all actions of men, especially their collective actions, subject to explicit, formal, and standardized rules of procedure, which are rationally—i.e., systematically—planned, calculated, and worked out in order to achieve explicitly agreed-upon goals.

The rationalization of life is the conscious inculcation of ideas, habits, and beliefs into individuals that results in the ability of individuals to control totally their own or others' emotions and inner life so that they might consistently, systematically, and rationally pursue preordained goals without irrational deflections, outbursts of emotion, deviation, or conflict. This form of rationalization is a peripheral but implicit issue in the discussion that is to follow.

In that discussion, we will attempt to extend Weber's discussion of both intellectual and formal rationalization and his discussion of music to the performing arts in general in order to summarize our previous discussion.

Intellectual Rationalization in the Performing Arts

Intellectual rationalization takes many forms. Included are attempts to embody in a particular performing art the underlying literary or programmatic "philosophy" content, or world view, of that program, independent of the idiom and techniques of any particular performing art. Thus, if a performing art is romantic, naturalistic, religious, nationalist, or "avant garde," it is subject to the ongoing attempt in other fields of knowledge and culture to make the underlying assumptions of the fields explicit, consistent, and reflective of its original and evolving assumptions. Since these other fields and styles are continually undergoing change, a performing art may often "borrow" programmatic content from continually changing fields and can vary the sources of its borrowings. This is only to say that the performing arts participate in, and may contribute to, the total, changing flow of knowledge and ideas that are constantly undergoing rationalization in their culture and society. They embody not only the "rationalization" of these programmatic and aesthetic assumptions, but counterrationalizations and irrationality as well, when one set of programmatic styles comes into conflict with others. Thus, a nationalistic or religious style may come into conflict with, respectively, a universalistic or secular style. The performing arts are subject to continual conflict and change as a result of changes that occur outside their respective domains but that they incorporate and implement.

The rationalization of the performing arts also includes the precise ways they embody and incorporate literary and programmatic themes, the creation of appropriate techniques, "images," and styles for so doing, their standardization and their elaboration. Thus, if there is to be a romantic ballet or romantic music, these styles are more than the borrowing of literary or programmatic themes. They become embodied in the very structure of the dance, its choreography and techniques, and in the selection, composition, and performance of music for the dance, as well as in the design of costumes, scenery, and lighting.

But this rationalization of literary and programmatic style involves more than embodiment of external assumptions and presuppositions in an art. In attempting to make "composition" and performance rational, systematic, methodical, and self-consistent, concern with the art form itself becomes increasingly prominent; and it becomes prominent at the level of creative and performing technique.

At the level of creative technique, the composer, playwright, or choreographer examines, "theorizes," and formalizes what he regards as the elements intrinsic to his medium. He formulates "rules,"i.e., a paradigm, and creates an intrinsic style, which he then tries to fill out through the creation of specific works, illustrations, and paradigms of that style. In the succession of works composed within the parameters of a creative style, the various possibilities of the style are examined, elaborated, fulfilled, and then abandoned. When it appears that no more can be said with that style, the style itself may be abandoned. This is to say that assumptions and limits of style may be so altered that the style is no longer recognizable in the terms of its original assumptions. The overall process of rationalization may be so continuous, so varied, and so multidimensional (different creators may be concentrating on the elaboration and development of different elements of a style) that it may not be possible to recognize the overall style at particular moments in its development.

The composer working within the bounds of a powerful, dominant tradition may even be unaware of the ongoing process of rationalization. He may take his tradition for granted even as he makes minor contributions to it; but the cumulation of minor changes may result in the collapse or transformation of a style. Only in retrospect or in specific moments of dramatic breakthough and conflict does the "concept" of a particular style become recognized and labeled. Moreover, at any given moment, creators may be working on a variety of styles, some old, some new, and some current; but in all cases variants of the hypothetical "ideal type" of their norm. Many variants, and the works that embody them, are stillborn—they lead to no further development. Many of these deadends become performed as curious museum pieces, after the passage of time. Still others become the bases of new stylistic innovation and development much later, after the main line of stylistic development has exhausted itself.

The rationalization of the intrinsic forms and styles of an art is thus not linear, nor is it evolutionary, leading to a single goal. Neither is it cyclical. At any time, a variety of styles is likely to be in the process of creation, and a still wider variety is likely to be performed. In the latter case, it is both because classics are valued and because the "experimental" work of the past can become the source of new experiments. The variety of styles persists because, in art, as in the humanities, there is no absolute form of nature or ultimate reality that can lead to a final, ultimate style. This is even true of music, which has a physical base in the harmonic resonance of overtones. Since style is based on the artificial, the "artful" construction of a set of limited assumptions, the specific content of the assumptions and their combination is the result of implicit or explicit conventions, implicit agreements between composers, composers and performers, and between both groups and their audiences and supporters. In the last analysis, then, audiences and other benefactors and supporters judge between alternative styles and decide—for the moment and in the long run—which will prevail in performance. Within these dynamics, however, one can discern a continual tendency toward formalization, even the formalization of a pure, nonprogrammatic art; but, so far, this formalization has not been the creation of an absolute, final, intrinsic art form. Rather, each successful style tends to develop a formal rationalization of its own assumptions before it, too, passes away. The processes of aesthetic rationalization are thus eternal and multidimensional, and lead to no final solution.

The Rationalization of Technique

The rationalization of technique is simpler than the rationalization of style, though at times it is hard to separate the two. One can illustrate the former by pointing simply to the development of systematic, standardized techniques of performance of the violin or piano, the systematic vocabularies of movement, steps, and mime in the dance, or the systematic development of techniques of breathing, vocal production, and practice in singing. At some levels, this form of rationalization of execution is purely technical, the result of self-conscious application of the technical means of producing the sounds, movements, and gestures of the arts in performance. At other levels, the rationalization of techniques is related to the literary or programmatic content of an art. A romantic ballet will demand a different set of techniques than, let us say, that demanded by psychological realism or a purely formal dance. And the theater of the absurd, or the plays of Brecht, demand different performing styles than the classic drama of Shakespeare or Molière.

Performing technique and style have a different meaning and vocabulary as related to the formalization of creative style apart from their explicit programmatic comment. Thus the performance of baroque music requires different techniques than that of classical, romantic, or the variety of postromantic styles; and performers, including conductors, can specialize and excel in the performance of one or more of these styles without being equally adept in all of them.

Yet, even within these larger parameters of performing styles and techniques, variations occur. Professionals, as a matter of principle, value pure technique and will judge each other in these terms; and they often create and develop pure performing techniques independent of cultural or programmatic style. Thus great creators of performing techniques emerge who rationalize performing technique according to given sets of explicit, rational assumptions. Thus, for instance, a Schnabel may "revolutionize" piano performance, Balanchine the dance, Stanislavski acting, Kolisch the string quartet, Toscanini conducting, and castrati the voice. Performing styles and technique become the object of "schools" in the wider sense of the term—German, French, Russian, and American piano playing—or the narrower—the ever-changing "Juilliard" school of piano playing, the "Adler-Clurman" school of acting, or the American Ballet School.

Yet the boundaries among the various forms of stylistic and technical rationalization are not clear. Some forms are related at the same time to programmatic assumptions, the formal rationalization of pure technique, and to pure professionalization, and others to a particular combination of these elements. A great choreographer like Martha Graham may create a totally new style and form of dance, new movements, gestures, extensions, steps, and floor work (and eliminate others). She has created her own schools, and choreography, and has embedded in them new programmatic themes and psychological orientations and values. Her work, like that of other great creators, is as technical as it is creative. Thus, at times, there is an intermingling of thematic, formal, and the purely technical processes of rationalization.

Such rationalizations, as Graham illustrates, can be embodied in an individual, or they can be institutionalized in an organization. As a result, the pluralistic, multidimensional rationalization of technical performance styles results, at this level, in a pluralistic competition of performing styles and techniques in ways that are not substantially different from those between programmatic and literary styles and between these and formal, pure, styles. In the short run, the resolution of these perpetual and endless conflicts results in particular balances and predominances of performing technique and styles, each of which, so far, has been continually upset by innovation and by the acceptance of even newer techniques by performers and audiences. Yet, of course, old styles persist and interpenetrate the new.

Formal Rationalization

Formal rationalization, the reduction of individual and collective action to self-conscious, systematically calculated rules and procedures, takes its most obvious form in the arts in rationalization of education and training. To the extent that education and training are the product of specific organizations, schools, academies, conservatories, universities, and rationally worked out apprenticeship programs, they undergo formal rationality. This entails, of course, consciously planned entrance examinations, curricula, and degrees, certificates and licenses based upon examinations and the completion of prescribed courses. It suggests the achievement of the "professional" status of the law or of medicine.

But formal rationalization implies much more than the rationalization of education in separate, formal associations. In addition to the breakdown of performance technique into its component elements and the perfection of each element, it implies, as we have noted, the development of systematically planned specialization. Thus, within any performing art, a plethora of subspecialties emerges, each having its own techniques, training, certificates, degrees, and career lines. Training to become a conductor, a stage manager, a soloist, a stage designer, etc., becomes increasingly the object of specialized schooling, training, and internship. Of course, the process is never complete: outstanding soloists seek to become conductors, and outstanding conductors take sabbaticals to compose. Moreover, older patterns persist, within which an outstanding but aging dancer may become a choreographer, ballet master or mistress, rehearsal director, or even costume designer. He or she may even become a company director or impresario. We have also noted that oustanding creative artists and organizers can create entire new companies in the pursuit of a style or of their personal demons, despite their lack of certified qualification. Yet these are great and eternal exceptions; the overall trend is specialization and subprofessionalization.

Specialization and professionalization involve more than the rationalization of training and technique. For, as soon as specialty begins to emerge, special interests also emerge. They are embodied in professional associations and trade unions that begin to exert pressures for their members, pressures directed at performing art companies as a whole, the public, and government. They attempt, among other things, to specify standards of training, apprenticeship, and entry into their subspecialty, and, in doing so, to create job monopolies over a specialty. They may exclude foreign actors, determine the length of apprenticeship and education, and supervise, or at least attempt to influence the manner and fairness of try-outs and examinations. It is in this sense that they contribute to the formal rationalization of the arts.

As specialization and subprofessionalization take place, the central role of the artistic administrator, coordinator, and impresario becomes even more important: they now emerge as the generalists, who coordinate the specialists. Yet they are specialized, bureaucratic generalists. In the past, depending on the era, the supreme arts administrator may have been a church official, a self-selected artist or businessman who served in the role of impresario, or a patrician, an amateur who devoted himself to an art by abandoning the family estate or business in order to serve art.

The past few decades have seen the rise of professional arts administrators, who often are trained in university arts administration programs or in business schools and who have served as officials in government and business. Their specialty is not an art but management itself. Their training is in accounting, finance, law, fund raising, journalism, publicity, and that indefinable specialty called management. They have a separate career line, which entails moving from one administrative position in the arts to another instead of from performance to administrative positions, as in the case of aging or mobility-oriented artists. They compete with Maecenases, with artists who have graduated into management, and with untrained "captains of arts" who have become impresarios, agents, or board members and officers of arts companies.

In part, the rise of professional arts managers, who themselves are subdivided into specialties, reflects the growing size of permanent companies in the performing arts. In part, administrative specialization reflects the corresponding increase in specialization of the nonartist world. Arts accountants have to deal, for instance, with government and nonarts accountants and public-relations men and with the representatives of technically complex media. In part, the requirements of dealing with government funding agencies and foundations require experts on grant applications and in law, accounting, and other counterpart occupations.

In this process, the arts administrator becomes a specialist. He develops a perspective of his own, which is necessarily different from that of the specialized professionals in an art and the gifted amateurs and impresarios who have traditionally been its self-selected managers.

In the past, the "bureaucrats" of the arts, the church or court official and the businessman, were the special objects of hostility of artists. Professional arts administrators are now often the heirs to this hostility, as are university administrators and the administrators of art councils.

This is perhaps a natural phenomenon, for, as we have seen, intellectual and formal rationalization of the arts involves a proliferation of specializations, styles, techniques, and literary programmatic goals for the arts; and these values and techniques involve specialized but intense loyalties, commitments, and—at times—even the sense of a mission similar to that of a charismatic prophet. Moreover, the ongoing processes of intellectual and formal rationalization within each style, "program," and technique of the arts throw out new content and techniques that conflict with past styles and techniques.

The professional administrator, perhaps committed to a continuous, stable evolution and integration of arts, and to operation and maintenance of established institutions, inevitably must be seen, in the face of continuous demands for change, as the represser of innovation, the denier of creativity, and the tool of the establishment, even when his ideology is that of "managed social change." The administrator must favor the accepted styles of the past and those which appear to be immediately profitable or fundable.

It is usually argued that the audience decides, in the long run, what is great art and what art will survive. By and large, this is true: the most performed art is usually the best. But if this is true, new creations in the arts require sufficient opportunity to be seen and heard. If one argues that the classical art of the past is the best art and uses that argument to restrict the possibility of new and unfamiliar art to be performed sufficiently for audiences to make a long-term judgment of it, then relying on the tastes of audiences is the means by which the arts become moribund. New classics, new styles, and new themes will fail to emerge.

Perhaps it is the charismatic artists and impresarios, the great innovators in style, programmatic content, and technique, who—risking all in creating new styles, art forms, techniques, and even companies—assure audiences that new and revived older arts have the opportunity to be the object of audience judgment. The very act of innovation inevitably invites a high rate of failure; but the risk of failure is the only avenue by which continual creativity in the arts is assured. Certainly, playing for short-term success and to established audience tastes is a form of failure itself. It leads to stagnation. There are, of course, times when the public, critics, and the arts establishments seem to tire of innovation and creativity. Too many changes appear to emerge in too short a period of time; and many of these seem to be trivial, sensational, or vulgar exploitations of the idea that change in itself is valuable. In such periods, performers, critics and the public—and even creators—may return to the classics and to abandoned styles and standards of the past.

Yet the processes of intellectual rationalization in all its forms along with the processes of formal rationalization with their conflicts, dead-ends, interruptions, and counterprocesses, are inevitable. The periods of reaction eventually end, and the processes of rationalization reemerge, often with altered assumptions or with new themes, styles, or techniques. Intellectual and formal rationalizations in the arts are inevitable so long as the arts are the result of self-conscious study and reflection by their creators and performers.

But, to repeat, these processes do not have a final goal; there is no final solution to the dilemmas and conflicts within the arts. Nor are the outcomes of these processes, in the long run, predictable, with or without a theory of artistic rationalization.

———•—

A theory of the performing arts based on these processes of rationalization can help to clarify the past and to specify some of the factors present in the contemporary arts, and can pose problems for the study of the future of the arts. In the long run, if this Introduction suggests a scheme of analysis, it is only a formal scheme. Its value may emerge in the fruits derived from its application to the specific performing arts in their respective times and places. It is what artists do as creators and performers and what managers, benefactors, and the public do that gives empirical substance to these processes. The theorists can only record effects, and—at most—describe the general processes of change.

SECTION TWO

The Performing Arts as Occupations

Pundits may talk of a conductor's "authority," his "beat" and his "knowledge of scores," but actual control of an orchestra is most frequently founded on the less gaudy basis of economics. When an orchestra is aware that the conductor has in his inside pocket a contract for the next season and the one after that, carrying with it the power to rearrange the personnel "for the best interests of the orchestra"—in other words, to hire and fire—its attitude is apt to be somewhat more respectful than if he is merely an interloper to be tolerated for a brief guest engagement.

Levant, 1940: 5–6

Performing artists sometimes resent the intrusion of sociology into their province, particularly when they are defined as practicing occupations rather than callings. Sociologists, on the other hand, sometimes fail to recognize the extent to which this sense of commitment is not merely public relations, but rather a definition of self with very real consequences.

Occupational commitment tends to be extremely intense in the performing arts. In order to be a ballet dancer, not necessarily a soloist with a major company, but even a member of the corps of a third-rate company, you have to practice virtually every day. The practice sessions are vigorous and long. They tend to structure other hours of your life, influencing whom you socialize with, on what schedule, and under what circumstances. The pervasive nature of the dancer's work also influences such minute details as whether or not the dancer is allowed to tan on the beach in the summer. The extent of commitment necessary to perform this work on any level makes dancing, as well as other performing arts, interesting to a sociologist.

Not only is commitment intense, but, in most cases, begins early. Virtually every instrumental soloist began music lessons early. The same is true of ballet dancers. You must, in other words, develop commitment at a young age or at least must be pushed into it early (the wings are filled with "stage mothers"). In theater, however, you can begin training much later, making an interesting contrast for study.

Because of the intensity and early age of commitment as well as certain elements of occupational subculture such as the notion of virtuosity, the performing arts are unlike many other occupations. On the other hand, whatever else they are (a "calling," an "art," a "way of life"), they are also occupations and may be studied in the same way and with the same concepts as other occupations. This is especially clear when the performing artist is viewed by outsiders (whether they be sociologists or the lay public). Then performing appears not so much an art as a way of earning a living. This is strikingly illustrated by the following excerpt from Judith Adler's (1979:115–16) study of the California Institute of the Arts.

> Looking for models of supreme professional "dedication" and disturbed by apparent absences of discipline, the lay staff favoured those arts which demanded organized cooperation and formal scheduling and whose performance was highly visible. They praised the dedication of institute dancers, whose work, in addition to being physically demanding, was collective and imposed hours similar to those of the clerical staff. Classical musicianship found favor for similar reasons: the expertise it demanded was immediately apprehensible to laymen and publicly "displayed."

A crucial task for sociologists studying artistic occupations is to relate changes in art styles to the social organization of those occupations. For example, work settings are investigated to show how they promote and/or inhibit creativity and how they contribute to artistic interpretations. The influence of macro factors, e.g., economic factors, the social position of the artist, the marketplace for artistic services, is discussed in later sections.

The first problem in studying artistic occupations is to decide which sociological category of occupations they fit into. A second problem is to study role careers in the arts. A number of studies have focused on occupational socialization (Kadushin, 1969; Federico, 1974) and occupational careers (Faulkner, 1973). In all such studies, it is crucial to explore the dynamic between the public and moral aspects of a career (Goffman, 1961: 127–28). The public career involves the publicly accessible features and events of the career in a role, whereas the moral career involves changes in both self-image and the bases used to judge performance in a role. Seen in this way, a major function of formal and informal training is the development of a self-image in an occupation. This process involves, among other things, the inculcation of standards for judging success and failure. A third focus involves seeing artistic occupations as interaction, a tack recommended by the approach of symbolic interactionism (Becker, 1974; Blumer, 1962; Freidson, 1976).

Each of the chapters in this section exemplifies one of these analytic focuses. Jack Kamerman attempts to classify symphony conducting in terms of traditional sociological models of occupations. Symphony conducting is examined to clarify the limits of the professional model in studying the performing arts. Ronald Federico, writing on the decision of dancers to stop performing, studies the consequences for identity of ending an occupational career; he deals indirectly with the problem of failure. Because the level of commitment is so great, so deeply ingrained, and so pervasive, the ballet dancer represents an almost ideal case for studying the effects of occupational identity on self-image. Robert Faulkner focuses on how expertise and authority are worked out in the interaction of musicians and conductor, rather than being explicable solely in terms of static role prerogatives. His study reminds us that our perception of the quality of others' work is often, at base, a judgment of how well they allow us to be good at what we do. Finally, the interview with Veronica Castang addresses a career in an artistic occupation from an artist's point of view.

The studies in this section have clearly benefited from work done elsewhere in sociology, particularly in social psychology and the sociology of occupations. In turn, perhaps because of the peculiarities of artistic work, studies of artistic occupations make reciprocal contributions to the field of sociology.

References

Adler, Judith. 1979. *Artists in Offices: An Ethnography of an Academic Art Scene.* New Brunswick, N.J.: Transaction Books.

Becker, Howard S. 1974. "Art as Collective Action." *American Sociological Review*, 39:767–76.

Blumer, Herbert. 1962. "Society as Symbolic Interaction." In *Human Behavior and Social Processes: An Interactionist Approach*, ed. Arnold Rose. Boston: Houghton Mifflin, pp. 179–92.

Federico, Ronald. 1974. "Recruitment, Training, and Performance: The Case of Ballet." In *Varieties of Work Experience: The Social Control of Occupational Groups and Roles*, ed. Phyllis L. Stewart and Muriel Cantor. New York: John Wiley.

Faulkner, Robert. 1973. "Career Concerns and Mobility Motivations of Orchestra Musicians." *Sociological Quarterly*, 14:334–49.

Freidson, Eliot. 1976. "The Division of Labor as Social Interaction." *Social Problems*, 23:304–13.

Goffman, Erving. 1961. *Asylums: Essays on the Social Situation of Mental Patients and Other Inmates*. Garden City, N.Y.: Anchor.

Kadushin, Charles. 1969. "The Professional Self-Concept of Music Students." *American Journal of Sociology*, 75:389–404.

Levant, Oscar. 1940. *A Smattering of Ignorance*. New York: Doubleday, Doran.

1

Symphony Conducting as an Occupation

JACK KAMERMAN

There are many equally valid ways to study symphony conducting. From a musicological approach, one can study the functions of the conductor and the techniques of conducting as well as the histories of those functions and techniques. In this chapter, on the other hand, I will analyze symphony conducting sociologically as an occupation. I will focus on the present, although a study might be done of any period in the history of the occupation.

There is of course nothing intrinsically dissonant about the two approaches, the musicological and the sociological. In fact, I hope that a harmonious, if not quite mellifluous, consonance can be achieved between this analysis and the musicological literature on conducting.

The Occupation of Conducting as It Is Today

There are three dimensions in the definition of an occupation: *occupation as activities performed*; *occupation as incumbents*, the group of people who perform those activities and who identify themselves or are identified by others as members of that occupation; and *occupation as paid positions*. These three are intertwined.

To portray the occupation as it is today, I will first describe the positions available to conductors including some idea of what conductors earn. This will be used to estimate the number of incumbents in conducting. I will briefly consider their training and will then describe what conductors actually   43 do. The conductor's sources of authority will be discussed and, finally, a summary statement will be made on conducting as an occupation as it is today.

Conducting: The Occupation as Incumbents and Positions

It is difficult, if not impossible, to estimate the number of conductors in the world. Statistics that would be useful are simply not kept. This would also be true if we were to limit our focus to the United States. The closest we could come to any defensible number would be to limit ourselves to conductors who hold permanent positions with professional orchestras. This would exclude conductors who are retired or unemployed, conductors of amateur orchestras, and guest conductors with no permanent post, and would miscount conductors who hold positions with more than one orchestra.

With those qualifications made, I will attempt to make some rough calculation of the number of professional, or paid, conductors in the United States.

One approach to the problem is to first specify the number of professional orchestras in the United States. Professional orchestras are generally defined as those "where all musicians are union and are paid union scale, no matter how small an annual amount that may be."[1] There are 143 orchestras with annual budgets above $100,000. This is the line above which all orchestras are probably professional by this definition and below which few if any are professional by this definition. These orchestras are broken down into three categories: 89 orchestras with budgets of between $100,000 and $500,000, 23 with budgets between $500,000 and $1.5 million, and 31 with budgets over $1.5 million.

While some conductors hold positions with more than one of the above orchestras, this is probably not true in more than a few cases. The number 143, then, would be a slightly high but roughly accurate count of the number of full-time chief conductors of symphony orchestras currently working in the United States.

To this number might be added assistant conductors.[2] The number of assistant conductors ranges from one per orchestra for professional orchestras with budgets below $500,000 to four or five for orchestras with budgets above $1.5 million. That would bring the total to somewhere between approximately 246 and 418 conductors.[3] If we expand the range to include orchestras with budgets below $100,000 as well as college and youth orchestras, the number jumps by about 1,350 to 2,250. There is also a sizable number of would-be conductors. As Holm (1978) noted, "That there are far more would-be conductors than positions is attested to by the fact that the smallest opening advertised—let's say assistant conductor at $8,000 a year with a re-location requirement—would bring 200–300 applications."

However, because there is no licensing of conductors and anyone who owns a baton or even a pair of hands can claim to be a conductor, it seems wise to limit the number to those who hold full-time positions as conductors. That would mean that the number of full-time symphony conductors in the United States is somewhere under 500. In other words, the occupation has relatively few full-time practitioners.

The number is small by virtue of the nature of the conductor's work. For a conductor to work, he needs an orchestra. There are relatively few orchestras compared, for example, with schools, organizations which teachers need to carry on their work. In addition, there is only one chief conductor per orchestra and few, if any, assistant conductors.

Conductors are paid well for their services. "In large orchestras, the amounts are kept very confidential and are hard to come by. In orchestras from $500,000 to $1.5 million, salaries range from about $20,000 to over $40,000. In the major orchestras, it would be higher, soaring into astronomical figures for the stars."[4] In addition to salaries, conductors earn fees for guest appearances with other orchestras, recording fees, royalties, etc. Even in orchestras with budgets below $100,000 conductors' earnings are impressive. They are as high as $1,500 per concert for each of three concerts in the season of an orchestra with a *total* annual budget of just over $30,000 (American Symphony Orchestra League, 1977:2).

Conductors, until thirty or forty years ago, were often instrumentalists who became conductors through apprenticeships to established conductors. They learned by working at it. Today, the process has become more "professionalized." Conservatories offer majors in conducting, and formal training usually precedes entry into an apprenticeship. In addition to conservatory training, some famous conductors hold summer master classes. There are also orchestral summer workshops, which provide a budding conductor with an opportunity for practice and training. There are competitions that conducting students may enter to win recognition and, in some cases, positions as assistant conductors with major orchestras. The New York Philharmonic, for example, selected many of its assistant conductors from among winners of the Dimitri Mitropolous Competition for Conductors (Rubin, 1974:44).

The Occupation as Activities: What Conductors Do

A conductor's activities are divided into those done preparatory to rehearsals, those done at rehearsals preparatory to performance, those done at performance, and those that lie outside these three areas.

Before rehearsal, a conductor must prepare the scores he will work on at rehearsal. This involves studying the score and in some cases making minor or major revisions. As Eugene Ormandy (1965:252), conductor of the Philadelphia Orchestra, tactfully put it, "When conducting older composers he must sometimes compensate for the technical inadequacies of the times by delicately rewriting certain passages in terms of today's more complete orchestras and more highly skilled players."

This study and rewriting are part of the process of *interpretation*, which is at the heart of a conductor's work as a performer. The English conductor Sir Henry Wood (1945:57) wrote, "It is the conductor's duty—his first and last duty—to see to it that the composer's score is fully carried out." Interpretation may be carried to a point of replacing a composer's indications in a score with the conductor's understanding of what a composer "really" meant to say. The subject of interpretation will be discussed in more detail later in this section. It will suffice to say here that scores, particularly the further back in time we go, do not provide performers with indisputable directions for performance. To one degree or another, all scores must be interpreted.

At rehearsals, the conductor attempts to get the orchestra to perform the interpretation he has made of a score. This may first involve arranging the seating plan of the orchestra to achieve the proper sound for the particular score being rehearsed. It may also involve changing the total number and proportion of instruments needed to effect his interpretation.

In addition, conductors explain to orchestra members exactly how they want certain passages played. They listen as players run through passages and pick out errors in playing. These errors may relate to tempi (the speed at which music is played), dynamics (the loudness or softness of the playing), intonation (whether notes are played on or off pitch), ensemble (instruments playing in unison), and other technical matters.

Conductors use several techniques to express their intentions to the orchestra. Verbal explanations are appropriate during rehearsals, but would be disruptive during a performance. Conductors use silent signals during performance to convey their wishes to the orchestra. These are given with the baton (held in the right hand), the left hand, the eyes (Culshaw, 1978:19–21), facial expressions, and body movements. Baton technique, at least, has become fairly standarized and is part of the formal training of all conductors. It is by far the major manner in which conductors direct the playing of an orchestra.

Mastering the technique of expressing intentions is only one of the requisites of good conducting. Another is getting the orchestra to carry the conductor's intentions out. This involves personal as well as organizational authority and is treated in greater detail in the next section.[5]

During a performance, the conductor uses the aforementioned silent techniques to remind players of the details worked out during rehearsals. The major part of the technical work is done during rehearsals. At the actual performance, the conductor is still important, because he makes sure the work done in rehearsal is not lost, and helps to generate the excitement that often characterizes performances. The conductor Charles Munch (1955:69) described this process:

> What is expected of the conductor during the concert? In principle he has a very simple role to play. He has carefully prepared everything in the most minute detail. He has done his work and is only a figurehead now. But it is not a useless tradition that keeps the chief at the head of his troops during the battle.
>
> In our day, an orchestra without a conductor is inconceivable. Our orchestras often consist of more than a hundred men whose actions must be integrated and co-ordinated, especially as new music becomes more and more complex.
>
> And the conductor must be there to instill in them the emotion that the music arouses in him.

Conductors sometimes change their directions during a performance from the "plan" worked out during rehearsal. This is usually one of the major crimes a conductor can commit from the point of view of orchestra members because unpredictability prevents players from successfully performing their roles.[6]

The fourth area of a conductor's activities covers those having nothing to do directly with rehearsals or performance. This includes planning programs, selecting guest soloists, engaging in public relations activities, and participating in hiring, firing, promoting, and other personnel decisions. These last powers have been curtailed through unionization. This is discussed more fully in the next section of this chapter on the sources of authority of the conductor.

To some extent these activities are as important as the actual competence of a conductor in achieving results with the orchestra. Programming, for example, may affect the size of audiences and subscription lists. These commercial considerations are likely to determine whether or not a conductor keeps his job.[7]

The previous two sections of this chapter have provided a brief description of the occupation of conductor as it exists today. It will now be possible, in the following two sections, to turn to some analytic features of conducting as an occupation.

Sources of a Conductor's Authority

In the current stratification of musical performers, conductors are almost always found at the top. The third-rate conductor of a minor orchestra sharing the stage with a celebrated instrumentalist or singer might seem an exception. Even in this extreme case, however, the authority that inheres in the conductor's office would lend legitimacy to his interpretive demands.

This is so because the conductor is the nominal director of a musical performance. Conductors are the final authority on stylistic matters and textual disputes that arise in attempting to discern a composer's wishes through interpretation of a score. Conductors are musical scholars who study scores, decide on their proper meaning, and translate that meaning into the performance of an orchestra and soloists.

Some of the authority exercised by conductors over members of an orchestra is charismatic. Weber (1968:3:114) held that the charismatic figure

> gains and retains it [charismatic authority] solely by proving his powers in practice. He must work miracles, if he wants to be a prophet. He must perform heroic deeds, if he wants to be a warlord. Most of all, his divine mission must prove itself by *bringing well-being* to his faithful followers; if they do not fare well, he obviously is not the god-sent master.

Compare Weber's words with the following descriptions of the conductor Arturo Toscanini:

> It was in [Richard Strauss's] *Don Quixote*— in the windmill variation. There are conductors who happen to know there is a mistake in a part at a certain point, and who stop at that point and tell the player: "You played this note, which should have been that one." But Maestro actually heard: with the *fortissimo* going in that windmill variation he stopped the orchestra and said to the second bassoon, "Weren't you playing B-flat?" "Yes, Maestro." "It's B-natural." I was sitting only three or four feet from this player, and I didn't hear it; and I don't think anyone else did. Only Toscanini did; and when a man shows this kind of perceptiveness you are drawn closer to him. [Wallenstein, 1967:178.]

> At one time, while rehearsing a Vivaldi concerto, he stopped the orchestra and turned abruptly to the first violin section. "Can't you see that those four notes are marked *staccato?*" he cried out. The concertmaster discreetly brought his music to the maestro and, pointing to the notes, showed him that there were no *staccato* notes in the passage. "But that's impossible!" Toscanini exclaimed. "It simply must be *staccato!*" An orchestral score was brought from the library, and after consultation it was found that this, too, did not have the debated *staccato* notes. "I can't understand it," Toscanini whined, almost to himself. "Those notes simply must be *staccato*. It can't be otherwise." It was quite true that Toscanini had not consulted the score for nearly ten years. But was it possible that his memory was beginning to play pranks? The following day, Toscanini triumphantly brought a different score of the Vivaldi Concerto, published some fifty years earlier than the one used in the previous rehearsal, and considered much more authoritative. "You see?" he exclaimed glowingly. "Didn't I tell you that those notes had

to be played *staccato?*" Toscanini had been right; the score published earlier had the questionable notes marked *staccato*. [Ewen, 1936:179–80.][8]

> But I would say the greatest experience, *playing* with a conductor, was with Toscanini. There was something that electrified you to a point where you had the feeling that you played better than you can play. I know that at *any concert* with him—maybe even a concert that did not sound so well outside—the players themselves on the stage, most of them, gave everything; and you came out saying "Ah!" You were proud of the way you played when you played with him; because you could not do anything but give your best: you always were enticed to give your best . . . you had only to look at his face: he was so inspired, that he had to inspire *you*. [Galimir, 1967:195.][9]

Whether these stories are true or apocryphal, the point is the same. These are tales of heroic exploits, a folklore of charisma.

From the other side, the orchestra's point of view, come tales of their ability to discern a conductor's charismatic mettle. The horn player, Franz Strauss, claimed, "When a new man faces the orchestra—from the way he walks up the steps to the podium and opens his score—before he even picks up his baton—we know whether he is the master or we" (Schonberg, 1967:15). Orchestra musicians frequently talk about testing a new conductor by intentionally playing wrong notes to see if he can spot the mistakes. As Faulkner (1973:151) remarks in his study of communication between conductor and orchestra, "At other times players witness a transformation of rehearsals into muted character contests in which musicians test the conductor's ear as well as his integrity and presented self."

In a certain sense these tests are solely for the benefit of the musicians themselves since, if successful, conductors would be unaware of either the test or its results. In addition, if the musicians either, to save face, perform well during the actual concert or make the same mistake—which is presumably so subtle that, if a conductor would fail to pick it up, so would an audience—then the joke has the subservient in-group quality of slaves playing games on masters. The imbalance of power isn't changed by the test. In other words, charismatic authority is not the only kind of authority conductors exercise.[10]

In addition to charismatic authority, conductors exercise legal authority. They have traditionally had the ability to hire and fire personnel, and promote or demote players within the orchestra. The former powers have been curtailed with the unionization of musicians during the course of this century. As Harold Schonberg wrote (1978:D19), "Gone are the days when a music director could hire and fire players at will, thanks to union protection and self-governing player committees."

Conductors still retain some degree of legal authority from their remaining powers in personnel decisions. Their reputation with audiences and its con sequent drawing power as well as their ability to bring in recording contracts and other sources of income to an orchestra are also sources of authority lying outside the charismatic domination of the musicians in an orchestra.[11]

In sum, the conductor has always had a mixture of charismatic and legal authority. As the nature of the work changed, so did the proportions of the two kinds of authority. It is also true that the office itself has come to be seen as charismatic, as the folklore of conducting and orchestra playing and the expectations of audiences reveal. But the conductor, for all his celebrity, is still basically the employee of a business enterprise, the symphony orchestra. As such, he is subject to the control of symphony boards of directors, audiences, and critics. This control as well as other features of conducting as an occupation will be treated next.

Features of Conducting as an Occupation

Most sociological studies of occupational development have dealt with professions. Professions, according to Freidson (1970:72), are occupations that have been "*deliberately* granted autonomy, including the exclusive right to determine who can legitimately do its work and how the work should be done." While the work of all occupations is evaluated to some degree by outsiders, "only the profession has the recognized right to declare such an 'outside' evaluation illegitimate and intolerable." Other occupations "like circus jugglers and magicians, possess a de facto autonomy by virtue of the esoteric or isolated character of their work. . ." but have no *recognized right* to declare outside evaluation "illegitimate and intolerable," their private feelings and public expressions notwithstanding. (Freidson, 1970:71.)[12]

Symphony conducting, by this or for that matter by any current sociological conceptualization of profession, cannot be considered a profession. Outside evaluation is the very basis of a performer's employment. That evaluation is done by audiences, critics, employers, and managers. Further, in spite of the wishes of some critics and audiences, no one in the past went to jail for conducting without a license, nor is anyone likely to go to jail in the future, because conductors have never been able to persuade anyone that the licensing of their craft is crucial to the welfare of society in general or any power group in particular. Nor, for that matter, have they attempted such persuasion.

While it appears that conductors command an esoteric theory and technique, audiences tend to honor conductors' claims to expertise for the wrong reasons. Audiences tend to think that the major part of a conductor's work is done during the concert when in fact a major task of the conductor, musically at any rate, is to remind musicians of the understandings reached during the real work sessions, rehearsals. Yet the conductor is judged by the audience on the basis of the performance, aurally, by the way the orchestra sounds, and visually, by the way the conductor looks as he conducts. This becomes the basis for the podium histrionics of certain conductors.[13] They have to display their abilities as performers in some way to an audience that may have little understanding of what a conductor actually does.[14]

Early in the career of modern conducting it was felt that any musician could conduct. As the specialty of conducting became more firmly established, it was felt that special training in the form of study and apprenticeship was necessary. Today music conservatories have degree programs in conducting. Yet throughout the history of modern conducting, people slipped into conducting from orchestral playing, solo instrumental playing, and even, in some cases, singing, composing, and the like. Entrance into conducting has always been a matter of opportunity rather than subject to formal regulation. In that sense conducting was not *formally granted* a monopoly over its services; what control it had initially was hard won and now it resembles more a monopoly by default than one established with government aid.

Conductors have always been subject to the whims of their employers by the very nature of their work. In order for a conductor to work, he needs an orchestra. Providing an orchestra is expensive beyond the means of all but a rare few conductors.[15] Conducting is a strange mixture of conductorial authority over an orchestra and a symphony board's directorial authority over a conductor. So in this sense, conductors are granted control over certain matters, sometimes programming,[16] always interpretation and technical decisions, and it is legitimate to study the circumstances of the granting of that control. It should always be remembered, however, that this granting is organizationally specific, i.e., individuals are granted control over particular orchestras rather than a whole profession being granted a formal monopoly over conducting in general.

Furthermore, even this control is over technical and interpretative matters and not over the terms and conditions of work. In addition, what little control conductors, with the backing of symphony boards, had over the terms and conditions of their work (and of the work of the musicians under them) has been severely curtailed in this century by unionization. For example, unionization limited the conductor's ability to hire and fire musicians on whim and limited the amount of rehearsal time a conductor could demand.

Most sociological models of occupational development, particularly of the professions, grant a key role to occupational associations in consolidating an occupation's position. However, conductors have never formed associations and their membership in the American musicians' unions in this country is more the result of union pressure than of conductor interest. Unions compelled conductors to join by threatening to deny them access to work if they did not. Consequently, sociological models that include the activities of occupational associations as a necessary condition of occupational development must be changed or ignored when applied to conductors.

Conducting is an occupation that resists organization into associations for several reasons. Compared with the total number of musicians in symphony-related organizations, there are few conductors. Conductors are, in the common sense of the term, leaders, and organizations of leaders are hardly the rule, particularly in the arts. Conductors, especially after the romantic period in music (the middle to late nineteenth century) were defined by audiences and critics as individualists, more like instrumental or vocal soloists than like symphony musicians or chorus members. More importantly, they have always had direct dealings with patrons and, later, with the upper echelons of the organizations that employ conductors, whereas the contact of orchestral musicians with employers has always been mediated through conductors or, later, through unions.

The individual drawing power of a conductor, his celebrity, is the source of his power. He has nothing to gain by forming an association and bargaining collectively. In fact, by pointing to his similarities with other conductors, one of the major functions of membership in associations, he has everything to lose.

To summarize this analysis of conducting today, I have argued that:

1. The sources of authority of a conductor are both charismatic and legal/rational and the proportion of the two has changed with unionization and other developments.
2. Conducting is not a profession by current sociological definition because its work is subject to almost exclusively outside evaluation.
3. A major part of its work is done "backstage"; its audience has little understanding of what goes on there, and consequently, conductors have a need to display their skills "onstage."
4. Training has become formalized to an extent with the advent of conservatory training programs in conducting, but, as with other crafts, apprenticeship remains a major training experience.
5. No occupational associations have been formed because conductors would have little to gain and much to lose by banding together; in that sense, conducting is an *individual* rather than a *collective* occupation, yet an occupation nevertheless.[17]

To reiterate, conducting is not a profession, nor does it have an occupational association. Some of the authority it exercises is charismatic. For all these reasons, it is different from most occupations sociologists have chosen to study. This makes it particularly interesting for sociologists to examine.

Notes

1. This definition, and the statistics that follow in the paragraphs on the number of professional orchestras and the number of paid conductors and their salaries, come from Holm (1978), unless otherwise noted.

The American Federation of Musicians (n.d.: Art. 22 sec. 1) defines a symphony orchestra as follows:

> The term "symphony orchestra" as used in this Article means and includes any orchestra organized as a philanthropic community project and maintained in substantial part by public subscriptions and contributions and being a full orchestra with a substantially permanent conductor and not less than sixty (60) players under personal service contracts for the season, and with a scheduled annual season of not less than fifteen (15) concerts of the character performed by symphony orchestras.

2. Excluded from this new total would be conductors of opera orchestras, musical show orchestras, ballet orchestras, pops orchestras, etc., who sometimes conduct symphony orchestras. A more serious, though very much smaller, exclusion would be guest conductors who hold no permanent position with any symphony orchestra.

3. If every professional orchestra had one assistant conductor, the total of chief and assistant conductors would be about 246. If a calculation were made using 1 assistant conductor for orchestras with budgets between $100,000 and $500,000, 2 for orchestras between $500,000 and $1.5 million, and 4.5 for orchestras above $1.5 million, the total would be about 418.

4. One estimate is as much as $150,000 per year (Rubin, 1974:42). In 1964, Alan Rich (1964:103) wrote that "the 'top four' [in the United States] (Boston, New York Philharmonic, Philadelphia and Chicago) pay from $75,000 to $100,000 a year."

5. One writer has even likened this aspect of a conductor's job to training porpoises because both involve operant conditioning.

> Reinforcing his musicians one step at a time, the conductor shapes the orchestra toward that elusive perfect performance of his dreams just as foot by foot I shape a porpoise toward a 20-foot leap hardly imaginable from its first small bounce out of the water [Pryor, 1977:64].

6. For a sampling of the views of orchestra members on the subject, see Faulkner (1973:154–55).

7. For example, Pierre Boulez, former conductor of the New York Philharmonic, was frequently criticized for the preponderance of contemporary works included in his programs. Among some musicians, this earned him the title of "The Twentieth Century Limited" (Rubin, 1973:32).

8. "*Staccato*" is "The shortened performance of a note (or group of notes) so that it sounds only for a moment, the major part of its written value being replaced by a rest" (Apel and Daniel, 1961:283).

9. Of the conductor Anton Seidl, the singers Jean and Edouard de Reszke (1899:259) wrote: ". . .when it came to the performance the artists had only to look

at his authoritative glance and the inspiring beat to gain absolute confidence, and feel that they would be ably steered through any difficulties that might arise." For an analysis of the shift from a charismatic to a noncharismatic conductor, see Arian (1971:13–50).

10. There are, of course, extreme cases when conductors lose their control of orchestras entirely. However, even extreme cases are, underneath, a mixture of sources of authority. The Dutch conductor Willem Mengelberg's loss of control over the New York Philharmonic in the late 1920s represents in part his charismatic delegitimation as the charisma of Arturo Toscanini, the conductor with whom he shared the Philharmonic, began to prevail. In part, it also represented the orchestra's prediction of Toscanini's eventual appointment as sole conductor. For an account of Mengelberg's fall, see Sargeant (1949:92–99).

11. A difficulty with some of Faulkner's analysis lies in his failure to specify the extent to which his data are time-bound. For example, "Communications and conductors are accepted ·to the extent they help members achieve their purposes" (1973:156). This is certainly truer after unionization than before.

12. Creative artists and performers, at least since the nineteenth century, have reputedly regarded their audiences and critics with disdain. Brahms once noted wryly that no statue had ever been erected to honor a critic. Becker (1963:85–91) makes a similar point about the disdain of dance musicians toward their audiences.

13. The famous nineteenth-century Wagnerian conductor Anton Seidl (1899:227) suggested that great conductors remained relatively inconspicuous during performances, while "time-beaters. . . wave wildly with their hands and stamp loudly with their feet, yet they accomplish little or nothing." Adorno (1976:105) also spoke of the difference between the work of the conductor in relation to the orchestra and the work of the conductor in relation to the audience. "Impressed by his medicine-man gestures, the listener thinks it takes just such as attitude to make players give their artistic best—a best that will be taken for something like the setting of a physical record. But the quality of the performance, the aspect of conducting faced by the orchestra, is largely separate from the one that beguiles the audience. Relative to the audience a conductor has, a priori, a propagandistic and demagogical touch. One is reminded of the old joke about the lady at a concert who asks the expert in the next seat to please let her know as soon as Nikisch starts spellbinding."

14. The conductor Zubin Mehta was once asked by a concertgoer whether he ever met with the orchestra *before* a concert. (Rubin, 1974:34.)

Goode (1961:313) points out that in most professions the client does not see what goes on backstage, but believes that "there *is* a backstage, that, in fact, complex intellectual activities go on when he is not there." Lawyers, among other professions, explicitly detail their backstage activities for clients in order to justify their fees. A lawyer may never in a sense go onstage if a case is settled out of court. In addition, most people have either been to a lawyer or know someone who has. This explains Goode's observation. Conductors, however, perform onstage and relatively few people have attended rehearsals. This explains my observation that conductors need to display their abilities as performers in some visible, understandable way.

15. In this century, Serge Koussevitsky was provided with an orchestra by his wealthy

wife and Sir Thomas Beecham by his inherited fortune. These are clearly exceptional cases.

16. However, even programming decisions are influenced by the tastes of audiences, critics, and symphony boards.

17. I do not of course mean that the occupation has no social organization. It is collective in that sense. I mean rather that whatever norms and values conductors share, they do not form associations.

References

Adorno, Theodor W. 1976. *Introduction to the Sociology of Music*, trans. E.B. Ashton. New York: Seabury Press.

American Federation of Musicians of the United States and Canada. 1977, *Constitution*. New York: American Federation of Musicians.

American Symphony Orchestra League, n.d. "Conductors' and Managers' Salaries: Urban/Community Symphony Orchestras, 1976–1977." Mimeographed. Vienna, Va.: American Symphony Orchestra League.

Apel, Willi, and Ralph J. Daniel. 1961. *The Harvard Brief Dictionary of Music*. New York: Washington Square Press.

Arian, Edward. 1971. *Bach, Beethoven, and Bureaucracy: The Case of the Philadelphia Orchestra*. University, Ala.: Univ. of Alabama Press.

Becker, Howard S. 1963. *Outsiders: Studies in the Sociology of Deviance*. New York: Free Press.

Culshaw, John. 1978. "Eyes." *High Fidelity*, August, pp. 19–21.

de Reszke, Jean, and Edouard de Reszke. 1899. "Tribute by Jean and Edouard de Reszke." In *Anton Seidl: A Memorial by His Friends*, ed. Henry J. Finck. New York: Charles Scribner's Sons, pp. 258–59.

Ewen, David. 1936. *The Man with the Baton: The Story of Conductors and Their Orchestras*. New York: Thomas Y. Crowell.

Faulkner, Robert. 1973. "Orchestra Interaction: Some Features of Communication in an Artistic Community." *Sociological Quarterly*, 14:147–57.

Freidson, Eliot. 1970. *Profession of Medicine: A Study of the Sociology of Applied Knowledge*. New York: Dodd, Mead.

Galimir, Felix. 1967. "Statement by Felix Galimir." *The Toscanini Musicians Knew*, ed. B. H. Haggin. New York: Horizon, pp. 191–201.

Goode, William J. 1961. "The Librarian: From Occupation to Profession?" *Library Quarterly*, 31:306–20.

Holm, Patricia (Director, Statistical Department, American Symphony Orchestra League). 1978. Personal communication to Jack Kamerman, 29 September.

Munch, Charles. 1955. *I Am a Conductor*, trans. Leonard Burkat. New York: Oxford Univ. Press.

Ormandy, Eugene. 1965. "Art of Conducting." In *The Conductor's Art*, ed. Carl Bamberger. New York: McGraw–Hill, pp. 251–56.

Pryor, Karen. 1977. "Orchestra Conductors Would Make Good Porpoise Trainers." *Psychology Today*, February, pp. 61–64.

Rich, Alan. 1964. *Careers and Opportunities in Music*. New York: E. P. Dutton.

Rubin, Stephen R. 1973. "The Iceberg Conducteth." *New York Times*, March 25, sec. 6, p. 32.

1974 "What Is a Maestro?" *New York Times*, September 29, sec. 6, p. 32.

Sargeant, Winthrop. 1949. *Geniuses, Goddesses and People*. New York: E. P. Dutton.

Schonberg, Harold C. 1967. *The Great Conductors*. New York: Simon & Schuster.

1978 "Why Conductors Are Treated Like Gods." *New York Times*, May 7, sec. 2, pp. D1, D19.

Seidl, Anton. 1899. "On Conducting." In *Anton Seidl: A Memorial by His Friends*, ed. Henry J. Finck. New York: Charles Scribner's Sons, pp. 215–40.

Sennet, Richard. 1975. "Charismatic De-Legitimation: A Case Study." *Theory and Society*, 2:171–81.

Wallenstein, Alfred. 1967. "Statement of Alfred Wallenstein." In *The Toscanini Musicians Knew*, ed. B. H. Haggin. New York: Horizon Press, pp. 175–85.

Weber, Max. 1968. *Economy and Society: An Outline of Interpretive Sociology*, ed. Guenther Roth and Claus Wittich, trans. Ephraim Fischoff et al. 3 vols. New York: Bedminster Press.

Wood, Sir Henry. 1945. *About Conducting*. London: Sylvan Press.

2

The Decision To End A Performing Career in Ballet

RONALD FEDERICO

Introduction

Ballet, like most artistic occupations, has received little sociological study. The major empirical study of the occupation (Federico, 1968, 1974; Sutherland, 1976) focused on recruitment, training, and early career experiences. This chapter attempts to extend earlier study by examining in a preliminary way later career experiences, focusing on the decision to stop performing. Since ballet is a performing art, dancers first aspire to success as a performer (Mazo, 1974:39) and most of their occupational socialization is performance oriented (DeMille, 1962). However, with few exceptions, ballet dancers have relatively short performing careers, which begin and end at an early age (Krause, 1971:265–66; Mazo, 1974:96; Federico, 1974:258). If the dancer is to have a career in ballet that spans the normal working years, s/he must be prepared to move from performing to non-performing dance activities. As will be seen, this shift in career is generally traumatic for the dancer, and is badly articulated with occupational socialization and other career structures.

Methodology

This research builds on data obtained in an earlier study of 146 professional performing ballet dancers (Federico, 1968). The dancers interviewed at that time were generally unable or unwilling to discuss the reality that they would sooner or later have to face the decison to stop performing. They would only 57 discuss their career socialization and their then active dancing careers. The primary data upon which this paper is based are from two personally conducted interviews with a well-known ballet dancer, four published interviews with individual dancers, and a published study of a ballet company that includes numerous excerpts from interviews with individual dancers. The personally interviewed dancer had been retired from performing for about a year at the time of the interviews. Of the published interviews, three were with dancers who were no longer performing, and one was with a dancer soon to retire. All of the interview excerpts from the study of the ballet company are from dancers then actively performing.

These data are obviously qualitative in nature, but they represent the best available data in an occupational area traditionally ignored by sociologists. Naturally this research has also drawn upon sociological and other appropriate sources to supplement and interpret the limited interview data. These include data about ballet from general sources, data about other artistic occupations, data about occupations that share certain characteristics with ballet, such as professional athletics, and the sociological literature on occupations.

Making the Decision Not To Perform

The decision not to perform becomes a very personal one, given the lack of occupational criteria for a dancer to use. A well-known dancer close to retirement from performing has spoken about her shifting perspective on retirement (Fonteyn, 1976), and a critic, even though noting that there are no criteria for a dancer to use, disagreed with one dancer's decision to stop performing at the time it was made (Barnes, 1973). Still another well-known dancer, in an unpublished interview, lamented that stars have great difficulty getting feedback that they can trust, and that it is epecially difficult for people to tell a star that s/he ought to stop performing. Yet the decision has to be made sooner or later, and there appear to be four major factors that affect it: (1) inability to attain one's personal artistic standards in performance; (2) inability to attain one's personal artistic standards because of roles available; (3) dissatisfaction with the performing life-style; and (4) the availability of alternatives to performing.

1. Inability To Attain One's Personal Artistic Standards in Performance

Each dancer has some personal concept of what his or her dancing should be like. This self-concept is made up of two parts: mastery of the physical dance technique of ballet, and the use of that technique to be expressive. Because ballet dancers almost never perform as solo artists, being employed instead in ballet companies, the technical and artistic preferences of the company's director(s) become significant determinants of each dancer's own vision (Mazo, 1974). Dancers, like musicians, must satisfy the standards of others in order to get and keep employment (Faulkner, 1974). As with all artists, dancers rely on the cooperation and support of many other people both inside and outside of the ballet world, and they can rarely afford to be totally independent artistically (Becker, 1974).

Nevertheless, the dancer must at some level satisfy his or her own artistic standards for performance to continue. There are several reasons why these standards may become unattainable and therefore the decision may be made to stop performing. One is the ever-present threat of physical injury. Ballet technique is extremely demanding physically, and the exigencies of the performing life frequently lead to injury that may force the dancer to retire temporarily or permanently (Mazo, 1974; Tobias, 1976).

A second reason that standards become unattainable is the physical decline that accompanies the aging process. It inevitably begins to affect anyone who relies on activity requiring youthful appearance, physical stamina, strength, and flexibility. Sooner or later, and it varies considerably from person to person, the body gives out. In general, this happens to male dancers earlier than female dancers because of the different nature of the physical demands placed on men and women in ballet. As one dancer expressed it, " . . . I had a vision of how I would like to dance. In Washington [where he gave his last performance], I didn't lose my vision. But my body would no longer respond." (Kisselgoff, 1972.) Others may feel that the dancer can still attain artistic excellence in spite of physical decline: "There are actual gains in artistry as the artist grows older, capable of overriding all other considerations." (Barnes, 1973.) But the final decision must always be the dancer's.

A third reason for artistic standards becoming unattainable is the artist's desire for alternate forms of artistic expression. It is well known that human development continues throughout the life cycle (Kalish, 1975:1), and this may include the desire for changed personal goals that require different occupational opportunities. "A vocational self-concept is a part of the global self-concept. It is the self-concept which guides the individual into and through his career experience. . . . The series of jobs a person holds represents a life-long search for a means of expressing himself in the world of work." (Zaccaria, 1970:53.) Especially in light of the artistic and personal constraints placed on a performing artist just noted, the dancer may decide that his or her personal artistic goals can best be attained in various nondancing activities. These may still be within ballet (teaching, choreography, directing, coaching, and so forth), or they may be attained outside of ballet (such as writing, acting, parenting, opening a shop).

2. Inability To Attain One's Personal Artistic Standards Because of Roles Available

Most ballet companies are divided, either formally or informally, into three strata. The lowest, the corps de ballet, is the largest and the one at which most dancers enter a company. The corps provides the backdrop for soloists and principal dancers, and corps dancing usually requires accuracy and uniformity rather than uniqueness and individual artistic expression. The middle rank is the soloist category, comprised of dancers who have roles that permit them to dance alone or in small groups. Soloists have considerably more freedom of expression than corps dancers, and their roles encourage the development of an artistic expressiveness and technical style unique to each dancer. Principal dancers are at the top of the role hierarchy. These are the "stars," the artists who dance the most demanding roles, which allow the greatest range of interpretation and communication with the audience.

Roles, then, affect the attainment of one's personal artistic standards in two ways. The first is the roles to which a dancer has access. A corps de ballet dancer has very little opportunity to express himself or herself because corps roles by definition do not encourage such expression. The corps dancers are usually young and willing to sacrifice artistic expression for performing experience and the opportunity to gain assurance and strength in their command of ballet technique. However, they aspire to eventually move up to soloist and, hopefully, principal roles where they will be able to develop artistic maturity. For most dancers, this never happens.

> Dancers generally join the company between the ages of sixteen and eighteen . . . . As a rule, . . . dancers start young and finish young—their average working life is ten years . . . . for most, at twenty-six or twenty-eight, or at the outside, thirty, it's all over. A performer who has not been promoted out of the corps by then never will be, and promotions are infrequent. [Mazo, 1974:96.]

Many dancers, then, are faced with the realization that they will never graduate to roles that allow artistic expression, and gradually lose interest in performing as a result. In a performing art, desirable roles represent success. When a dancer accepts the fact that they will never be attained, it is symptomatic of personal failure as well as lack of opportunity to mature artistically (Federico, 1968).

The second way in which roles affect the attainment of personal artistic standards lies in the nature of the roles themselves. Even those who are fortunate enough to obtain principal roles may find them insufficient for the attainment of personal artistic standards. Dancers frequently express the importance of roles being created for them in order to capitalize on their technical and artistic strengths (Fonteyn, 1976; Mazo, 1974). However, many of the most important standard classical roles, especially for men, are limited in emotional scope and heavily dependent on a youthful appearance. In unpublished interviews, a well-known retired male dancer talked at some length about this problem. He felt that many roles require that the dancer work "within the mind of a young man." This, combined with the youthful appearance and strength required to properly dance such roles, make them at once artistically uninteresting to the more mature male dancer and increasingly difficult and incongruous physically. He felt that older women, for whom the physical strength needed is different from that needed by the male dancer, could create the youthful illusion more successfully, although it remains to be seen how artistically rewarding dancing the role of a young woman is to a female dancer of greater years and artistic maturity. At any rate, when even the best roles no longer hold opportunities for artistic growth and integrity, the dancer may decide that performing is no longer possible within his or her own artistic standards and goals.

3. Dissatisfaction with the Performing Life-Style

Performing ballet dancers lead an extremely rigorous life. Rarely can a day go by without a technique class to continually refine the classical steps that the dancer uses in performance (DeMille, 1962:113–14). This is usually followed by rehearsals for several hours, also demanding of the dancer's physical energy and concentration, followed at night by the intensive, exhausting hours of performance. It can be a very closed world.

> In the company, as in the army, you don't have to think. People tell you what to wear, and where to go and what time to show up. . . . So all a dancer really has to do is dance, try for roles and aim at advancement inside the company. When you are seventeen, there is no outside. The important thing is to dance. [Mazo, 1974:100.]

The problem is that one doesn't stay seventeen forever, and, as noted above, perspectives and life goals shift. While at one point dancing may be enough, at another point one may yearn for a less restricted existence, and that may be incompatible with performing.

One ballerina who stopped dancing for a year expressed the problem and her solution in the following way:

> I loved my fans and all the people in the ballet and just suddenly it became too much in my life. I couldn't handle it all. [Draegin, 1976:42.]

> The dancing was engulfing me to the point where I really ceased to enjoy it. Once I came to this realization, I knew I had to stop completely . . . . I just lived a normal life, which I need very much . . . I enjoy a nice home, and friends, and I suddenly found myself with time for such things . . . .I met people who had nothing to do with the dance world—this was really a new experience for me. . . . my own attitude [now] is, I go in, I do my job and I leave. [Kriegsman, 1976:E-1 ff.]

The latter dancer had the star power to be able to negotiate a performing life on her own terms—few have that power (Peters, 1974:46). Most dancers are still struggling for recognition and better roles. In an overcrowded profession, they are in no position to negotiate such a happy compromise as the above dancer achieved. For most dancers, then, when the demands of constant physical struggle, living up to one's own and the audience's technical and artistic demands, and the narrowness of the performing dancer's world become too much, the only viable alternative is to stop performing.

The above discussion may help to explain why so many dancers stop performing by the age of thirty (of the sample sudied in 1966–67, 87 percent were twenty-nine years old or younger) (Federico, 1974:258). Clearly, dancers do not retire because they have reached an age where performing is no longer feasible. There are self-identified reasons that stop them. Injury is no doubt a major cause. However, the effects of artistic values and changing life-style preferences suggested here are probably the most significant. If this is true, one would expect that a significant intervening variable might be friendships and love relationships that either reinforce or weaken occupational commitments. The Mazo and Kriegsman references would tentatively support this argument. My earlier research showed a dichotomy between dancers whose friendships and love relationships were either within or outside of the dance world. This factor as it relates to the decision to stop performing would be a fruitful area for future research.

4. The Availability of Alternatives to Performing

Ballet dancing is both a job and a dedication. Although ballet dancers support themselves through their dancing, when things are going well they would almost pay to perform. When things are not going well, however, dancing may become primarily a means of financial support (Mazo, 1974). The decision to stop performing, then, becomes an economic decision, as well as one with deep emotional meaning to dancers who have usually spent most of their lives preparing themselves to dance (Federico, 1968). The economic and emotional aspects of the decision are both eased if there is either a dance-related or a performing-related alternative readily available—directing a ballet company, or acting, for example. When such alternatives are available, it may be considerably easier for the dancer to decide to stop performing as a dancer.

Nondance and nonperforming alternatives tend to be much less attractive to dancers. As one dancer said in an interview, learning to dance is like building a statue that one gets increasingly reluctant to "break" by stopping dancing (Federico, 1968). Another, also in an interview (unpublished), said, "I have been on stage so long that I can't completely ignore the audience." One alternative that is neither dance related nor performance related is available to women—marriage (assuming economic support by the husband). This seems to be a meaningful alternative for some female dancers who wish to stop performing. For most dancers, though, the lack of dance or performance-related alternatives creates anxiety when grappling with the decision whether or not to stop performing.

This is especially so since earlier research has shown that most dancers have given very little advance thought to the postperforming years (Federico, 1968). They seem to find it very difficult to admit that they will not be able to dance forever, yet of course they know that they cannot. The motivation to dance has to be very strong to overcome the considerable obstacles to a performing dance career, and admitting the reality that the career may be a short one, or even that it has to end sometime, may be perceived as potentially jeopardizing. This is one of the major ways ballet as a career differs from similar careers, such as professional athletics. While athletes and dancers both face limited numbers of "performing" years, athletes have the opportunity and the encouragement to plan for the "postperforming" years (Charnofsky, 1974). Dancers do not. The dancer's view is well expressed by the same ballerina quoted at length earlier. "I suppose I'll dance for another five years; I don't really know. I'm just going to go by the day, or the year. . . .For now, I just want to dance as well as I can and enjoy it. . . . "(Draegin, 1976).

The Effects of the Decision Not To Perform

A dispassionate social science analysis of the decision by a ballet dancer to stop performing mutes much of the personal conflict and sense of loss that seems to accompany this action. It is important to realize that none of the factors discussed here are supported by occupationally structured processes or procedures. Ending the performing phase of one's career is generally a decision made by each dancer, and then carried out with no predictable, structured activity or resources to help in the transition from performer to non-performer. Although it eventually happens to every dancer, the occupation refuses to institutionalize the event. Performing and all of its attendant demands become an ingrained part of the dancer. Without it s/he may feel quite threatened:

> My life was so concentrated on the exigencies of dancing that I was utterly lost, aimless, without direction or purpose [when she could not dance for a prolonged period due to an injury]. When I was fully occupied with class, rehearsals and performances, I thought of a million things I would do if I had time, but as soon as the time was thrust upon me I had no idea how to organize myself to use it, and my spirit was too low to care. [Fonteyn, 1976:108.]

The ballerina who retired temporarily reacted in a less fearful way, but in an equally driven manner. "I was enjoying life so much I actually began to feel guilty. I was so used to a rigid regime and constant discipline. In the back of my mind, I felt I should be doing something, accomplishing something." (Kriegsman, 1976.)

A third dancer reacted to retirement from the stage with relief, but also with a statement that well captures the intense emotional involvement that performing entails:

> Two days after my decision to retire, I felt as if someone had stepped off my chest. . . . It's been a long love affair so passionate that it has taken all my time. Being old-fashioned, I haven't had time for another affair. It was a love–hate affair that goes on and on. Now it has stopped. I feel relieved. I have a freedom I have not known or wanted until now. [Kisselgoff, 1972.]

However, this dancer does not mention here, in an interview right after he stopped performing, what he shared in an unpublished interview a year later. In the later interview the dancer admitted that the first year after he stopped performing was psychologically traumatic and characterized by a severe loss of motivation and sense of purpose.

The meaning of the decision to stop performing is heavily dependent on the occupational definition of and preparation for such an action. As noted earlier, dancers are not prepared for a short performing career—their occupational socialization is limited almost exclusively to preparation for performing, and it is so intensive as to exclude most other kinds of occupationally useful socialization (Federico, 1968). For example, young dancers are advised, "If you wish a career as a professional dancer, you will probably have to forego college" (DeMille, 1962:42). As another example, Mazo says:

> When you spend your early teens cutting class in order to go to ballet lessons, and your late teens dancing, when almost all of the people you know are dancers who also cut alot of classes, you get to know alot about

dance but you don't think much about Ibsen. You certainly don't care whether you think about him or not. . . . There is no world but the company. [Mazo, 1974:54.]

This kind of socialization appears to be poor preparation for the performing and non-performing career reality. In addition, in an overcrowded profession the chances of getting a ballet job, and certainly a job that offers artistically fulfilling principal roles, are remote. All of these factors tend to make the decision to stop performing a very problematic one for ballet dancers.

Riding the Crest

Ballet as a career is being influenced by the current popularity of dance in general and ballet in particular. For example, it is estimated that the dance audience has grown from two million to sixteen million over the past fifteen years. The number of dance companies has grown from 35 to 350 during the same period (*Dance Magazine*, May 1981:3). Much of the popularity is the result of exposure through the media, especially television programs such as "Dance in America" and "Live from Lincoln Center." For the first time, ballet dancers are media stars. Dancers like Margot Fonteyn, Rudolph Nureyev, Cynthia Gregory, Natalia Makarova, and Alexander Godunov are widely known and are powerful box-office attractions. They, of course, need companies to dance with, thereby increasing the need for dancers who are less well known. The results have been dramatic on the realities of ballet as a career. Cynthia Gregory has stopped performing on more than one occasion because of dissatisfaction with the roles and partners offered her. In the past, she would have been replaced and would have found it hard to get another job. Now she has enough star power to come and go at will, with no question about whether she will be welcomed back and given concessions. Even dancers with less star power benefit. Gelsey Kirkland and Patrick Bissell, fired for uncooperative behavior and unreliability, were reinstated after considerable media publicity. When all the dancers at American Ballet Theater went on strike in 1980, their cause was widely publicized and many of their demands were met.

The popularity of ballet and greater media exposure have made ballet a somewhat more secure and more lucrative occupation, although it has not reduced the competitive aspects of the career structure. Postperforming opportunities have also been affected. Films like *Valentino*, *Nijinsky*, and *The Turning Point* have created new opportunities for nondancing performing opportunities. The demand for dance has increased the demand for choreographers, company managers, persons who can properly film and produce dance, and persons to stage popular ballets all over the world. Training facilities have become more serious in order to prepare dancers for companies that require a very high level of technical facility in ballet and other forms of dance. This has created booming opportunities for teachers and persons to organize and work in organizations that specialize in developing and delivering materials for dance teachers.

The popularity of ballet (and dance in general) has also been felt in other non-performance areas. Dance has become part of society's revived interest in physical fitness and exercise. Alwin Nikolais, for example, has developed a well-known exercise system as an extension of his highly respected modern-dance performing career. Other dancers have done the same. Dancers have also become active in working with professional athletes and in other levels of physical education. Indeed, a dance company was formed recently to incorporate gymnastic movement into dance (Robertson, 1981). Related to the popularity of dance and its spillover into physical exercise and fitness is the development of dance-influenced fashions. This relationship has gone two ways. Dance wear has become more colorful, stylish, and available in a wider variety of fabrics. In the other direction, dance styles have influenced leisure and exercise wear. A number of dancers have been involved in these activities after they stop performing. Nadine Revene, for example, has built a very successful business that specializes in dance and leisure wear (Friedman, 1981).

Postperforming options for dancers have also been influenced by the money that popularity has brought. Whereas previously dancers were very poorly paid (Federico, 1968), today financial security is a more attainable goal. The performing years are still likely to be short, but at least while performing the pay allows some financial planning for the postperforming years. Corps de ballet dancers in major ballet companies, the lowest-paid dancers in those companies, can now expect union scale of about $350 a week when performing (less during rehearsals). For stars, the sky can be the limit. Data are scarce, but Valentina and Leonid Kozlov, two ballet dancers who defected from the Bolshoi Ballet in 1979, by early 1981 had purchased a $250,000 home "which they are slowly filling with exquisite pieces of furniture and rugs" (Pikula, 1981:65). Also in 1981, it was reported that Natalia Makorova's fees for performing twenty-eight times during the Broadway season of a small company she had formed and was directing exceeded $107,000 (*Dance Magazine*, August 1981:6). Money is also obtainable other ways, at least for stars: Margot Fonteyn and Rudolf Nureyev have both done nationally run ads for mink coats. Opportunities to plan for postperforming years, then, are greater than they have ever been because of greater work opportunities and increased financial security for many ballet dancers.

Conclusion

It seems clear that the decision to stop performing is closely tied to social-ization into the occupation. Retirement from the stage, like the performing phase of the career, is made problematic by a recruitment and training system that lacks a structure tying it to performing and postperforming activities in a useful and productive way (Federico, 1974). The costs of this structural discontinuity are great to the individuals involved, and to the long-term stability of the occupation itself. It is difficult for an occupation to obtain and use societal resources efficiently when it is confronted with massive expenditures of resources for member socialization, which never really result in a stable occupational population. For example, when trained but still young dancers feel forced to stop performing because of the factors discussed in this chapter, performance standards suffer as new dancers are gradually trained for the vacant roles. When this is a chronic situation, artistic and organizational stability are jeopardized.

The question then arises whether the occupational structure could be made more efficient in utilizing its human resources. This is a question well beyond the scope of this chapter, and extremely difficult to answer in any case. Without attempting to answer it in any substantial manner, some issues can at least be raised. One is that creativity is very poorly understood. It is much easier to train a dancer in ballet technique than in artistic expressiveness, so the socialization system tends to emphasize the former. This in turn tends to hide issues such as preparing a dancer for the non-performing part of his or her career, since that is not clearly related to mastery of ballet technique. Another issue is that the occupation itself has traditionally been relatively unconcerned with activities other than teaching and performing. Choreog-raphers, directors, choreologists, etc., have tended to emerge rather than be created through training. This has resulted in the haphazard availability of talented people for these jobs as well as the career discontinuity already mentioned.

Yet another issue is that the arts have traditionally been starved for funds in the United States. This has discouraged the establishment of state-supported training institutions for dancers, which, in other societies, has encouraged the development of postperforming career opportunities and, ultimately, pen-sions. This has led to the present free-enterprise system of dance training and socialization, which, whatever its benefits, certainly exacerbates the problems involved in creating a continuous career pattern for dancers. However, as noted in the last section of this chapter, the surge in popularity of ballet and other forms of dance is exerting powerful forces that are changing aspects of the profession. Funds to support dance have been increasing from both government and business (Laine, 1981; Arcomano, 1981), although this may change (*Dance Magazine*, August 1981:6–7). With more money coming into dance, there may develop efforts to make the whole occupational structure more predictable in terms of its output.

Obviously, each issue is extremely complex, having many sides and raising many related issues. The basic point is that the decision to stop performing is a difficult and often painful one for the professional ballet dancer. In spite of recent changes related to the current popularity of the occupation, it is likely to remain so for the foreseeable future because of the structure of the occupation.

References

Arcomano, Nicholas. 1981. "The Business Committee for the Arts." *Dance Magazine*, June: 70–71.

Barnes, Clive. 1973. "The Rockette Who Became a Prima Ballerina." *New York Times*, April 29: D–12.

Becker, Howard S. 1974. "Art as Collective Action." *American Sociological Review*, 39:767–76.

Charnovsky, Harold. 1974. "Ballplayers, Occupational Image, and the Maximization of Profit." In *Varieties of Work Experience*, ed. Phyllis Stewart and Muriel Cantor. New York: John Wiley, pp. 262–73.

DeMille, Agnes. 1962. *To a Young Dancer*. Boston: Little, Brown.

Draegin, Lois. 1976. "Cynthia Gregory Returns." *Dance Magazine*, December: 42.

Faulkner, Robert. 1974. "Making Us Sound Bad: Performer Compliance and Interaction in the Symphony Orchestra." In *Varieties of Work Experience*, ed. Phyllis Stewart and Muriel Cantor. New York: John Wiley, pp. 238–48.

Federico, Ronald. 1968. "Ballet as an Occupation." Ph.D. diss., Northwestern University, Evanston, Ill.

  1974 "Recruitment, Training, and Performance: The Case of Ballet." In *Varieties of Work Experience*, ed. Phyllis Stewart and Muriel Cantor. New York: John Wiley, pp. 249–61.

Fonteyn, Margot. 1976. *Autobiography*. New York: Alfred A. Knopf.

Friedman, Aileen Robbins. 1981. "Nadine Revene's Designs on Dancers." *Dance Magazine*, July:47.

Kalish, Richard. 1975. *Late Adulthood: Perspectives on Human Development*. Monterey, Cal.: Brooks–Cole.

Kisselgoff, Anna. 1972. "For Bruhn in Retirement, Tributes and New Plans." *New York Times*, January 14:18.

Krause, Elliot. 1971. *The Sociology of Occupations*. Boston: Little, Brown.

Kriegsman, Alan. 1976. "The Unretiring Gregory." *Washington Post*, December 5:E–1.

Laine, Barry. 1981. "The NEA's Dance Program." *Dance Magazine*, May:60.

Mazo, Joseph. 1974. *Dance Is a Contact Sport*. New York: Saturday Review Press.

Peters, Anne. 1974. "Aspiring Hollywood Actresses: A Sociological Perspective." In *Varieties of Work Experience*, ed. Phyllis Stewart and Muriel Cantor. New York: John Wiley, pp. 39–48.

Pikula, Joan. 1981. "Coming of Age in the West." *Dance Magazine*, June:64–69.

Robertson, Michael. 1981. "Musawwir Gymnastic Dance Company." *Dance Magazine*, June:88–89.

Sutherland, David. 1976. "Ballet as a Career." *Society*, November–December:40–45.

Tobias, Tobi. 1976. "Alexander Grant." *Dance Magazine*, November:42–47.

Zaccaria, Joseph. 1970. *Theories of Occupational Choice and Vocational Development*. New York: Houghton–Mifflin.

3

Orchestra Interaction: Communication and Authority in an Artistic Organization

ROBERT FAULKNER

In his classic treatment of authority in organizations, Chester I. Barnard directs attention to the persistent, stable, and reproducible features of inter-action in deliberately created social structures (Barnard, 1962). He focuses on the problematic features of compliance by organizational subordinates and, specifically, on the interpretive contexts in which directives from su-periors are scrutinized, evaluated, and translated into appropriate behavior by members. In his formulation, communications are viewed as situated work contingencies: factors upon which the legitimation of authority depends. Following Weber, the probability that an authority will be given obedience is dependent in part upon the extent to which his communications are viewed as authoritative (Barnard, 1962; Weber, 1964; Silverman, 1970). In other words, authoritative directives are socially constructed and sustained (Berger and Luckmann, 1966; Rose, 1962; Blumer, 1969). This theoretical emphasis concerns itself with the perspectives of subordinates (Shibutani, 1955), their standards for what they construe as clear and understandable directives, the propriety and compatibility of communications with their beliefs, and their sense of achieved competence in being able to comply with these directives.

The description and analysis that follow focus on symphony orchestra performers' perceptions of the problematics of making music and their in-teraction with conductors. These occupational members have organized their work experiences into procedures and perspectives for engaging in collective   71 lines of action to accomplish their purposes, and for dealing with the exigencies of role performance. Making music together is a practical organizational achievement that rests on recognized and sanctioned ways of doing things. Conductors' directives, in rehearsals and final performances, build upon those features that enhance the spontaneous playing of the musicians and reduce areas of ambiguity and unpredictability for them. Players themselves claim considerable expertise in assessing the wisdom, interpretive powers, consistency, and controlled spontaneity of the conductor. Because the specific musical task has most likely been performed previously, under other conductors, musicians have had a chance to develop generalized work standards for evaluating the ability of any one maestro to move a group of high-powered virtuosi to perform as he wishes. This special world of concerted action that emerges between performers and conductors reveals many problematic features relevant to the sociological study of authority. This study analyzes the ways in which performers, as "lower-level participants" in artistic organizations (Etzioni, 1961), perceive and construct definitions of interaction with conductors and proceed to respond to situations created for them.

Methods

This study is based on seven months of observation and fifty interviews, lasting from one to four hours, with members of one of the top fifteen symphony orchestras in the United States. During the orchestra season, rehearsals were attended and interviews were tape recorded, either after the morning's work or later in the performer's home. Some reinterviewing was done in order to generate more complete evaluations of the succession of maestros. The open-ended questions asked of these musicians were first discovered from the musicians. Performers were questioned in their own language and were encouraged to talk about the various conductors and work experiences faced over the season, to express their own ideas of work contingencies that could make their job tough, unpleasant, and at times degrading.

The musicians were frank respondents when it came to the generalities of making music, but getting at their troubles with particular conductors was difficult and at times required subtle and indirect interviewing tactics. These consisted of beginning the questions about their work by asking the musicians to define the ideal conductor; once the interview was under way, respondents were asked to compare the merits of the conductors under whom they had worked during the season. This tactic put players in the position of describing specific work experiences that either approached or fell short of their own conceptions and image of the ideal. It also elicited detailed interpretations of those work situations in which the fracture between ideals and reality was most obvious, role expectations were violated, and performer tensions and complaints were viewed as "caused" by certain forms of interaction between musician and conductor.

Setting

The symphony world today offers a number of organizational settings in which subordinates are frequently under the direction and command of guest conductors. Musicians in both the "Big Five" orchestras (Cleveland, Chicago, New York, Boston, Philadelphia) and in the organizations a notch below these ranks are likely to experience higher rates of conductor succession over the musical season. Peripatetic guest conductors travel from orchestra to orchestra, rehearsing a week or two, giving concerts, and then moving on to another setting. Their tours of duty put them before orchestras with different talent, technique, and temperament. Musicians hear a great deal about the reputation and style of these maestros and know something about their ability to handle an orchestra and to make music.

An occupational lore develops around performers' problems and work adventures with conductors. They may play under more than twenty or twenty-five in succession over the concert season; some are recognized as skilled but not too inspiring, others are seen as extraordinary and even charismatic leaders; still others are viewed as mediocre or worse. Similiar standards are applied to permanent conductors. Such structural instability may well affect an organization's performance. Variations in leadership, due to constant succession, should have an impact on subordinates' perceptions of authority and compliance. In fact, this variability offers the organizational theorist something of an extreme case in the dynamics of work, in that the positions or offices in the formal structure are stable, but the incumbency of superiors changes rapidly and their mastery of communicative efforts and competence is closely scrutinized by subordinates. The conductor is supposed to be a leader, he sets the tempo, maintains proper ensemble and balances, and impresses his will over a group of virtuosi. Musicians agree that it takes about ten or fifteen minutes for an orchestra faced with a new maestro to determine whether he is a fake, a phony, a brilliant technician, a charismatic personality, or a poseur (see Schonberg, 1967). Between the orchestra and the conductor must lie respect, reciprocity, and trust.

The conductor is the focal participant in the ensemble's efforts, for the ongoing musical experience is continually shared and sifted through members' evaluative standards and their stock of preconstituted knowledge about the particulars of concerted playing. When asked specifically what they look for in the person on the podium, it becomes clear that both words and actions are closely attended to and scrutinized for their practical content. Communications and directives that are inadequate, incomprehensible, shallow, and incompatible with the purposive action of performers can carry little authoritativeness. A conductor must create respect. He is not accorded a fixed distribution of deference because of the position he occupies. From the moment a conductor steps on the podium a special world is in the process of being constructed. Performers respond to the person and his cues, they develop interpretations into situational definitions, and project lines of concerted action on the basis of these constructions.

Making music is an act of collaboration and practical decision making, and not a routine to which performers merely accommodate themselves as players. Moreover, musicians have ideas of the possibilities in any piece of music, and beyond that, an idea of the maestro as an agent of their own behavior. One of their major preoccupations and concerns is the authoritativeness, the controlling force, of his directives as the orchestra plays through them, not once but many times. In "playing through" a conductor's translation of musical symbols into meaningful sound, the effects of interaction, such as shared meanings, become objectified (Berger and Luckmann, 1967:34). A musical world of meaning is built up and sustained, for better or for worse: as players put it, "you're either making music or just playing notes." They agree that each maestro reads the symbols differently. They also agree that those expressive signs that fail to communicate a sum total of information allowing members to engage in lines of action and interaction can have little, if any, authoritativeness within the orchestra. This is a process of defining the situation (Ball, 1969; Stebbins, 1969) in which communicative competence and wisdom is attributed to the conductor's error-correcting ability, his knowledge of the performance problems faced by musicians, and, in general, his interpretive skill in transforming the occasion from one of merely playing notes and "experiencing things" to a situation of genuinely creative cooperation and "having an experience" (Dewey, 1958:35–37; 1926:382–91).

Defining the Situation: Conductor Directives and Concerted Action

Turning to the situational definitions constructed out of the cues and cognitions from the podium, the acts that spring from these constructions, and the standards they hold a conductor to, we can ask what given "communication problems" imply about and entail for the purposes of making music. In the interpretive construction and maintenance of orchestral performances, two conditions appear to be a recurrent topic among orchestra performers.

First, these respondents stress the ideas that meanings emerge from interaction and that some directives are open to various interpretations, and, especially, fail to specify in advance the desired musical outcome produced by an individual musician, a section of the orchestra, or the entire ensemble. As members of the orchestra attempt to respond selectively and appropriately to cues, ambiguity of expressive signs results in uncertainty. These conditions generate lowered expectancies for a player's sense of control and mastery of his performance, at the same time reducing his ability to forecast or adjust to what his like-situated colleagues will in turn perform.

A second and related contingency is found under those conditions where directives are viewed as unpredictable and inconsistent, and as combining competing instructions for the players. Performers' depictions of the meanings of such a conductor's actions stress the negative consequences of equivocation. They see behind a series of expressive signs an underlying pattern in which the conductor cannot decide what he wants.

As the following interviews illustrate, what is specific to the responses of these players is not some type of absolute obedience toward the conductor. By virtue of what the players identify as extraordinary qualities and directives, the conductor exercises not only a type of inspiration but also an exemplary persuasiveness in demonstrating to them that his interpretation is correct. By these features he exercises a kind of domination over performers (Weber, 1964: 324–28). As these excerpts demonstrate, this does not involve some kind of automatic acquiescence of musicians to the director's views. Nor does it exclude the possibility that they disagree with him on his musical interpretations, phrasing, and tempo. This is all the more relevant since the conductor, as innovator, at times challenges these expert performers' ways of thinking and playing music. Like all professionals, musicians jealously guard their prerogatives and "working prejudices" from outside interference (Becker, 1963: 85–100).

As Weber reminds us, the crucial tests of charisma and expertise can be found not only in communicative strength and persuasiveness but also in the responses of organizational subordinates. Conductors call for new ways of thinking and playing; that performers are receptive to this is recognized in the recurring phrase, "He has to show us what he wants, he has to have that personality, then we'll follow him." Resistance to the demands of some conductors is a concrete indication of perspectives and sentiments that can be found among every performer in the orchestra. Here are some examples of the scrutiny given to definitions of the situation and the standards to which players hold conductors.

Asked to compare several of the conductors he had worked with over the season, a middle-aged woodwind player responded as follows:

> *R. is very good, this week has been enjoyable, but T. to my mind is second-rate. There are a lot of things a second-rate conductor doesn't even begin to realize. It's easy for a conductor to be a charlatan. The whole thing is based on his being a musician's musician. You see, the musician needs someone who has leadership, a sense of beauty, intelligence . . . but leadership is not enough, you just can't force us to play. You can have a bull up there on the podium but that isn't going to bring you anything of beauty. He has to be more than that. R. knows what he wants and can convey it to us. A conductor has to have, well, ability, just technical ability with the stick, he must tell us what he wants with the stick. We have to have confidence in him because if he can't convince us with the stick, then he's lacking in his own convictions somewhere.*

A percussionist with a penchant for musical particulars judged one of the less talented conductors against these standards and interpreted him as displaying exceedingly vague directives, which then led to some incompatibility between maestro and musicians.

> *The conductor must know what he wants and then convince me, convince the orchestra, that he is right; now that's important. We all have our own ideas and it's difficult if he doesn't know himself. Now, Y., he was with us last week, is horrible, just totally inadequate. He doesn't communicate with technique or with words. He sort of looks surprised when we play. That's when the troubles start, it lacks authority, his beat lacks it. He follows us and you can't follow somebody who is following you. He can't tell us, so what can we do? We were very depressed about the whole thing, we ended up sounding bad.*

Not surprisingly, inadequately defined cues and cognitions not only lack authoritativeness; they are themselves generators or causes of subsequent conduct such as open disrespect, sullenness, deliberately lowered work effort, selective inattention, sarcasm, and in general the making and taking of role distance (Goffman, 1961: 105–15). At other times players witness a transformation of rehearsals into muted character contests in which musicians test the conductor's ear as well as his integrity and presented self (see Goffman, 1967: 239–58). A young reed player who had started his career in the orchestra world a few years back was considerably more opinionated than his colleagues. He made several allusions to the above-mentioned conductor and then went on to discuss another. He objected to a frozen communicative style, a constricted expressivity, and limited understanding of the proper use of rehearsals. He was asked if there were differences between the conductors over the season.

> *Sure. A lot of them have a very small range of emotional expression, how shall I put it, they have two or three expressions and they use them all the time so they get up and huff and puff and it doesn't mean a thing. They don't communicate. They are of no use to us. And then maybe they're too distant, you can never tell whether you're doing it right or wrong, they never respond when you respond to them. I guess after a while you stop watching them, you stop paying attention to*

what they're doing, you start making subtle jokes, things like that. E. (I shouldn't mention names), but he doesn't have anything to offer, he isn't saying anything up there, he just is beating time—nothing happens. You play and you play, it's just notes followed by his beating time. We resent this. Anyone can beat time, but you've got to communicate.

Inept orders result in a sensed lack of effective coordination as well as a decline, as Barnard puts it, in the net inducement for accepting conductor orders and directives as having authority (Barnard, 1962: 166). Moreover, performers are highly skeptical of conductors who employ a kind of verbal overkill where expressions are vapid, do not define clearly the particularized role information necessary for compliance, and do not foster a continuity of shared meanings between musicians.

Q: *What are some of the work problems you faced over the past weeks with W., T., and S.?*

A: *Well, take S. The other day we rehearsed this one work and his idea was to take it bar by bar and he never accomplished anything, no phrases, no understanding of the music, no nothing, it was a disappointing show. We all hate him. When he stops and makes comments, he gets nothing done. With W., this week, you do, he knows what to say, just the few words to say to us. Then he lets us play. But with S., it's words followed by. . .*

Q: *Music?*

A: *No. . . words followed by notes. It didn't mean anything, just notes. He stops and I think he doesn't even know what to say to us, or maybe how to say it. I was talking with my stand partner yesterday at the break and he said that with S. or E. you could stop the music anywhere and put a cadence in at any bar and it wouldn't matter at all. You could end it in the last movement in the second bar. Now, that kind of conductor you don't need.*

A brass player discussed some of the consequences of inadequate communications and the attentiveness of his colleagues to signs or proof of a conductor's exceptional leadership abilities as well as personal qualities. These excerpts from an interview that lasted over three hours suggest the inclination of members to view authority in personalistic terms.

I think W. has that personality, he has that quality. He knows exactly what he wants us to do and he conveys it. The concert last night was exciting, really. He has that charisma. It's just their personality, that's the mark of a good conductor. He can make you want to play as good as you can for him, he gives you that confidence. I think you can tell when a man gets up there whether or not he has it, they just have a certain personal magnetism, it's hard to explain. Like T., he'll make you play, whether you want to or not. We can tell right away. . . And then I would put the other side of this by saying, if there's not an outstanding personality up there, well, why knock yourself out? Sure. . . it's not worth the effort, the physical and mental effort of paying attention, of concentrating, of listening, of constantly adjusting. All of this is hard work. I think if the guy doesn't have it, you play with indifference. If he can't tell you, forget it. There's the efficient and inefficient way of doing a rehearsal; it's not unlimited time. So we feel that you might as well stop watching him closely, start dreaming or something.

The distinction between expertise and the person exercising it has for most of these musicians a reduced importance; it is not a clear-cut dichotomy but rather a blending of imputed authority of competence, charismatic leadership, and performance effort. The content of their knowledge turns on several well-developed clichés and an immensely factual spectrum of conductor types, styles of leadership, and varieties of skill. Morover, players, with the ease of seasoned veterans, claim to be able to compare and assess conductors. Although there is some disagreement about just how quickly a musician can accurately assess and "psych out" the expertise and personality of a conductor, it was generally agreed that authoritativeness and the more elusive ability to take command can be established within a few minutes, if not sooner. All claim to know, and to know a great deal, about what to look for in terms of musical erudition, the meanings of expressive signs for their own role performances, and especially the meshing of a particular conductor's authority at his first rehearsal with their own reconstructions of past work experiences under others.

The following player is representative of many in emphasizing that his grasp of and control over his own performance is primarily commensurate with the conductor's control over his, with the conductor's expertise and leadership skills. Facial expressions, directives, and inflections are closely attended to and carefully scrutinized as the player tunes in to the podium performance and the directives given and given off by the conductor. He could tell right away

. . .what the man has. You know with the first downbeat. In other words, he's taking command. If he doesn't take command, then you know he'll heel back. But if he takes command and has that personality and that ability, you know, with the first beat. Then you sit up and give your attention. He's got to be inspiring, he must convince us that his way, his concept, is the right one. If he does, we'll follow him, if he proves he can weld the players into a unit.

Next is a respondent who slides immediately from the problems of inadequate information to his ideas about unpredictability between performances and the trouble with contradictory expressive signs. He was talking about a conductor he especially enjoyed working with:

When W. gets up there and conducts, he acts out the emotions of the piece at the time. You know exactly what it's supposed to sound like, and what exactly you're supposed to do. This is it. But some conductors don't communicate, they are very limited and can only act out one kind of emotion and they do that for every type of music. J. cannot give you a feeling of happiness or joy or gaiety. You see, a big problem is that these guys can't convey it through the stick, facial expressions, the whole body. I'd say we're confronted with too many conductors who are too competent for their own mediocrity. T. is an excellent musician, he rarely makes a mistake in the score, but he just doesn't communicate to me. The standard joke is the conductor who goes "faster, faster,". . . but his beat gets slower and slower— the guy who says one thing and does another, or who can't communicate, who gives gestures of expression but they're not showing us his meaning. He is of no use. Uninspired conductors and uninspired performances—that's the problem. . . We get upset when this happens.

Musicians hold the conductor accountable for correcting errors and increasing the scope of collaborative consensus; work pressures build up under conditions where performance outcomes are doubtful. A brass player had this to say about rehearsals and sensed mastery over the part he had to play.

A: *I've played the same composition several times under different conductors, like the Hindemith we did last night, and sometimes it's very easy and sometimes it's very difficult. It all depends on the conductor—and this is the same music.*

Q: *Could you give me some examples of this problem?*

A: *It's their technique of the baton, that more than anything else. The baton doesn't make any sound, but if you're really watching, it can confuse you. Like Q., he can make it difficult for you to play. He can create pressure on you. If he's inadequate as far as his knowledge (and we see some like that), then what he does can make life miserable, awfully miserable. Most of the tension and pressure comes from poor rehearsal techniques, that's a problem. Some of them just don't seem to be able to budget their time, and quite frequently, for the last rehearsal, I feel that we don't know the piece of music that well. I don't know my part well enough; it's not properly rehearsed; the balances are unclear; tempos are not clear: the whole thing is poorly done. This is where the pressure always comes right back to me. I don't like this, because if the guy on the podium did a better job of budgeting his time and clearly telling me what he wants, then we wouldn't have this last-minute frenzy, this big panic. If he was better as a conductor and could show us what he wanted, we wouldn't have this, and I wouldn't be suffering because of it.*

Several of these musicians point to instances where conductors, under pressure of the concert, seriously affect the sum of information musicians receive from the podium. Moreover, persistent discrepancies appeared between what the performers anticipated on the basis of a conductor's gestural signs and imputed attributes, and what the unfolding events actually showed him to be. A player with quite opinionated views about the attributes required for suitable communication from the podium became somewhat unrestrained in his account of one particular maestro.

You expect certain kinds of things to happen, and when they don't, well, the tempo may be completely different than what has been rehearsed for five rehearsals. Some conductors fall apart during concerts. I'm thinking of one man who was so erratic—one day it's here, another rehearsal it's there, and then during the concert he's doing it entirely different. We don't know what to expect. . . That's one of the troubles with T. From the first day he came here I called him one of the biggest fakers in the business. He had everything that a conductor's supposed to have. He looked like one, he knew how to work his frustrations out on the orchestra all week long. He was nastier than anybody you would want to have on the podium and he had a tremendous amount of showmanship. But when the chips were down on the night of the concert, he just couldn't deliver. He'd get lost, he would ride roughshod over things he'd worked on all week long. You can't respect a man like that. I would express my opinion to his face. I don't care. He was a faker.

Incompetence, charlatanism, abuse of players, and excessive posturing are viewed in terms of imputed expertise and conductor character. Maestros who prevent performers from successfully predicting behavioral outcomes—both the conductor's and their co-performers'—and who abuse the mandate of position come in for some of the harshest appraisals in the interviews. Ambiguous definitions of the situation and inconsistent directives not only decrease players' expectations of being able to interpret collective action, but undermine the conditions under which they can comply with directives. To the recipients of such communications, this increases their work pressures and heightens overall tension within the ensemble. As for the impact on making music and the attachment players experience in working for an indifferent or bad conductor, one player had this to say:

These guys make us sound bad, they make the orchestra angry, they make me sound bad, and then some of the more discontent and lazy players take over and you wonder after a few rehearsals of fighting with the man and the stick why the hell he's up there in the first place. You see, the man must know what he's doing and be able to tell us how to do it, and then we'll play.

As for trust as a condition for concerted action, a principal in the woodwind section had this to say:

With the conductor last week . . . like if I have a solo to play, I know I can play as expressively as I know how and I know he won't go off and leave me and he knows I won't go off and leave him. There's a component of faith in what happens between us and a conductor. If it's there, the music is there. . . . You learn to size a conductor up, to see what he can do—this takes a rehearsal before you know. You sort of get a feel for him. With some of these guys, you must stop listening, you just stop being attentive because there's no reward, I would say, in being especially attentive.

For these musicians, ambiguity and equivocation create discrepancies between the role mastery a player expects and the degree of control he achieves. Under inept conductors, communications and directives become, in effect, poor predictors of concerted action by reducing the minimal standards for clarity in decision making and thereby resulting in a particular kind of alienation at work. Another problem is introduced by the musician just quoted. Whereas ambiguity and equivocation can be seen as problems of inadequate communicative gestures and role prescriptions, there is a problem of what players view as illegitimate directives and role prescriptions, that is, unwarranted attempts of the maestro to extend his influence and power into the performer's own sphere of professional expertise. In this instance too much control, rather than not enough, is viewed as exerted. These communications are often defined as incompatible with a player's personal and professional interest as a whole. Of course, it is the ability of the conductor to convince his musicians that he is right, that his interpretation is the authoritative one. His authority therefore builds upon those features that enhance the spontaneous playing of musicians and substantially reduce areas of unpredictability while, at the same time, as one player put it, they "inspire confidence in your own playing of what *he* wants."

Conclusions

I have presented orchestra performers as organizational members who experience work problems with conductors to the degree that directives are vaguely defined, grossly incompatible with performers' standards, unconvincing as musical interpretations, and technically unsound as guides for the successful execution of the music. The system of authority in the orchestra, I have argued, is more than a pattern of static roles and statuses. It is a network of interacting human beings, each transmitting information to the other, sifting their transactions through an evaluative screen of beliefs and standards, and appraising the meaning and credibility of conductor directives. The orchestra, as the most complex musical instrument, is composed of performers who communicate with one another, establish definitions of the situation under successive maestros, and thereby affect one another's tacit and explicit understandings about music and music making under various conductors.

This picture discloses certain ideas of general relevance for the study of organizational authority. In the first place, an organization like the symphony can be seen as a system of social control in which members bring to bear a set of interpretive schemes for sizing up and evaluating the "focal superior," the conductor. This creates an organizational climate and work setting in which communications and shared meanings of exemplary performances are the conditions under which the conductor legitimizes his authority.

Second, like professionals in other organizations, these performers resist illegitimate intrusions into their sphere of competence and feel maligned under imputed incompetence. Communications and conductors are accepted to the extent they help members achieve their purposes. As in other performing arts, and sports organizations, organizational success and effectiveness are closely tied to the efforts of the "team leader." But unlike the film director, field manager, or ballet mistress or master, the conductor is directly involved and implicated in the organizational execution of the performance. Thus, like a "crew leader," his role performance has an impact on members' culture markedly different from that exerted by expert supervisors in industry.

Finally, I have argued that the authoritativeness of communications in organizations is not only situationally approved, but socially created and maintained. To this end, I have focused on performers' definitions of the situation and what they construe as information that allows them to engage in lines of concerted action. This suggests the general proposition that part of the sum total of recognized musical knowledge is generated in ongoing organizational action. In his perceptive piece "Making Music Together," Alfred Schutz writes:

> Within this socially derived knowledge there stands out the knowledge transmitted from those upon whom the prestige of authenticity and authority has been bestowed, that is, from the great masters among the composers and the acknowledged interpreters of their work. Musical knowledge transmitted by them is not only socially derived; it is also socially approved, being regarded as authentic and therefore more qualified to become a pattern for others than knowledge originating elsewhere. [Schutz, 1964: 168–69.]

It is the validation and confirmation of this knowledge and expertise that are problematic within the transaction between conductor as interpreter and musicians as performers. And it is this imputed authenticity upon which the excellence of an orchestra depends, as well as upon which the authoritativeness of communications and conductors rests.

References

Ball, Donald W. 1969. "The Definition of the Situation: Some Theoretical and Methodological Consequences of Taking W. I. Thomas Seriously." Mimeographed. University of Victoria, B.C.

Barnard, Chester I. 1962. *The Function of the Executive*. Cambridge, Mass.: Harvard Univ. Press.

Becker, Howard S. 1963. *Outsiders: Studies in the Sociology of Deviance*. New York: Free Press.

Berger, Peter, and Thomas Luckmann. 1966. *The Social Construction of Reality*. Garden City, N.Y.: Doubleday.

Blumer, Herbert. 1969. *Symbolic Interactionism: Perspective and Method*. Englewood Cliffs, N.J.: Prentice–Hall.

Dewey, John. 1926. "The Nature of Aesthetic Experience." *International Journal of Ethics*, 36:382–91.

1958 *Art as Experience*. New York: Capricorn Books.

Etzioni, Amitai. 1961. *A Comparative Analysis of Complex Organizations*. Glencoe, Ill.: Free Press.

Goffman, Erving. 1959. *The Presentation of Self in Everyday Life*. Garden City, N.Y.: Doubleday.

1961 *Encounters: Two Studies in the Sociology of Interaction*. Indianapolis: Bobbs–Merrill Co.

1967 *Interaction Ritual: Essays on Face-To-Face Behavior*. Chicago: Aldine.

Rose, Arnold (ed.). 1962. *Human Behavior and Social Processes: An Interactionist Approach*. Boston: Houghton–Mifflin.

Schonberg, Harold C. 1967. *The Great Conductors*. New York: Simon & Schuster.

Schutz, Alfred. 1964. "Making Music Together." In *Collected Papers II: Studies in Social Theory*, ed. Arvid Broderson. The Hague: Martinus Nijhoff, pp. 159–78.

Shibutani, Tamotsu. 1955. "Reference Groups as Perspectives." *American Journal of Sociology*, 60: 562–69.

Silverman, David. 1970. *The Theory of Organizations*. London: Heinemann.

Stebbins, Robert A. 1969. "Studying the Definition of the Situation: Theory and Field Research Strategies." *Canadian Review of Sociology and Anthropology*, 4:193–211.

Weber, Max. 1964. *The Theory of Social and Economic Organization*. New York: Free Press.

4

Interview:
Veronica Castang

Learning To Act and Learning To Be an Actress

J.K. *When did you first become interested in becoming an actress?*
V.C. *I think I always have been, but I was too embarrassed to tell anybody. It seemed like a very silly way to try to make a living. I always did plays in my spare time, from the time I was about fourteen. I belonged to various amateur groups and children's acting groups. I'd always been taken to the theater, since I was a small child. My mother was interested in the theater. She had actually studied theater, but had had to give it up. And certainly, when it came time to think about what I was going to do in the future, she thought it was a pretty dumb idea to want to be an actress. So, I did something else for a while. I went to school and studied art history and French and worked in the art field for quite a few years. Then, when I came to America twenty years ago, I was working at the San Francisco Art Institute and doing plays in my spare time there. I realized I was staying up until four in the morning and getting up at seven to go to work. I thought, I'd better do this or I'm going to be upset with myself. So I did. I mean, I had no idea what to do. Somebody told me there was a book on summer stock theaters, so I just wrote to all these theaters, sent a resumé and a photograph. I didn't even know you were supposed to send an eight-*

Veronica Castang has appeared in numerous Broadway and off-Broadway plays. She has also appeared at most major regional theaters in the United States. She was interviewed by Jack Kamerman at her home in New York City in March 1982.

by-ten photo; I sent a five-by-seven, and got a job as an apprentice in summer stock in Pennsylvania. I did twelve dreadful plays in twelve weeks, acting in them and changing the sets for the next show, and building the sets, and sweeping the dressing rooms. I learned a lot. Some of it may have been terrible, but I certainly learned.

J.K.   Did you have any formal training in acting?

V.C.   Well, not really. I did go to the theater in England. There's a great schism in England between the amateur and the professional theater. It's not considered a terrible thing in England to be an amateur actor or actress. There are actually some very, very good amateur theaters. There's one called the Questors Theatre near where I used to live as a child... I did take a course there for a year, which was my first introduction to Stanislavski and any kind of formal training. I auditioned for the regular company and I got turned down. I was devastated that I was turned down for an amateur company. So I thought, maybe I ought to do something about it. I joined this student group, which was actually very thorough. I mean, it was all in your spare time, but it was literally all my spare time. There were some very good people. You had to audition to get in. But they were not thrilled by the idea of anyone who wanted to be a professional. They thought it was fine to want to be an amateur. The man who ran the theater spent his whole life working in insurance. Actually, he's quite famous in England for running that theater, but it was always an avocation. So when I started to get itchy, so that it looked as though I might want to be a professional actress, that was rather looked down on. It's funny because it's so different here. Anybody who's ever acted seems to want to be a professional.

And I took some classes when I first came to New York, too. But I'm not a great believer in classes; they never did much for me.

J.K.   That's interesting. In the U.S., training is sometimes more formalized. Colleges have programs...

V.C.   Yes, well, I don't see that at all. From what I've seen of it, it certainly doesn't necessarily produce very good actors or actresses. It may produce very well-informed, intelligent people who know a great deal about the theater. But I don't think it really prepares you for what it might be like to work in a professional theater. For one thing, from what I've seen of it, it's an extremely protected atmosphere. When I first came here I lived in San Francisco, and I was thinking at one time of going back to school and taking graduate work [in theater] at San Francisco State, which has the most beautiful facilities, the most gorgeous theater with an incredible light board. People who go there find it difficult when they have to go out into the real world.

The Public and Moral Aspects of an Acting Career

J.K.   *How do you prepare a role?*

V.C.   *It's funny, after a while there are certain roles that you don't need to do very much preparation for. There are certain parts that just jump out of the page at you. It depends on what the role is. A few months ago, I left the show I'm doing now [**Cloud 9**] for a while to do another play [**After the Prize**]. In it I played a Nobel Prize-winning scientist. I had to do quite a bit of reading for that so as not to appear like a dummy when I talked about the things for which I'd won the Nobel Prize. It was important to me that people should believe that this woman was a scientist. Now that doesn't necessarily mean that you have to know everything there is to know about black holes or whatever. But you have to be able to make people believe that this **woman** knows everything there is to know about black holes, enough to have won a Nobel Prize for it. It's not quite the same as knowing all about it yourself. You just have to convince the audience of that. And that was very important to me. I would have hated it if people had said, it's obvious that this woman is not a scientist. And that was something I asked people. I don't read reviews anymore, but I did ask people if anybody had said that. I think one person did say it, and of course that will be the one I'll remember for the rest of my life, rather than all the people who didn't say it.*

J.K.   *Why don't you read reviews?*

V.C.   *Well, I stopped reading them about two years ago, because they're too upsetting even if they're wonderful (which one hopes that they are). They affect you. I did a play about five years ago in which I played a model in a life class. It was a difficult thing to do, something which I'd not done before. One reviewer, who's a wonderful woman whom I admire a great deal, said it was "a beautifully unself-conscious per-formance." I read that review, and of course the next few days I was so self-conscious. I thought, "What did I do to make myself unself-conscious?" I had no idea what I was doing. And the bad ones you memorize; they're etched in your brain. Most actors are like that. You can have ten good ones and one bad one, and you'll remember the one bad one. So I just decided it was not a good idea to read them.*

J.K.   *My understanding as an outsider of what it's like to be an actor is to have to get used to being turned down. To go to many, many auditions and, in some cases, to be turned down time after time.*

V.C.   *It's terribly difficult. It's very, very difficult not to think that it's you personally and your whole work and your whole persona that's being rejected. So many times you're turned down for some quirky, odd little reason, and it's really nice to know about that. I like to know specifically why I've been turned down, not just because they think I'm untalented, but because I'm the wrong height or I'm the wrong age or my hair's the wrong color or something like that. I like to know those things because they're less devastating than, "you should give up the business and go back to what you were doing before."*

J.K.   *Will people tell you that?*

V.C.   *Sometimes they do and sometimes they don't. If you know them, they'll tell you. If you ask, they'll tell you. Not everybody, of course, wants to know. I do. Because there have been times when—this hasn't happened to me for a while, because I've been working very steadily for the last five years—but there was a time, I used to have my annual "getting-out-of-the-business" time. The thing that really kept me going was that I've always been really a character actress. I was never really the American idea of the ingenue. And I knew that I'd work more as I got older, which is what has happened. I've become more useful. And as more people know me, they become more imaginative. They use you in things that somebody wouldn't use you in if you'd just walked in the door and they'd never seen you work. If you work with people and they know that they like to work with you, then they'll work with you again rather than go with an unknown who might look right, but they don't know whether they can get on with that particular person.*

J.K.   *Do you ever get, or did you ever get, stage fright?*

V.C.   *Oh, God, yes. Funnily enough, I get it much more as I get older (and a lot of people have said that). I think it has to do with commitment, because, when you're young, you get stage fright for different reasons. You get it, I think, because you think you don't know what you're doing, and you're going to trip over the furniture and forget your lines, and those sorts of things. When you get older, you pretty much know you're not going to do that (although you do, sometimes). To me, as I get older, the need is my demand on myself to do really good work, because now I've been doing this for a long time and I'm not going to give up and go back to what I did before. This is what I do, and it's important to me that I should be really good.*

J.K.   *Can you imagine any circumstances under which you would no longer act?*

V.C.   *Oh, I don't know. I think of that sometimes. What would happen to me if I were in a car accident and lost my leg? There aren't too many one-legged parts. Well, I don't know, really, what I'd do. I don't know whether I'd be able to work under some theater-related circumstance, because I think that it would be terribly hard for me to deal with watching other people acting, and not be able to act myself. On the* *other hand, I've felt that I would like to do some directing. I probably wouldn't get around to doing it unless somebody asked me, or if I had to because I couldn't act anymore. But I'd prefer not to think about it. I'd deal with it if I had to.*

J.K.   *Is your acting the most important thing in your life?*

V.C.   *Yes, I guess it is. It's a difficult question. I think it's an especially difficult question for women, because of what it involves, being a woman whose work is so important. I've not really let myself say this to myself or anybody else for a long time. I was married for quite a long time. I was married to an actor, and it was very difficult. I was dividing myself, but not really giving enough attention to my work. A lot of it was out of fear, I guess, because if I looked after somebody else, it meant that I didn't have to look after myself. Since I'm not married anymore, I'm much more selfish. I just had to be. I said to myself, well, if I'm going to do this, I'd better really do it. No messing around, I've given up too much not to really do it properly. So, yes, it is the most important thing in my life, but there are other important things. But they're all part of it somehow. When you're an actor you can't shut off any part of your life as not being part of your acting. It's all part of your acting. It all makes you who you are as an actor.*

SECTION THREE

Managing Performers and Performances

A good administrator is one who rules with a Prussian hand in an Italian glove.

Anonymous

If the overall objective of this book is to reveal the relationship between art and society, the purpose of this section is to explore the social organization of the settings in which performances are made. This association is based on the sociological assumption that the performing arts are not determined exclusively by the interaction of performers, but also by extra-aesthetic aspects that support or hamper the entire production process.

Performances rely on individual virtuosity, exchange of ideas among performers, and the assistance of a cadre of support personnel, including those individuals involved in the nonartistic tasks of a company (fund raising, managing, bookkeeping, etc.). The division of labor within performing art companies varies according to the particular requirements of dance, theater, or music; however, most agree that their tasks could be divided into "artistic" and "administrative." For the purposes of this presentation, let us consider "artistic" all roles that are directly involved with the performance seen by an audience. These will include the roles of conductor, choreographer, and playwright, because of their autonomy over artistic decisions with regard to interpretation and style. The hierarchy of authority and the status of performers are contingent upon the nature of their tasks, with regard to both the aesthetic requirements of their art form and their social position within the organization. It is interesting to the sociologist to view the effect of professional status upon organization tasks, and vice versa. In accomplishing organizational goals, both artistic and nonartistic tasks come into play, and these, in turn, reflect upon the status of the individual. Such status is dictated by the normative order of both the profession itself and the specific organization.

In general, this section deals with the nonartistic aspects of arts organizations, focusing on their budgets, planning, and long- and short-range objectives. The range of performing arts companies is indeed diverse. Symphony orchestras and opera companies are multimillion-dollar operations; theater and dance companies have much smaller budgets, shorter seasons, and part-time musicians, and are often without a permanent home. Although the larger organizations are more than likely to employ managers with diversified accounting skills, they share, to a greater or lesser degree, the economic difficulties of smaller companies.

The nonprofit nature of the classical performing arts organizations described in this book distinguishes them clearly from other types of business organizations. Although much attention has been given to profit economics in the United States, little work has been done analyzing and problem solving for the not-for-profit organization in health, education, welfare, or the arts. In fact, until the late 1960s, performing arts organizations knew little of the nature of their deficits, and hardly ever conducted audience surveys. It was not until the role of government as a patron of the arts expanded, and double-digit inflation occurred between 1970 and 1980, that the arts took cognizance of the need to analyze their budgets, conduct audience studies, seek other sources of untapped income, and so on. In the past, when deficits appeared in a season's budget analysis, the cure was to tap private patrons, and apply for further government subsidy. As these funds became more scarce and production costs escalated, arts organizations began to look at more rational management practices, such as cost efficiency, the development of better market practices, and the establishment of specific goals and short- and long-range plans. The resignation of performing arts organizations to such strategies is evidenced by proliferation of arts management programs and the employment of arts managers across the nation. This trend, however, has not been without its effect upon the manager's expertise, and it remains to be seen just how this ascendant role determines the choice and quality of performances.

The discussion that follows will show how the very nature of the performing arts organization creates dilemmas over fulfilling community needs, maintaining artistic quality, coordinating the multiplicity of performing and non-performing roles, and maintaining the financial solvency of a company. In each of these articles, the focus of attention becomes the critical role of the manager in affecting artistic decision making and the final outcome of the artistic product.

Rosanne Martorella raises the important issue of the ambivalent nature of the performing arts organization, which must serve community needs and fulfill artistic goals, yet sustain itself as an organization. Consequently, in describing the role of management within the performing arts organizations, Martorella reveals how organizational goals (e.g., the selection of repertoire) are translated to include goals that are not solely artistic, but involve the needs of the organization itself (for example, box office income).

Stephen R. Couch compares two major orchestras, the London Philharmonic and the New York Philharmonic, revealing the influence of social factors (for instance, patronage) on the structure of the organizations, and on the musical nature of these symphony orchestras. He argues that the organization of each orchestra directly affects its musical styles.

The experiences of ballet dancer and choreographer Edward Villella, set forth in the interview at the end of the section, exemplify the dual function of a choreographer—a role that must manage creativity by devising mechanisms for both autonomy and the full integration and coordination of tasks within the framework defined by the choreographer for the dancers. Villella also discusses the relationship between artistic and financial decision making in a ballet company. Stinchcombe's model of "craft-administration" (1959) accounted for work in which actual decision making could not be accomplished without those individuals directly involved in the actual work. Similarly, performing arts organizations develop mechanisms of decentralization by limiting their control of the nonartistic aspects of production to the work level, the rehearsal time. As Villella shows, the choreographer, the conductor, or the stage director must possess artistic integrity within a hierarchy of authority emanating from within the profession, thereby facilitating the development of mechanisms of autonomy, responsibility, isolation and de-centralization from the nonartistic support personnel.

Reference

Stinchcombe, Arthur L. 1959. "Bureaucratic and Craft Administration of Production: A Comparative Study." *Administrative Science Quarterly*, 4:168–87.

5

Rationality in the Artistic Management of Performing Arts Organizations

ROSANNE MARTORELLA

Introduction

Research in the arts has focused primarily on popular culture and classical painting and literature; less attention has been given to serious music and the performing arts. This chapter examines the role of the arts administrator in dance, music, opera, and theater. After an initial discussion of the changing structure of performing arts organizations, which addresses the issues of their increased size, complexity, and economic insecurity, some of the consequences of these organizational changes upon the occupational role of the administrator will be explored. Since the organization is the work milieu of performers today, I have chosen to focus on the managerial role, in the hope of shedding some light on the nature of performance.

A theoretical framework is provided by sociological studies of organizations interacting with their environments (Hirsch, 1975; Thompson, 1967), analyses of nonprofit administrations (Baldridge, 1971), and studies of occupational ideologies (Bensman, 1967; Caplow, 1954; Strauss, 1971). Whereas Hirsch (1975) and Jarvie (1970) comment on the interplay between art and commerce, Baldridge (1971) and others concentrate on the conflicting role of the administrator in organizations that serve communal needs and that have traditionally dissociated themselves from "vulgar" and economic considerations. Education, social work, and medicine, for example, are caught in the ambivalence of serving community needs and yet sustaining themselves and the organizations they work for. Consequently, organizational goals often take precedence over the clients the organizations are intended to serve.

The client nature of artistic organizations offers an analogy. Unlike commercial rock music or Hollywood movies, serious art cannot sustain itself financially. Increasingly, however, it functions like commercial art by having a star system, occupational formalization and organizational complexity. On the other hand, it is distinctive primarily in adhering vehemently to Renaissance notions of individuality, artistic genius, and art for art's sake, and in underplaying audience demand and the profit motive. Along with the traditional service orientation of the arts is an increasing sense of professionalism, which gets translated into an additional set of goals beyond the client, and which includes client interests within the interests of the institution. The interesting sociological question becomes one of a conflict of interests generated by the ambivalent nature of any public representative task. Public service occupations attempt to seize control over their work, and, at the same time, profess to serve their clients. Who ultimately controls is determined by the prevailing economic system and the nature of the task. For the arts, the situation is further complicated by the aesthetic definitions and requirements of the specific medium.

The person who defines his work by criteria beyond the situation of the particular performance is the arts administrator. He has come to mediate the conflict between artistic standards and the public representative nature of the performing art. Given the increasing professionalization of his role, ideologies evolve to legitimate his decision-making power in a work setting whose traditions offer constant challenges to his "rational" behavior. In this chapter, I will attempt to relate the performing arts organizational structure with the ideologies expressed by managers and administrators, and will offer some clues to the future impact of this rapidly evolving role.

Social Change in the Arts

The nature of the arts today must be understood in light of demographic, economic, and organizational changes of twentieth-century America. With the rise of urban centers and an influx of immigrant populations since the middle of the nineteenth century (Raynor, 1976), secular music has become increasingly middle class, with strong European preferences. Population heterogeneity and urbanization coincided with economic and political changes that have affected the arts. In the early twentieth century, economic security in the arts was threatened by social changes; by midcentury this situation was aggravated, by the accelerating costs of arts productions. Financial backing shifted from individual patronage to greater reliance on mass audiences, ticket sales, subscriptions, and, more recently, on foundations, businesses, and the federal government. Increasing occupational specialization and professionalization have been brought about by both the developing middle-class audience and the unionization of the arts.

The 1960s witnessed an enormous nation-wide expansion of activity in the arts. Many independent organizations and large art centers have been organized since 1960. An enormous growth of cultural life in the nine-year period 1960–1969 accounted for the creation of one-fifth of the existing music organizations, and one-half of all dance and theater organizations. A total of 242 art centers and theaters were established. All have experienced an increase in attendance, facilities, number of performances, paid personnel, and maintenance fees in the past decade. Ironically, as a result of this growth and expansion, costs of production have exceeded artistic salaries in some of the performing arts (Ford Foundation, 1974:47).

The income–expense gap and the effects of inflation on the arts have been documented for some time (e.g., by Baumol and Bowen, 1966; Martorella, 1982), but it remains to be seen how this gap, and increasing government support, have affected the internal structure of arts organizations. Deficits continue to be the norm. Attempts are made to manipulate art's productivity level and "efficiency." Managers and arts administrators have responded to these developments by attempting to apply business expertise.

The importance of the role of the arts administrator has been directly influenced by increased organizational complexity in the arts and by the economic impasse, which, by the early 1970s, forced government funding. Although government support for the arts is small in the United States, compared with that in other nations, it has increased enormously since the creation of the National Endowment for the Arts in 1965. Approximately $120 million was slated for total national distribution in 1979, which included direct grants to state councils and expansion programs and grants-in-aid to artists, schools, and so on. Every state is now represented by a state arts council, and community arts agencies number over twelve hundred. However, the Reagan Administration has reduced NEA funding by half. The Ford Foundation reported that the total expenditure for 1970–1971 of all professional, nonprofit, performing arts companies in the country was over $159 million, with symphony orchestras having expenditures greater than those of all other art forms combined (Ford Foundation, 1974:41). By 1980, expenditures had jumped to $425 million. The total arts sector in the United States, including commercial enterprises, totaled approximately $11.5 billion, employing over 735,000 artists and representing about 1 percent of the nonfarm economy in 1972 (Netzer, 1978:9–11).

The foregoing discussion has emphasized the major changes in the arts and in the context in which arts organizations function. After briefly analyzing some economic and structural changes that have occurred within arts organizations, we will turn to the nature of the administrative role.

The Social Structure of Performing Arts Organizations

Each of the performing arts (dance, theater, symphony music, and opera) and non-performing arts (visual and literary) has evolved differently, and is presently at a different level of organizational complexity. As the arts have expanded, and as their economic sources have changed and become less secure, personnel have been assigned to coordinate varied activities. Expertise in tax laws, union negotiation, and other dimensions of nonprofit administration has become a prerequisite for the administrator. The days of the single impresario—in charge of financing, repertoire, casting decisions, policy making, and composing—are gone. Ideally, but in rarer and rarer cases, the top administrative position embodies an individual who combines artistic training with business sensitivity, who has technical knowledge of music, a sense of organization, and a knowledge of the talent market. Administrative decisions more often depend now on the input of a cadre of administrators and assistants. The extent to which top management formalizes the hierarchy and decision-making process has been a historical accident—a response to the size of the organization rather than adherence to musical tradition.

Prior to the development of the present complex structure in arts organizations, leadership of a performing ensemble was assumed by an artist. The nature and aesthetics of the art form, from its emergence until the mid-twentieth century, dictated who would be primarily responsible for coordinating specialized tasks and aesthetic interpretations of style. By the late nineteenth century, performing roles became highly specialized (Martorella, 1982). The critic and impresario who had musical training served in transitional roles. By the mid-twentieth century, the arts administrator emerged as a fully independent occupational role in the arts.

Analysis of the role of arts administrator must include analysis of the organizational structure, and must allude to the consequences of this structure for the role. Divisions of labor between performing artists, non-performing artists, and ancillary personnel define role boundaries. In most companies a twofold scheme exists, "artistic" and "nonartistic." Perhaps this is an oversimplification, but initially such a bifurcation prevails, with the "artistic" category including performing and non-performing artists directly involved in the creation of the product (e.g., stage directors, designers, choreographers, and composers). There is much diversity in the classification of artists, with gradations of pay, prestige, and power over aesthetic interpretations reflecting the hierarchy of involvement and importance of one artist over another. Star or solo performing roles are negotiated on a "fee per performance" basis, but orchestral musicians, corps de ballet, chorus, and stage crew have annual contracts.

With increasing complexity of the organization and its production staff (e.g., stage crew, backstage maintenance), support personnel have become specialized into artistic, technical, stage and shop, financial, and stage management functions. Artistically related tasks for support personnel include working with performers, negotiating performers' contracts, and acting as a liaison with union representatives (or with the chorus, corps de ballet, orchestra musicians, and personal managers and agents), as well as allocating time for rehearsals and resolving stylistic conflicts as they arise. Technical responsibilities include coordinating the activities of ushers and maintenance staff and allocating space for rehearsals. Stage and shop operations cover working with stage crews, engineers, carpenters, hair and wig stylists, makeup artists, wardrobe mistresses, lighting, and film. Those responsible for the financial operations analyze budgets, oversee the box office and gift shop, and prepare reports for the board. Stage management includes the coordination of activities onstage, making sure artists are on time, escorting prima donnas, having promoters and supernumeraries in place at the right time, and arranging for rehearsals and stage placements. Administering arts organizations requires sophisticated managerial skills to deal with the professionalization and changing financial support of the arts.

A Biographical Profile

The top management position is usually filled by an artist (conductor, choreographer, director, etc.), who has assistants with more managerial expertise. In the larger organizations, one can find almost two distinct hierarchies: artistic and nonartistic, with decisions being shared by manager and artist. The professional commitment of managers is reflected in their titles, so that a conductor may be called "musical director," whereas a nonmusician may be called "executive director" or "general manager."

Analyses of the previous jobs held by administrative and artistic directors are presented in Tables 2 and 3. Table 2 lists jobs previously held by administrative directors of music organizations—rock, jazz, opera, choral—in New York State and shows how these jobs vary with the size of the organizations' budgets. It appears that the highest percentage of administrative directors, 27 percent, previously held positions as producers, managers, or art administrators. The second largest group of today's administrators, with 23 percent, had been artists, and those who had been educators make up approximately 25 percent of current administrators.

Table 2. Last Job before Becoming Administrative Director of Music Organization (New York), 1971–72 (in Percentages)

| | Performing Arts | | Size of Budgets* | | |
Previous Positions of Current Administrators	Total	Music	$ 5,000 to $49,999	$ 50,000 to $249,999	$250,000 and Over
Arts Administrator, Producer, Manager	26*	27*	19*	24*	43*
The Arts (Director, Writer, Composer, Choreographer, Painter, Architect)	25	23	20	25	14
Education	18	25	22	15	18
Business	14	16	19	12	9
Administrator or Executive of Non-Arts Service Organization	1	1	3	6	3
Professional	6	2	5	4	3
Government	2	0	2	4	3
Communications (TV, Radio, Newspaper)	1	1	2	3	2
Student	1	1	1	1	1
Housewife	1	1	2	1	0
Other	5	3	5	5	4

SOURCE: National Council of the Arts (1973:31).
*Figure includes all visual and performing arts organizations.

In comparing music organizations with other performing arts organizations, music groups—more than dance, theater, and other presenters—have a tendency to employ art administrators, educators, and businessmen rather than musicians, composers, or singers. The more complex structure of music groups, discussed previously, demands such recruitment policies. This is confirmed further when top positions are correlated with company size, as measured by the companies' annual budgets. Forty-three percent of the administrators in organizations with budgets over $250,000 had previous experience as administrators, producers, or managers. The largest proportion of administrators in smaller organizations came from education and the arts. With the growth of their budgets, and the establishment of liaison and constant communication with unions and funding agencies, organizations have come to employ men and women who have been educated and/or trained as arts managers and administrators. Smaller organizations probably serve as training grounds for upcoming arts administrators.

Table 3 lists the last job administrators held before they became artistic directors in all the performing arts organizations in New York State. The organizations with larger budgets more consistently hire artistic directors who were previously employed as arts administrators, producers, or managers. The sheer size and complexity of these organizations seem to dictate requirements for specialized skills in management. Tables 2 and 3 seem to confirm that "professional" arts managers perfect their skills in smaller companies and move up from these companies.

Table 3. Last Job before Becoming Artistic Director of Music Organization (New York), 1971 (in Percentages)

| | Performing Arts | | Size of 1970–1971 Budget* | | |
Previous Position of Artistic Directors	Total (160)	Music (68)	$ 5,000 to $49,000 (134)	$ 50,000 to $249,999 (48)	$250,000 and over (59)
			%	%	%
Music	29	61	22	20	21
Theater	20	5	16	23	6
Arts Administrator, Producer, Manager	12	5	9	11	30
Education	11	15	16	7	4
Dance	16	0	10	11	9
Visual Arts	1	0	3	11	13
Student	4	5	9	7	4
Other Art	0	0	3	0	0
Communications (TV, Radio, Newspaper)	0	0	0	4	0
Other	4	7	9	4	9
Unavailable	3	2	3	2	4

SOURCE: National Council of the Arts (1973:81–82).
*Figures are based on organizations with separate artistic director and on total performing and visual arts organizations.

Specialized education programs in performing arts administration attest to the dramatic increase in administrators being employed by arts organizations. Of the twenty-six graduate-level programs, dating from 1966, eighteen were fully operational by 1976 and were offering a graduate degree with a major concentration in arts administration. The majority were established in the mid-1970s and remain in schools of management rather than fine arts. At least a third of the curriculum is set aside for art electives and/or internships in local arts centers or performing arts organizations. Typical management courses include statistics, model building, economics, computer programming, and organizational theory, while art-related courses include law and the arts, labor negotiation, nonprofit administration, box-office management, community and press relations, theater design, planning, and grantsmanship (Donner, 1975). Arts Management, a national news service for those who finance, manage and communicate the arts, proudly reports on the employment of marketing, promotion, and consumer experts by arts organizations across the nation (Arts Management, 1976).

The business and legal backgrounds of administrators of large companies, the development of graduate arts-management curricula, and the employment of nonartistic personnel all support the argument that arts organizations are becoming increasingly formalized.

Rationality in Artistic Decision Making

Managers of the nineteenth and early twentieth centuries were either artists themselves or "impresarios," a title connoting status and power. Their claim to legitimacy was either their personality, talent, or lineage, established by kinship, tradition, or a network of personal contacts within the art community. By the mid-twentieth century, the impresario became almost extinct. Given the tradition of "managerialism" in America, it was not surprising that the concepts of scientific management were seen as resolutions to the economic problems facing the arts. Donal Henahan (1979) laments the consequence of this:

> The managerial revolution in the arts, recently growing so evident, has deep roots in this country, which has always prized organizational ability over the creative impulse. . . . They are professional, efficient and well-informed, as a rule, but it does seem unlikely, given the foundational, endowmental origins of their careers, that in them we are about to witness the birth of a generation of Huroks, not to mention Diaghilevs or Lincoln Kirsteins. [Sec. 2, p. 1.]

Although Max Weber's analysis of the decline of charisma was associated with a philosophy of history and social movements, he always linked the type and extent of charisma to some institutional order.

> A charismatic movement may be routinized into traditionalism or into bureaucratization. Which course is taken does not depend primarily upon the subjective intentions of the followers or of the leader; it is dependent upon the institutional framework of the movement, and especially upon the economic order. The routinization of charisma, in quite essential respects, is identical with adjustment to the conditions of the economy. . . [Weber, 1958:54.]

The institutional base of charisma stems from both the internal hierarchical structure of the arts organization and the external environment comprised of artists, critics, and audiences, all of whom define art. Although the external institutional basis has greater historical and aesthetic precedence, the organization is the work milieu of the performer, and one that has posed dilemmas for the individual performer. The increased size and complexity of artistic organizations has encouraged a "routinization of charisma." There are examples of this trend in all the performing arts of dance, theater, and music, in which organizational goals may have originally reflected a highly personalized style but must become "routinized" if the organization is to grow (Raymond and Greyser, 1978:28). An examination of specific casting and repertoire decisions will reveal how economic concerns take precedence over artistic values in establishing priorities for decision making.

Simon (1957) writes: "The rational administrator is concerned with the selection of these effective means" (p.61). Such effective means, including production values geared to lower costs and increased productivity, and cost-benefit analysis, are revealed to be the major preoccupation of arts administrators today and greatly affect artistic decision making. One music critic, Henahan (1979:22), has written:

> Almost invariably, these organizational experts find themselves involved in making decisions about the arts themselves, often with little prior knowledge or even awareness of the arts they must oversee. . . .Nederlander. . . .neatly sums up the modern manager's priorities: "take care of the real estate and the arts will take care of themselves."

In another instance, the Seattle Opera Company's general director, acclaimed as "arts administrator of the year," was praised as follows on the basis of his business expertise: "One of the greatest entrepreneurs I have ever known. We admire him because as businessmen we admire entrepreneurs. He won our respect and his credibility partly because of his ability to speak our language and exhibit one of the most cherished characteristics we admire" (Salem, 1976:49).

Besides the influx of managers who have been trained by and recruited from business, choreographers, conductors, and producers openly involve themselves in and discuss the effects of economics on their art form. John

Dexter's highly publicized new production of Meyerbeer's *Le Prophete* received notoriety for having saved the Met $200,000 by borrowing scenery and costumes from other productions. In an interview with the *New York Times*, Dexter commented: "In terms of economics, the unit set is easier to handle. One thing we must do here is to lighten the physical load. We have some monster productions. A realistic set means we have to tie up the stage for two days sometimes. And our maintenance bill is phenomenal" (Braun, 1977:13).

Analogous studies in dance (Barnes, 1975) and theater (Gussow, 1975) reveal how repertoire and casting reflect attempts to raise box office receipts. Murray Louis, a noted modern dance choreographer, placed the ambivalence between art and money in terms of artistic freedoms and the increased reliance upon "outside" sources for audiences and federal subsidies. He laments:

> I do not wish to imply that this isolation was welcomed. The clamoring for funds, audience and opportunity was as active then as it is today, with of course one small exception. We had none of those things then and today we have them all. But what also made that period different from today was a germinal difference, an intrinsic difference, a basic difference. Before, the art was shaped and dealt with from within, and today it is being fashioned from without. What constituted the art then was the dancer, the teacher, the choreographer and the small devoted audiences one managed to attract. These things were within our grasp. Classes, creating, rehearsals and teaching all occurred within the only security we knew, the studio. Everything made sense in that studio, everything fell apart and came together there. . . . I feel, however, that the strains are real. The studio is no longer in control. The dancer, teacher, choreographer can no longer call the shots. We have out-priced ourselves and over-expanded the profession too quickly, and the decisions for the remedy are all coming from the "outside."

Managers or directors, who are non-performers, are more prone to criticism. They are often seen as conservative and bourgeois by musicians and sophisticated audiences, who are critical of their priorities: production issues, budget, and box office sales. Harold Schonberg, music critic of the *New York Times*, in reviewing Rudolph Bing's regime and the 1972 season, wrote:

> And Mr. Bing's tastes are conventional, all the more in that he has made no secret of letting box office considerations dictate his repertory. . . .But many feel that the Metropolitan Opera repertory has been unadventurous and stagnant. And there have been constant complaints about the quality of musical preparation. Mr. Bing seems honestly insensitive to musical values. He always has been more concerned with production and administrative values. [1972:13.]

The interplay of art and money has been explored. Repertoire and casting decisions within the world of the performing arts were found to be influenced by market factors. Over a ten-year period, repertoire trends were found to reflect the audience composition. Box-office favorites appeared, season after season, enjoying the most elaborate and expensive of setting and costuming. Experimental and new productions, considered risky and expensive, were at a minimum. The number of productions per season was also lowered in an attempt to lower the costs of production. Efficient coordination was assured, and allocation of rehearsal time and scheduling were made more predictable with fewer productions per season. In casting, managers hired a group of loyal performers who did not command the fees of the international star market. Criteria for casting became objective. Such a "routinization of charisma" became expressed in terms of reliability, accessibility, tolerable personalities, and often fulfilled reciprocal obligations between administrator and performer. Given the importance of box office receipts, a performer's artistry was measured in terms of box office sales, and virtuosity in terms of its suitability for a technological age (Martorella, 1982).[1]

Arian, in *Bach, Beethoven and Bureaucracy* (1971), analyzed how organizational changes in the Philadelphia Orchestra increasingly led to a reliance on box office receipts and record royalties. This "bureaucratic era" of the Philadelphia Orchestra decreased innovativeness in repertoire and increased alienation among orchestra musicians. This trend is accelerating as administrators attempt to lower production costs and to generate greater federal subsidies.

Toward an Ideology for Rational Administrative Behavior

Analogously to other public service occupations, the job of arts administrator is viewed as essential and serving communal needs. The rewards are more than financial, including high social status and recognition for dedicating one's life to artistic ideals. Low salaries are compensated for by altruism and the nonmaterial contingencies of the work (Bensman, 1967). With increasing income sources from public funds, the arts administrator is viewed as "accountable" to the public. Such client control in the arts includes environmental pressures (for example, audiences' tastes, critics' responses, superstars' preferences, deficits), which become the organizational uncertainties, and the most problematic features of organizational stability. The major areas of decision and policy making—repertoire, casting, financing—are manipulated so that organizational goals are minimally met, while uncertainties are controlled. A concern with audience preference and a tendency to cast superstars insure box office returns; at the same time, limiting the number of productions in a season and casting less expensive artists as "covers" lower staging and personnel expenses. Such decision making reveals how efficient "levels of production" are met by the administrator who employs techniques of rationality in arts administration. The administrator, who claims to fulfill artistic goals, is actually the person most removed from the creation of the artistic product, especially if the position is solely in management.

The governance of a company by artists or right-wing administrators affects the nature and style of the creative product, and directly reflects organizational priorities as prescribed by top management. In a performing arts organization, it becomes a significant factor in determining aesthetic styles and artistic standards. More intensive study is needed analyzing artistic and nonartistic leadership within the performing arts organization. Future research should compare decision making by artists and by managers, given their commitment to artistic or business priorities, respectively.[2]

Summary

The occupational ideology of administrators has been shown to be part of the rationalization of production. "Accountability" and "organizational survival" serve to legitimate administrative decisions, while artistic standards and innovative repertoire are preempted. The future effects of administrative management on the arts will certainly not result in boldness in repertoire. On the contrary, "rationality" in artistic management, expressed by the employment of business techniques, will result in the standardization of repertoire, the routinization of charisma.

Notes

1. Commentators have criticized the high Cs of singers and the gymnastic quality of today's dancers as attempts to attract a mass audience.
2. It would be interesting to do a comparative history of companies whose leaders have been both artists and administrators.

References

Arian, Edward. 1971. *Bach, Beethoven and Bureaucracy: The Case of the Philadelphia Orchestra.* University, Alabama: Univ. of Alabama Press.

Baldridge, J. Victor. 1971. *Power and Conflict in the University*. New York: John Wiley.

Baumol, William J., and William G. Bowen. 1966. *The Performing Arts: The Economic Dilemma*. New York: Twentieth Century Fund.

Bensman, Joseph. 1967. *Dollars and Sense: Ideology, Ethics, and the Meaning of Work in Profit and Nonprofit Organizations*. New York: Macmillan.

Braun, Richard M. 1977. "Dexter: An Artist Who Pinches Pennies." *New York Times*. January 16, p. 13.

Caplow, Theodore. 1954. *The Sociology of Work*. Minneapolis: Univ. of Minnesota Press.

Donner, William H. 1975. *A Survey of Art Administration Training in the U.S. and Canada*. New York: Donner Foundation.

Ford Foundation. 1974. *The Finances of the Performing Arts*, vol. 1. New York: Ford Foundation.

Gussow, Mel. 1975. "A Playwright's Invention Named Papp." *New York Times*, November 9, p. 12.

Henahan, Donal. 1979. "The New Impresarios: Still in the Shadow of Sol Hurok." *New York Times*, March 18, sec. 2, pp. 1, 22.

Hirsch, Paul. 1975. "Organizational Effectiveness and the Institutional Environment." *Administrative Science Quarterly*, 20:327–44.

Jarvie, I. C. 1970. *Movies and Society*. New York: Basic Books.

Martorella, Rosanne. 1982. *The Sociology of Opera*. South Hadley, Mass.: J. F. Bergin.

National Council of the Arts. 1973. *A Study of Non-Profit Arts and Cultural Industry in New York State*. New York: Cranford Wood.

Netzer, Dick. 1978. *The Subsidized Muse: Public Support for the Arts in the United States*. New York: Cambridge Univ. Press.

Raymond, Thomas J. C., and Stephen A. Greyser. 1978. "The Business of Managing the Arts." *Harvard Business Review*, 56:23–31.

Raynor, Henry. 1972. *A Social History of Music from the Middle Ages to Beethoven*. New York: Schocken.

Rockefeller Fund. 1965. *The Performing Arts: Problems and Prospects*. New York: McGraw–Hill.

Salem, Mahmoud. 1976. *Organizational Survival in the Performing Arts: The Making of the Seattle Opera*. New York: Praeger.

Schonberg, Harold C. 1972. "He Ran His House as an Autocrat." *New York Times*, April 16, p. 13.

Simon, Herbert A. 1945. *Administrative Behavior*. New York: Free Press.

Strauss, Anselm. 1971. *Professions, Work, and Careers*. San Francisco: Sociology Press.

Thompson, James. 1967. *Organizations in Action*. New York: McGraw–Hill.

Weber, Max. 1958. *From Max Weber: Essays in Sociology*, trans. and ed. H. H. Gerth and C. Wright Mills. New York: Oxford Univ. Press.

6

Patronage and Organizational Structure in Symphony Orchestras in London and New York

STEPHEN R. COUCH

The sociological study of the arts has been receiving increased attention in the United States in recent years. A fair number of scholars have been realizing that by studying the interdependent influences of social structure and artistic style, we can learn much about the more general question of how the patterned organization of social life influences, and is influenced by, the values and meanings attached to life by persons and groups, and the artifacts that embody them.

However, understanding the linkage between social structure and artistic style must be seen as the pot of gold at the end of a very long and elusive rainbow. We need to learn much more about the social structure of art worlds before it will be possible to systematically explicate the nature of the relationship between that structure and the culture it produces.

Consider, for example, the symphony orchestra. It does not simply depend on the "needs" of music composed for it, but greatly influences the development of music itself. As John Mueller (1951:7) so aptly stated, the "very form and logic of music grows out of its performance history." The very definition of "music" with which composers begin to work is formed through socialization to the culture in which they live. That definition itself is arrived at through performance, and the nature of performance—its technology, its participants, its own social structures and culture—is very much influenced by sociocultural patterns operating at higher, more general levels of analysis. 109

Music itself not only influences organizations that perform it but is influenced by them. Therefore, discovering factors that influence the structural development of performing groups is a critical prelude to discovering the relationships between social structure and musical style itself. This chapter attempts to accomplish some of this preliminary work by examining some aspects of the organizational development of the symphony orchestra in London and New York.

The symphony orchestra is America's most successful and prestigious performing arts institution. Along with its success, the most striking feature of American symphony orchestras is their organizational structure. Professional symphony orchestras in this country are run by boards of directors composed of prestigious individuals who in most cases either possess a good deal of wealth or have access to people or organizations with such wealth. Administration of the orchestras' affairs is handled by a professional management staff engaged by and beholden to the board, while artistic affairs are within the purview of a musical director–conductor also engaged by the directors. The orchestras' musicians are unionized employees hired by the board on the recommendation of the musical director.

Although this is the organizational pattern almost all American professional orchestras have come to follow, it is by no means universal. Rather, the American system represents but one of a number of options used to structure symphony orchestras (Taubman, 1970). A particularly interesting contrast is found in the case presented by the four privately run symphony orchestras of London. They are organized as producer cooperatives, with the musicians electing a board of directors from among themselves. Management personnel, musical directors, and conductors are hired by the musicians, who ultimately are responsible for all artistic and policy matters.

In terms of the development of organizational structures, these differences are significant. How is it that organizations in countries with the same basic dominant economic structure (capitalism), producing the same product (or repertoire), using the same human and mechanical technology, and possessing the same type of workplace power structure (authoritarian control exercised by the conductor during the working day), have such different organizational structures?

This chapter attempts to answer that question by comparing the London situation with that of the New York Philharmonic, which began as a cooperative but later changed its structure to its present lay-board form. The histories of the Philharmonic Societies of New York and London, and of the present-day London orchestras, will be used to show how the organization of the symphony orchestra is connected with social forces that extend far beyond the cultural spheres of the orchestras themselves.

The organizing framework for examining these cases is quite simple. Two different kinds of influences can be seen as acting on orchestral structures throughout their histories. One concerns large-scale social forces. The second in effect mediates between these general social forces and orchestral structures. To illustrate, the rise of monopoly capitalism, a large-scale social force, both required and resulted in the accumulation of great wealth in the hands of a few people. Some of them in turn used personal wealth to help support orchestras, an intervening influence—namely, the pattern of patronage. In doing so, they gained a measure of control over the operations of the orchestras, a matter of orchestral structure. This chapter is specifically concerned with explaining orchestral structures in terms of the major intervening influences, and with explaining the intervening influences in terms of large-scale social forces.

Throughout the social history of the orchestra, a basic fact emerges—since the seventeenth century, the orchestra has been appropriated from the court-centered aristocrats by the bourgeoisie. The connection of this appropriation to larger social forces seems obvious—it occurred during the period of rise and entrenchment of the bourgeois class, a time when bourgeois power in all fields became dominant. The appropriation of the orchestra, however, cannot be seen in terms of a simple social class analysis, but is subtle enough to require more detailed examination. The appropriation with which this analysis is concerned is the appropriation of the orchestra from the musicians themselves by the business and social elite. Interestingly enough, this process can be seen as a proletarianization of the performing orchestral musician over the past century, and therefore as part of a much more general social occurrence (Couch, 1979). The musician began this process as an independent businessperson (in musical jargon, a freelancer) and, in most cases, ended it being assimilated into the working class, selling his or her labor to those who have (or have access to) capital. Both the New York and London Philharmonics began this process as cooperatives, with the musicians controlling their own organizations. The New York Philharmonic became in time an organization controlled by a lay board of directors, with the musicians being employees. The Philharmonic Society of London became not an orchestra but a concert-sponsoring organization—the present London orchestras are not directly related to the Philharmonic Society, but developed separately in more recent times.

During the eighteenth century, the patronage system by which the arts were supported in Europe went through a period of dissolution. The rise of the bourgeoisie and the attendant decline in aristocratic wealth resulted in many continental courts' no longer being able to support court orchestras. Musicians gained their freedom from the restrictions of court service only to be thrown on their own in an attempt to make a living through music (Raynor, 1972).

In England, a process took place which was both similar and different. England never had the multitude of aristocratic courts that existed on the continent. Patronage of the arts in England had traditionally fallen more substantially on the middle classes (this being well illustrated by Shakespearean theater). However, the church had been a most important patron of the musician. With the advent of the Commonwealth, however, church patronage was suddenly curtailed. The musicians who had enjoyed church patronage had to seek a living by other methods, including performing in taverns. Late in the seventeenth century, musicians began to sponsor their own concerts in taverns or "music rooms"—hence, the beginning of public concert life in England (Nettel, 1946).

During the eighteenth century, as the wealth of the middle class grew, public concerts became more institutionalized. Composers and performers would sponsor concerts, hoping to make a success of the event not only artistically but financially. The musical structure became one in which entrepreneurs would hire musicians (themselves independent businessmen jockeying for musical odd jobs in order to make a living) and produce concerts (Raynor, 1972). Though the audience was still a relatively elite one, the development of the public concert (that is, with an admission fee) saw the musical performance take on a commodity character. From that point on, musical performance entered more and more into the commodity market, with the musicians themselves coming to expend their labor as employees.

Although this process made it possible for many musicians to earn at least some money from playing music, it presented both musicians and wealthy bourgeoisie with a major problem. Unlike court concerts, to which audiences were invited because of their privileged relationship to the prince, music of the "best" kind could now be heard by anyone possessing enough money to buy a ticket. But this "democratization" of music was not what was desired by the wealthy bourgeoisie. They were attempting to justify their new class position by taking over, not destroying, aristocratic culture. It was the ordering of the stratification system that was being changed, not the stratification system itself. As there was exclusivity within the aristocracy, so was there exclusivity within the bourgeoisie. Only bourgeoisie worthy to hear and able to understand great music should be allowed at concerts. Concerts were still social events, as they had been at the courts. But practically, given the public concert, how is a cultural heathen with the price of admission to be turned away? As for the musicians themselves, many looked with disdain on the mixing of music with money. The making of music was a gentlemanly affair, not to be mixed with pecuniary motives. In addition, the admission of paying audiences without regard to social class position could only adversely affect what music was performed, as well as disrupt the performances themselves.

The formation of the Philharmonic Society of London can be seen as an attempt to resolve this problem.[1] Professional musicians in London around 1800 made their living primarily by teaching music, supplemented by free-lancing. There were concerts of the newly fashionable "symphony" music, but the appeal was not as great as that of opera or choral music. The society began in 1813, not as a money-making venture but as a cooperative of musicians jointly producing a few concerts each year. The cooperative organization of the society and the professed desire of the members not to emphasize money over music can be seen as a gentlemanly reaction to the public concert run for money.

Although democracy for one and all was seen as far too radical by these musicians, democracy among peers was already part of the gentlemanly code, and was emphasized. Equity among the musicians of the society was the rule. Members rotated as conductors. No soloists were hired. Exclusivity of members and audience was, however, equally emphasized—both members and subscribers had to be approved by the society before being admitted.

This situation did not last long. Middle-class wealth continued to grow throughout the first half of the nineteenth century. Such wealth was sufficient to support much musical activity, including orchestral concerts. But the Philharmonic did not benefit from this growing wealth. Instead, competition grew in the form of concerts featuring orchestral music that was lighter than the Philharmonic's repertoire—what we know today as "pops." This type of music was more immediately appealing and entertaining to larger numbers of people than the Philharmonic's repertoire—the Philharmonic's music and policies were seen by many as "stodgy" and "snobbish." The competition of these "pops" concerts strained the financial position of the Philharmonic to the point where it became necessary for it to appeal to a broader base for support, and therefore to abandon some of its original policies for the sake of "box office draw." Soloists were admitted to the Philharmonic's programs. Concerts were held in larger halls, with extra tickets being sold to anyone with the money to pay for them, regardless of social position. At the same time, advertising and conscious use of the "snob" appeal of symphony concerts were used to increase support, rather than diminish it.

The situation in New York was similar.[2] A group of musicians formed the Philharmonic Society of New York in 1942 as a cooperative somewhat similar to the society of London. The New York Philharmonic soon felt the pressure of competition and responded by seeking the support of a broader base of the community.

Increased popularity of the Philharmonics, however, did not solve the orchestras' financial problems. The latter part of the nineteenth century saw both Philharmonics plagued by increasing financial crises. Competition spawned artistic improvements and expansion in such areas as advertising. Yet expenses continued to mount. As has been shown by Baumol and Bowen's

(1966) classic study of arts financing, the arts are in a poor position financially in both an expanding and a receding capitalist economy, needing increased subsidies in order to survive. By the end of the century, it was clear that a financial base firmer than that of the box office had to be found. The great wealth amassed by monopoly capitalists during this period provided that firmer base.

The Boston Symphony provided a model (Hart, 1973:48–70). In 1881, the wealthy Henry Lee Higginson offered to cover all debts incurred by the Boston Symphony, provided that the musicians of the symphony be contracted so as to give the symphony the major part of their time throughout the course of the season. The offer was accepted. With the musicians playing together consistently, it did not take long for the Boston Symphony to become the model orchestral ensemble in the country. The success of the Boston Symphony inspired the wealthy of other cities to band together and privately finance professional orchestras.

Returning to a consideration of the New York scene, visits of the Boston Symphony to New York had much influence on the New York musical community. In addition, competition in orchestral music had increased with the founding of the New York Symphony, under the sponsorship and control of various wealthy New Yorkers. The Philharmonic in its part-time, cooperative form could not maintain its eminent position as the leader of orchestral performance in New York. In 1911, wealthy patrons offered to greatly increase the number of Philharmonic concerts, and to pay for Philharmonic deficits, in return for control of the organization of the orchestra. The offer was accepted. The musicians had traded control for financial security. The cooperative was dead, with organizational power being put in the hands of a board of directors from among the ranks of the patrons. The musicians had lost control of the orchestra.

Why would the musicians settle for this trade? The temptations were great. It offered a living wage through the performance of music, something symphonic musicians in New York had never enjoyed. In terms of the continuance of the Philharmonic, their only alternative seemed to be the relegation of their orchestra to a permanently secondary status and quality, given the trends of the day. The case of the New York Philharmonic seems to be a classic example of the difficulty institutions have in attempting to maintain economic and political forms that are out of step with the dominant economic and political structures.

In London, a similar situation occurred. During the First World War, funding for the Philharmonic Society of London dropped. Even with its small number of concerts, it found it impossible to continue operations. Sir Thomas Beecham, the eminent English conductor and a gentleman with a good deal of inherited wealth, offered to bail out the Philharmonic in return for political control of the orchestra. His offer was accepted, and the London Philharmonic Society ceased to be a cooperative orchestra.

It is at this point, however, that differences between the New York and London situations became apparent. In 1918, the London musicians, who were dissatisfied with the one-man rule of Sir Thomas, retook control of the orchestra, which again became a cooperative. That they would (and could) do so reflects a difference in the situations of London and New York which can be traced to a number of factors.

In the first place, it is significant to note that the wealth of Sir Thomas was not "new" wealth, but inherited. The new base of wealth for support of the orchestra was not as broad in London as in New York. In addition, the conception in London of a "permanent" orchestra was not as grand. It was always assumed that a good deal of freelancing would still be necessary for members of a permanent orchestra in London to be able to make a living wage, even during concert season. Expanding the season to a point where employment with the Philharmonic Society of London would constitute the major part of one's total employment was not practical. The base of support was just not there. Instead, a "permanent" orchestra was an orchestra consisting of the same personnel at every rehearsal and concert, with adequate rehearsal time for each concert. Beecham's offer, therefore, did not provide the same financial security as that offered by his New York counterparts.

Between the First and Second World Wars, a number of complicated factors were involved in shaping the London orchestral scene. Beecham continued to attempt to found his own orchestra, and to make various arrangements with the Philharmonic Society, but each effort failed. At the same time, competition was increased through the formation of the BBC Orchestra, supported by the growing power of the broadcasting and recording industries, and then by the British Government. Still, the growth of broadcasting and recording created enough work so that the BBC Orchestra did not gain a monopoly in the London orchestral world.

Beecham did, in 1932, finally succeed in forming his permanent orchestra—the London Philharmonic Orchestra (not to be confused with the Philharmonic Society of London). It drew many of the best players away from the Philharmonic Society. The society's financial backing had also nearly collapsed. The society decided to engage the new London Philharmonic Orchestra for their season of concerts. The society's own orchestra was thereby defunct; the society, still a cooperative, was now a cooperative concert-sponsoring society and no longer a cooperative orchestra.

The focus in London must now shift away from the society to the London orchestras that were left. What is found is that the system of private patronage broke down completely with World War II. The case of Beecham's London Philharmonic Orchestra is typical. With the war, its financial position collapsed. It ceased operations in 1939. However, it was quickly reformed by the musicians as a cooperative, both sponsoring concerts itself and acting as its own agent by securing concerts for itself sponsored by others. The cooperative form, while not giving the orchestra enough financial backing to be a permanent group, at least allowed it to continue to function. This type of organization, anticipated by the London Symphony Orchestra in 1904, became the model for London orchestras (Pearton, 1974; Smyth, 1970).

This cooperative form of organization was helped immeasurably after the war, when Britain entered into its program of government subsidies to the arts. The large-scale social force of the development of state capitalism in Britain has served to protect the cooperatives from the influence of wealthy patrons. What is more, the Arts Council of Great Britain—which decides on government funding for arts groups—is set up in such a way as to minimize direct governmental interference with the policies of the orchestras. There is, as should be expected, political pressure put on the orchestras by those who hold the purse strings, but the pressure has not seemed to be partisanly political. However, the situation is not stable in London today. There are five orchestras operating in the city, with a demand that really does not call for five (Arts Council of Great Britain, 1970; Committee on the London Orchestras, 1965).

The cooperatives as seen in the context of patronage and power under capitalism may only be a stopgap measure. The cooperatives survive because they operate in a highly unstable patronage environment where no one group has been able to offer the musicians a stable, year-round income in return for control of the orchestras. As long as a more stable patronage system is not found, the cooperative form is liable to remain. But if one is found, it is likely that there will be a trade of power for security, and the musicians' cooperatives may become a form of the past.

In New York, the situation in this century has not been so complex. The early part of the century saw the New York Philharmonic follow a pattern similar to that followed by the large businesses of the time—the acquisition of a monopoly. It merged with a number of other New York orchestras and, with the help of its rich patrons, drove others out of business.

The century has not, however, seen the Philharmonic bask in a period of financial stability. Costs soared greatly, due in part to the push by musicians to turn the Philharmonic into truly full-year employment and to receive a wage comparable to that received by other skilled workers. At the same time, it has become more difficult for a few wealthy patrons to cope with the huge deficits amassed. In addition, the United States government (as well as that of New York State) has only recently begun to fund the arts, including the New York Philharmonic, and the amount of governmental funding is still relatively small. Consequently, power within the orchestra has remained with the wealthy, or with those who have access to the support of the wealthy.

In summary, three stages of patronage (the major mediating influence between large-scale social forces and orchestral structure) can be seen as having taken place. The first was the breakdown of court and church patronage caused by the rise of capitalism and resulting in the rise of the public concert, the broadening of the commodity form in music, and attendant reactions against this form. The second was the partial stabilization of the patronage system through the development of monopoly capitalism and the appropriation of the orchestra (completely in America, partially in London) by wealthy patrons. Finally, the rise of state capitalism, a stage which has only recently begun in England and America, finds the state entering directly into arts patronage. In America, this has had little effect on orchestral structure; in England, it may be what has allowed the London orchestras to remain as cooperatives to this point.

This investigation has shown how differences in the development of capitalism in England and the United States created different possibilities and constraints on the patronage support available to symphony orchestras, which in turn influenced the orchestras' organizational structures. One question remains to be considered: what are some of the consequences of these forms of organization? This chapter will conclude with an examination of the influence of orchestra structure on four areas: musical programming, orchestra economics, musician alienation and job satisfaction, and the social nature of the music itself.

First, an examination of the repertoire of the New York Philharmonic, other American orchestras, and the orchestras of London, indicates surprisingly few differences (J. Mueller, 1951; K. Mueller, 1973; London Orchestral Concert Board, 1968–1975). Especially striking is the dominance of the "standard" repertoire of the eighteenth and nineteenth centuries (especially the latter) and the relative paucity of innovative works. It seems that London musicians program works quite similar to those programmed by American symphony orchestras; the London orchestras' structure does not lead to a significant increase in innovative programming. The most plausible explanation for this lies in the market situation in which London and American orchestras find themselves. In both cases, box office appeal is financially essential, and there is a great fear that too much of a deviation from the standard repertoire will result in the loss of necessary box office revenues (Zolberg, 1980).

Second, although I have argued in this chapter that economic conditions have influenced the development of different orchestral-organization structures, those structures in turn influence the ability of orchestras to tap available financial resources in an ever-changing economic environment. In London, the lack of large-scale stable support for orchestras has made it necessary for London orchestral musicians to work extremely hard in order for their orchestras to survive. The amount of work done by each of those orchestras surpasses that of almost all orchestras in the United States (London Orchestral Concert Board, 1968–1975). The musicians themselves decide on how many services the orchestra will play. It is hard to imagine most American musicians, operating in an adversarial labor-relations structure with boards of directors, accepting the amount of work performed by London musicians.

On the other hand, cooperative permanent professional orchestras are unlikely to be able to survive for long in the United States. Here, where private contributions from individuals and corporations are essential, a cooperative orchestra is unlikely to receive nearly the support that can be secured by the work and contributions of boards made up of businessmen and bankers. During the 1960s and 1970s, as government support for the arts increased dramatically in this country, the possibility grew for a sharing of control over orchestras among traditional board members and musicians, workers, and racial and ethnic minorities. But with today's massive federal cuts for arts support, bringing with them the need for even greater amounts of private contributed money, a consolidation of power by the traditional elite boards will likely result (DiMaggio and Useem, 1978:389).

Third, does orchestral structure influence the job satisfaction of musicians? The answer to this interesting question is not known. No rigorous study of worker satisfaction in symphony orchestras has been conducted. It is known that orchestral musicians in the United States have become increasingly militant during the past two decades, winning better pay and longer seasons through struggles at the collective bargaining table. Perhaps one cause of this militancy is the powerlessness of musicians within orchestras. Only recently have orchestras begun to utilize the advice of their musicians in such areas as auditions, conductor selection, and artistic policy, and even here, musician participation has usually come about after protracted struggle. Indeed, only since the 1960s have orchestra musicians won the right to negotiate and ratify their own contracts. The powerlessness of American orchestra musicians within their work environment combines with physical and mental stress factors inherent in playing long seasons in professional orchestras and helps provide an explanation for the very high rate of physical and psychological problems found among professional orchestra players (Tucker et al., 1971; Shaw, 1978).

In London, the hard-fought struggles by musicians to keep the identity and structure of the cooperative orchestras against many adverse circumstances indicate the strong belief held by many musicians that orchestral democracy is beneficial (Pearton, 1974). At the same time, anecdotal accounts by London musicians reveal some ambivalence toward the cooperative structure (Smyth, 1970; Previn, 1979). In light of theoretical formulations about workplace democracy, and of growing empirical evidence that workers' control increases job satisfaction (Blumberg, 1968; Hunnius, 1973; Greenberg, 1980), a comparative study of work satisfaction among orchestra members in London and the United States would be an enlightening and important contribution to the study of the social organization of artistic work.

Finally, let us return to the relationship between organizations and the music itself. The arguments presented here lead to the conclusion that the orchestra is basically an elite institution. Is symphony music, then, inherently an elite art? Studies show that audiences at symphony concerts are largely composed of highly educated upper-middle-class persons (DiMaggio et al., 1978). These social characteristics hold true even when free outdoor concerts are held (Shanet, 1975:398). One argument used to explain this is that lower-class persons do not have the education or training to appreciate complex art forms.

Although this may be true to some extent, another hypothesis is at least as plausible. It flows directly from the fact that the symphony orchestra is class-based. Therefore, symphonic music is seen as "high art," the property of the privileged class. Most people are not expected to be able to understand symphonic art. This breeds feelings either of inferiority or of jealous resentment against this art of the elite.

Perhaps, then, symphonic music is an elite art not mainly for any musical or educational reason, but because of the social class connotations attached to symphonic art. If this is true, then attempts at broadening the base of support for symphony orchestras and their music are bound to fail unless they include serious efforts at removing these class connotations. And the removal of such connotations is unlikely to occur unless control of the orchestras is held not only by an elite board of directors, or by the musicians themselves, but is shared with broad segments of the entire community in which the orchestras reside.

Notes

1. Material on the history of the Philharmonic Society of London has been drawn primarily from Elkin (1946), Foster (1912), Nettel (1946), and Royal Philharmonic Society (1970).

2. Historical information on the New York Philharmonic has been obtained from Shanet (1975), Erskine (1943), Huneker (1917), Krehbiel (1892), Philharmonic Society of New York (1853), and from the Philharmonic's annual reports and programs.

References

American Federation of Musicians. 1980. *Wage Scales and Conditions in the Symphony Orchestra, 1979–1980 Season.* New York: American Federation of Musicians.

Arts Council of Great Britain. 1970. *A Report on Orchestral Resources in Great Britain, 1970.* London: Arts Council of Great Britain.

Baumol, William J., and William G. Bowen. 1966. *The Performing Arts: An Economic Dilemma.* New York: Twentieth Century Fund.

Blumberg, Paul. 1968. *Industrial Democracy.* New York: Schocken.

Committee on the London Orchestras. 1965. *Report.* London: St. Clements.

Couch, Stephen R. 1976. "Class, Politics and Symphony Orchestras." *Society,* 14:24–29.

————— 1979 "The Orchestra as Factory." Paper presented at the American Sociological Society Annual Meetings, Boston, August 28.

DiMaggio, Paul, and Michael Useem. 1978. "Cultural Property and Public Policy: Emerging Tensions in Government Support for the Arts." *Social Research,* 45:356–89.

DiMaggio, Paul, Michael Useem, and Paula Brown. 1978. *Audience Studies of the Performing Arts and Museums: A Critical Review.* Washington: National Endowment for the Arts.

Elkin, Robert. 1946. *Royal Philharmonic.* London: Rider.

Erskine, John. 1943 *The Philharmonic-Symphony Society of New York.* New York: Macmillan.

Foster, Miles Birket. 1912. *The History of the Philharmonic Society of London, 1813–1912.* London: John Lane.

Greenberg, Edward S. 1980. "Participation in Industrial Decision Making and Work Satisfaction: The Case of Producer Cooperatives." *Social Science Quarterly,* 60:551–69.

Hart, Philip. 1973. *Orpheus in the New World.* New York: W. W. Norton.

Hauser, Arnold. 1972. "Alienation as the Key to Mannerism." In *Marxism and Art,* ed. Berel Lang and Forrest Williams. New York: John McKay.

Huneker, James G. 1917. *The Philharmonic Society of New York.* New York: Privately printed.

Hunnius, Gerry, David Garson, and John Case (eds.). 1973. *Workers' Control.* New York: Vintage.

International Conference of Symphony and Opera Musicians. 1980. *Compiled Index 1973–1980 Senza Sordino.* Cincinnati: ICSOM.

Krehbiel, Henry. 1892. *The Philharmonic Society of New York.* New York: Novello, Ewer.

London Orchestral Concert Board. 1968–1975. *Annual Reports of the Board of Management.* London: London Orchestral Concert Board.

Mueller, John H. 1951. *The American Symphony Orchestra.* Bloomington: Indiana Univ. Press.

Mueller, Kate H. 1973. *Twenty-Seven Major Symphony Orchestras.* Bloomington: Indiana Univ. Press.

Nettel, Reginald. 1946. *The Orchestra in England.* London: Jonathan Cape.

Pearton, Maurice. 1974. *The LSO at 70: A History of the Orchestra.* London: Victor Gollancz.

Philharmonic Society of New York. 1853. *Constitution and By-Laws.* New York: William C. Martin.

Previn, Andre. 1979. *Orchestra.* Garden City, N.Y.: Doubleday.

Raynor, Henry. 1972. A *Social History of Music.* New York: Schocken.

Royal Philharmonic Society. 1970. *Memorandum and Articles of Association.* London: Royal Philharmonic Society.

Shanet, Howard. 1975. *The Philharmonic.* Garden City: Doubleday.

Shaw, Henry. 1978. "Our Decibel Dilemma." *Senza Sordino,* 16:1–2.

Smyth, Alan (ed.). 1970. *To Speak for Ourselves: The London Symphony Orchestra.* London: William Kimber.

Taubman, Howard. 1970. *The Symphony Orchestra Abroad.* Vienna, Va.: American Symphony Orchestra League.

Tucker, Alan, Maurice E. Falkner, and Steven M. Horvath. 1971. "Electrocardiography and Lung Function in Brass Instrument Players." *Archives of Environmental Health,* 23:327–34.

Zolberg, Vera L. 1980. "Displayed Art and Performed Music: Selective Innovation and the Structure of Artistic Media." *Sociological Quarterly,* 21:219–31.

7

Interview:
Edward Villella

---•---

Choreography as Management

J.K.   When you choreographed, did you get any sense of problems you weren't aware of when you danced?

E.V.   Choreography is not dancing. Naturally, you have to dance to choreograph, but you can't think the same way. It's totally different. It's a completely different approach to an art form and it's an investigation of a different manner. You investigate style and music and invention. As a dancer you investigate your physicality to personify what other people have digested in terms of the art form.

J.K.   I was just wondering if there are any problems in trying to get the other people to do what you want them to do.

E.V.   Oh, sure, from many points of view. If you're an accomplished dancer, you are probably dealing with people who may not be as accomplished as you are, especially if you're a choreographer just starting out. If you're an established choreographer, it's just the reverse. You may have danced pretty well, but if you're really good, you're working with the very best people.

   As a choreographer, you can't just have people move the way you move. You see, you have to understand the people that you're working with. So if you work with a person who's trained for two years, you

---

Edward Villella was a principal dancer and choreographer with the New York City Ballet from 1959 to 1979. He is the host of the public television series *Dance in America*. He was interviewed by Jack Kamerman at his home in New York City in November 1981.

approach it quite a bit differently than with somebody who's danced for ten years. Or if you deal with somebody in the corps de ballet, you deal differently than with a soloist who's been a soloist for five years. You have to understand what's in front of you. You have to investigate not only the music and the style and the thematic lines, et cetera, but you also have to have in your mind **who** is going to do this. And then, from there, it's a question of personalities, sensitivities, intelligences, backgrounds, experiences, insecurities, securities. You know, as a choreographer you become sort of everything: you're the producer, you're the director, you're the choreographer, you're the costume designer, you're the set designer. You don't **do** all of those things, but you have to have them in your mind enough to converse with those people.

You know, one of the most difficult things for a choreographer who has never choreographed before is simply to **stand** in front of people. It's an experience, to stand in front of people to make them do your will. It's like the first time you become a private, and then you become a corporal, and then suddenly you're a drill sergeant. It's a very human art form and you have to approach it from human points of view.

J.K.   How did you like it?

E.V.   *I loved it!* I like the idea of standing in front of people and being able to tell them what I know. But the thing is, when you stand in front of people like that, you have to know more than they know. That's the big challenge.

Arts Administration

J.K.   You were with the New York City Cultural Affairs Commission. Did you see things as an administrator that you didn't see as a dancer?

E.V.   I think it's a very bad example. That entire structure was to me—how to put it diplomatically—like a very thin line. I had spent a long time as a member of the President's National Council on the Arts, and I had spent a lot of time with various panels on the National Endowment [for the Arts]. So, basically, I was dealing on a federal level. To go from a federal level, not even to a state level, but to a municipal level, even though it was the City of New York. . . I was shocked by the lack of structure there. And so I didn't find it an exhilarating experience, and I didn't find it a particularly rewarding idea in terms of administrating, because there was little or nothing to administrate. You know, it's an honorary job; it's a donation of time. What I was led to believe was that there was structure enough that I could lead the rest of my life and *still be able to function that way. But apparently not. In the past they had been, I guess, something like political appointments, and political appointments usually are people who have donated time and energy or, specifically, money, or people who are in positions in certain financial, corporate structures. And I guess the assumption was that when a chairman of this or that comes along, he comes along also with his infrastructure. I have no infrastructure. This is it, you're looking at it. My suggestion there was that unless there was money enough to put a structure together, I simply couldn't function, because I did not come with an office and a corporation behind me. That was unfortunately my experience. So I was not pleased with that, and simply had to leave after six months. So, it's a very, very bad example to base anything on.*

J.K.   *Sometimes things make financial sense if you're an administrator that may not make artistic sense if you're in the artistic end of an organization.*

E.V.   *The function of the administration of any cultural and/or artistic organization is to allow the artistic directors to function. That is, in my estimation, their sole purpose. It is not their purpose to define activities. It is for the artistic director to define those activities in consultation with the administrator, who then can tell you whether it's financially feasible or not. That, I think, is the major complication.*

There are priorities in anything. But the financial priority—which is obvious to an administrator who has no artistic background—is not obvious to an artistic director. I think it's essential that administrators have total and complete command of the art form. My recommendation is that if it's going to be dance or music or theater, you get a dance person or a music person or a theater person and train those people to be administrators. You are then not taking these administrators by the hand and saying, "Look, you can't dance in this theater, and here are the seventeen reasons why." It may make great economic sense that they're going to pay us $10,000, but what you may not know is that there are no lights and there is no orchestra and there are no backstage facilities, no place to rehearse, a cement stage. There are other considerations, so you can't say, "We're getting $10,000. We have to dance there." It's nonsense.

J.K.   *There's often the same conflict in other situations between administrative and professional staff.*

E.V.   *My recommendation to the National Endowment for the Arts was this: in terms of the ongoing idea of this art form, we should encourage the development and education of dancers, musicians, theater people, in their own particular art forms, and as their careers are ending there is a normal transition that they move into an administrative area. That* to me makes great sense, rather than hiring someone out of a university who has brilliant and wonderful marks in accounting and who can't hear a note or can't see a step. It doesn't make sense.

J.K.   Who has the power in a ballet company?

E.V.   It depends on the ballet company; it depends on the individuals. The ideal situation is to be a George Balanchine and to have a Lincoln Kirstein. That's ideal. Lincoln Kirstein told me that one of his main functions was to allow Balanchine to do what he does. That's crucial. Balanchine knows everything about theater and somebody has to be there to support his developing a product. If it's the New York City Ballet, it's not an accountant or a lawyer, that kind of administrative idea. Certainly you need that kind of support, but you need that support with an understanding. In terms of a ballet company, it should be the vision of the artistic director. And then it should be the administrative function to allow that vision to come to fruition. That's basic.

J.K.   Who would have the power [in a company] with a less charismatic figure than Balanchine?

E.V.   Well, if you have an artistic director who doesn't have a background and an experience, and you hire an administrator who does, certainly it's going to be the administrator. It's going to be the person with the most knowledge. It's not even charisma. I know a lot of people who simply shrink away from a camera or a microphone or a photographer, or simply don't want to be out in the public eye, but who are brilliant artists. It's really the knowledge of the art form and the vision you have and where you are going to go with this art form, where you are going to go with this particular company, how you understand that and then see where that's going to take you. The worst thing is to get into any kind of strictly bottom-line budget-locking idea. I've been through many circumstances where funding was not available to do the costumes that we wanted to do. You find another way to do it. Look what Balanchine did. Balanchine didn't have the money to have elaborate sets or costumes, so he choreographed in a way that he didn't need them. Now it's being imitated the world round. You see people in black tights and white T-shirts and girls in leotards and small skirts, practice clothes. It's now a style. Where did that come from? It came from Balanchine.

J.K.   Do ballet companies have requirements as companies that, for example, theater companies wouldn't?

E.V.   Absolutely. Completely. Stage: you need a stage. You can do theater in this room. You can't do ballet in this room. If you need an audience of twenty-five, you could do singing, or chamber music, or you could be a comedian. But if you're a ballet dancer, a single ballet dancer, you couldn't do ballet in a room this size. You just can't. So, number *one, you need a stage, but what about this stage? You can't have cement, you can't have hardwood, it can't be slippery. These are very basic, simple things. Not only that, what about lighting? Well, what do you mean, lighting? Theater lighting or ballet lighting? In theater, you can light an area and then you can light another area and it gets very close and intimate and dramatic.*

Dance is not that way. It's big and it's open and it moves. It's all about moving. You need the whole stage. So certainly it's different. What do you need with an orchestra? You need a bunch of guys and ladies who can get up and sit in front of a stand that has a light on it, and they're rehearsed and prepared. The hall has to be warm enough so that their fingers aren't cold, and not too warm so it doesn't affect the strings. That's all you need, and a proper shell and acoustics. What we need is much, much more than that. We need pipes hanging overhead; you have to be able to fly things in and out. If you need just a backdrop— not even scenery, but a backdrop—you've got to get it in and out. You need side lighting. Orchestras, what do they need? Just some front lighting and overhead lighting and some stand lights. We need side lighting and follow lights, and different gels and different colors. It's a far more complex idea. The only thing you can really compare it to, maybe, is opera, in terms of dimension and requirements.

J.K. *In your experience, how do conflicts get settled within companies?*

E.V. *It depends on the company. Five years ago in ABT [American Ballet Theater] the conflict was decided upon if you were the most recent defector who had the biggest publicity and were going to sell the tickets. If you wanted to dance the first **Giselle**, everybody fought amongst themselves and with the management, and the management just had to decide who was the biggest box office draw at that time. . . if that's the kind of conflict you're talking about. If you talk about a New York City Ballet, the conflicts are rather restrained because there is a central artistic director, somebody who controls that company, somebody who has a vision—not only a vision, but knowledge beyond almost everything and everybody. You respect that knowledge. The reason people dance at the New York City Ballet is not just to dance, but because the attraction is knowledge and quality. That's finally what you want as an artist. I don't think it makes much sense to stand in front of some dinky production and be paid a great deal of money and have a lot of people come and applaud and tell you you're great. That's cheating yourself. It's also cheating your art form. The wonderful thing is to stand up in front of an audience with your complete knowledge and technique and abilities and the rest of it, and be supported on the same level in the pit, in the costume shop, in the scenery shop, in the lighting design.*

It's all a huge collaboration, and the person who has all of that knowledge and can pull all of that together is an artistic director. And when you find a person like that, that's the person you should work for. You shouldn't work for the guy who's going to pay you $5000 more a week, because in the end, when it's all over, you're going to look at your bank account. . . Are you really going to be happy with it? It's a momentary idea, and if you sacrifice the quality for a lot of money, it's not a very pleasant thing to look back on. Unless you really like to look at your Mercedes out in front of your house and the Cadillac in the backyard. If that's what you're really about, maybe you're not an artist anyway. I don't really know the definition of the word. I don't know Webster's definition, but I have my own sense of what it is and what it's about. What it is is that there's an area that you live, it's not a job that you do, not an occupation. It's not even an art form. It's a life-style. And if that's your life-style, live it.

SECTION FOUR

THE SOCIAL DETERMINANTS OF PERFORMING STYLES

At one of these concerts [April 19–21, 1821] I asked Christian Kramer, the master of King George IV's famous band, how it was that the King was so perfectly satisfied with the tempi taken of all Haydn's Sinfonias, His Majesty being so fastidious. "Why," said Kramer, "His Majesty always beats time to every movement. I watch him and beat the same time to the orchestra."

(Smart, 1971: 57)

Occasionally, the connection between style and political and economic factors is as direct and straightforward as the introductory quotation to this section suggests. Usually, however, the relationship is more subtle and complex.

Factors that influence style may inhere in the inner dynamics of the art itself or they may be external to the art and affect cultural phenomena in general. The former include changes in styles and aesthetic assumptions. These changes are often thought to result from the creative genius of great figures in the history of the art, e.g., Haydn "inventing" the symphony; Nijinsky elevating the importance of the male dancer in ballet; Paganini extending the limits of violin playing. Artists, for obvious reasons, are fond of this approach. The latter include factors that sociologists feel more comfortable with: social and economic influences (such as changes in patronage), considerations of power, etc.

Of course it is in their interrelationship and the recognition of the validity of both approaches that the most promising analysis lies. For example, the increasing complexity of orchestral scores was a function of the creative leaps of composers like Beethoven and Berlioz. However, the increased size of the orchestral forces their scores demanded was both made possible and necessitated by the growth of the public concert. The growth of the public concert was in part a result of the erosion of aristocratic power and the consequent entry of performing artists into the open market.

The key task of sociological analysis of the performing arts is to specify the conditions under which these factors operate. One way to approach this is to study style movements in the arts, recognizing that large-scale factors are filtered through interpretive screens. This screening process results in "groups within the same actual generation which work up the material of their common experience in different specific ways" (Mannheim, 1952: 303–4). One kind of interpretive screen derives from membership in a particular occupational group. These memberships must be coordinated with other memberships—class, for example—if the specific effect of large-scale factors is to be understood. Also, the same occupational group may be differentially susceptible to the influence of these factors in different periods, depending on its current occupational self-image. For example, artists were probably more deeply affected by philosophies like romanticism in historical periods like the nineteenth century, during which they were grouped with intellectuals, than when they were defined as craftsmen, as they were in centuries prior to the eighteenth.

The goal of this analysis is the systematic explanation of style changes. The case studies in this section represent initial steps toward that goal. Karen Gaylord analyzes the basic nature of style itself and argues that aesthetic conventions are responsive to conventions of everyday life. This is clearly seen when aesthetic conventions lag behind everyday conventions, making theater appear artificial and "staged." June Riess Goldner, in her examination of the early history of the solo singer, studies performing style by focusing on the institutional factors that influenced the emergence of the role of solo singer. Jack Kamerman ties shifts in conductors' interpretive styles to factors like unionization and relates this specific case to the larger process of rationalization. The excerpt from Dmitri Shostakovich's memoirs reminds us that developments in the performing arts can sometimes have clear ideological antecedents, particularly with the exercise of raw power in totalitarian regimes. We are also reminded that subtle causation is often a luxury of democratic societies. Finally, in the interview with playwright John Bishop, influences on performing styles emanating from within the arts themselves are examined.

References

Mannheim, Karl. 1952. *Essays on the Sociology of Knowledge*, trans. and ed. Paul Kecskemeti. London: Routledge & Kegan Paul.
Smart, Sir George. 1971. *Leaves from the Journals of Sir George Smart* (1907), ed. Bertram and C. L. E. Cox. New York: Da Capo.

8

Theatrical Performances: Structure and Process, Tradition and Revolt

KAREN GAYLORD

This chapter explores the sociology of theatrical performance and performance styles. The work of selected directors and playwrights, specific performances, genres, and theatrical periods is discussed, and ancient Greek theatre is used to illustrate the theoretical points made.

***

In drama, the audience is confronted with a version of humanity in one version of the world. Each kind of play presents a different attitude toward life, shaped by the intent of playwright and/or production. Different visions are expressed in different styles, often based on different conventions, and make different demands upon actors and audiences. And if the drama is, according to Aristotle's definition, essentially an imitation of an action in the form of an action—thus doubly symbolic, being meaningful and affective but not instrumental or effective—then the theatrical performance within which it is embodied is a special kind of public ceremony and "social object." For, as Erwin Piscator (1949:286) pointed out, "There is no theatre without an audience." The actor becomes the mirror in which the audience can see themselves. "The mirror in the case of the actor is the audience. But the faithful and real picture can only be created by both actor and audience" (ibid.: 289). Theater, that is, can exist without costumes, sets, music, lighting effects, even a text, but never without actors and spectators. Jerzy Grotowski, founder–director of the Polish Laboratory Theater, has written, "We can thus define the theatre as 'what takes place between spectator and actor.' All the other things are supplementary" (1968:32).

From this perspective, a theatrical performance is a total social phenomenon. It involves a collective totality created dialectically by the combination of its constituent elements, most crucially its living participants. It is a collective representation in vivo and representations, as Tiryakian observed:

> become social only through the action of distinctive forces operating in association with other members of the collectivity. These members also contribute their own ideas and feelings, which, in turn, modify and check those of the individual. From this combination and alteration of private feelings, the result is a new social synthesis [1962:17].

It is the moment-by-moment interaction between performers and spectators, and the synthesis they mutually achieve out of action and response, that explains why—no two audiences being identical—no two live performances will ever be exactly the same. It is because of the inevitable impact on performance that actors hope for a warm house and dread a cold one. There are good and bad audiences, as there are good and bad performers.

To stress this interaction between spectator and performer is to point to certain sociological paradoxes of performance. To be a member of the audience is to have taken on the role of "attendant" and the obligation of abiding by the conventional rules of conduct that structure the forms of attendance. These norms and forms are not only culturally, subculturally, or class specific but also have changed over time. (For example, the usually docile, passive, middle-class audience of today has been socialized into conforming to a far more restrained set of attendance rules than was the case for popular audiences in the past.) In like manner, to be a member of the cast is to have taken on the role of performer and that role also is shaped by cultural expectations. Moreover, within the drama itself the performer will take on still another role by enacting his assigned part. The hope inherent in the occasion is that the initially uncommitted attendant–spectator will further be willing and able to settle into what might be called the role of the witness. In this role, the spectator serves as a psychological participant and empathetic collaborator in the maintenance and "truth" of the fictive world onstage, is "taken out of himself" and becomes for the time part of an ad hoc collective consciousness, ready to find meaning and significance in the events taking place on stage.

Thus the theatrical occasion involves a double consciousness for all concerned. The performance takes place on at least two levels of "reality" simultaneously and within at least two frames. The outer frame always embraces both audience and performers. The inner frame demarcates the playing space. Again, rules or conventions of various kinds distinguish between the two frames and structure their contents in terms of time, space, and behavior. Some rules may be explicitly stated to meet the needs of a particular production (e.g., "No one will be seated after the curtain rises"). Many, if not most, rules are implicit and, if part of a theatrical tradition, will be taken for granted and remain largely out of awareness unless violated. These rules, too, vary historically and culturally and some of the most interesting ones have to do with structuring "permissable violations" of general practice regarding the distinction between the two frames. For instance, when a Broadway audience follows the custom of applauding the first appearance of the star onstage, they are, as attendants, applauding the skilled performer qua performer. In the process, they break the frame of the specific dramatic event and, momentarily, "bracket" the illusion of the constructed reality on the stage.

On the other hand, such conventions of presentation as direct address, the aside, and even the soliloquy, alter without breaking the dramatic frame to quite another purpose. And such devices as "planting" an actor in the audience and having him perform from there obviously extend the frame encapsulating the dramatic action by extending the playing space itself. On the level of the dramatized reality this can function to merge audience as witnesses with actors as characters. Jerzy Grotowski's work demonstrates just how deliberately and painstakingly worked out the manipulation of the forms and conventions structuring the intricacies of the dual framework of the audience–performer relationship can be. Grotowski feels that this relationship should be one of "perceptual, direct, 'live' communion" as well as expressive of the conceptual core of the drama. One of his major concerns is "finding the proper spectator–actor relationship for each type of performance and embodying the decision in physical arrangements . . . For each production a new space is designed for the actors and spectators" (1968:19,20). Hence in Wyspianski's *Akropolis* the audience was "completely ignored, because they represent the living while the actors are ghosts. The actors speak while gliding between the spectators, but there can be no contact.[But] in Mickiewicz' *The Ancestors* they [the audience] are made to participate in the harvest and crop ritual. An actor becomes the Chorus Leader and the audience the chorus" (Barba, 1963:162). At the same time, in this production, "individual spectators were isolated, facing in different directions, and the action took place among them. Peformance and audience interpenetrated, both filling the entire hall" (Kirby, 1969:277).

Grotowski's name is almost emblematic of the leading edge of a modern theater grown sharply self-conscious of its methodology and having unprecedented freedom to choose from stage conventions and performance techniques developed over thousands of years and around the globe. If the choices have been right, the audience is expected to respond as the offered circumstances dictate with an intense, involuntary form of collective participation. "Gut reactions," the sudden surfacing of deep and/or elemental emotions expressed in tears, gasps, or outbursts of laughter are here freely given as proper validation and authentication of a shared experience. In contrast, according to the norms governing the public etiquette of individual response in everyday life, one is usually expected to modulate or suppress such primitive responses.

At the same time, the very abundance of possibility and the practice of borrowing presentation devices and conventions from many traditions can engender problems of style. Style, as Goffman defines it, is "the maintenance of expressive identifiability" (1974:288). What cannot be identified cannot be understood, but in theater today the facets of such "expressive identifiability" become extremely complex. We may speak of the style of a particular actor, theatrical group, theatrical period, not to mention the style of different theatrical genres within a historical period, and of a particular play within a given genre. For example, the brilliance of Olga Knipper–Chekhova's portrayal of Masha in the Moscow Art Theatre's production of Anton Chekhov's *The Three Sisters* drew special acclaim even as the ensemble acting style of the MAT set new standards for that approach. The MAT's naturalistic acting style also proved theatrically right for the presentation of Chekhov's dramas of milieu—which, in turn, are distinctively different from Ibsen's realistic plays, though both are part of the same genre. And the overall realist style of both is vastly different from the symbolist style of Maeterlinck, though all belong to the same period.

It is generally assumed today that a theatrical production must take the various aspects of style into account with the goal of using them to achieve dramatic "truth" and aesthetic unity. The style of a particular production is now seen as "not something added to the play as a decoration: it is the basic manner of expression and its control is one of the most powerful means of achieving unity in a presentation" (Kernodle, 1967:344). But, while stylistic coherence of the production as a whole has become a sine qua non of effective communication, there is no necessary demand for consistency in the combination of conventions used. An enormous range of theatrical forms is available. Even deliberate violations of traditional modes of presentation, which actually express and cohere with an internal unity of meaning, are entirely permissible. For example, modern middle-class audiences have learned to expect that period plays will usually be done in period style. Confronted with Shakespeare in modern dress, they will accept that departure from established custom but will then search for its symbolic significance.

Interestingly, the concern for historical accuracy underlying that particular convention is a relatively recent development. When Charles Kemble presented *King John* at Covent Garden in 1823, he had J. R. Planché, a playwright and antiquarian, design the first "historical" production of Shakespeare with the entire cast dressed according to period. This development can be seen as a somewhat tardy reflection in theater of the growing historical consciousness of the late eighteenth and early nineteenth centuries. Theatrically, this production, in its combined emphasis on scenic spectacle and historical accuracy, also reflects the flamboyant staging characteristic of the romantic movement and foreshadows the attention to detail that would soon become a hallmark of the first realists. At any rate, Kemble's innovation paid off handsomely at the box office and, as Planché himself later reported:

> When the curtain rose and discovered King John dressed as his effigy appears in Worcester Cathedral, surrounded by his barons sheathed in mail, with cylindrical helmets and correct armorial shields, and his courtiers in the long tunics and mantles of the 13th century, there was a roar of approbation, accompanied by four distinct rounds of applause, so general and so hearty, that the actors were astonished...A complete reformation of dramatic costume became from that moment inevitable upon the English stage. [1959:462.]

A new dramatic convention had been born.

It was noted earlier that contemporary theatrical performances often present an eclectic but purposeful mélange of stage conventions, which originated in quite different traditions and which have now been retailored to suit the needs of particular directors or the vision of particular playwrights. So, for example, Thornton Wilder borrowed heavily from the conventional stagecraft of Oriental theater. And, to transcend the strict limits imposed by the style of traditional realism, Bertolt Brecht, as both dramatist and director, brilliantly violated its established canons and employed a range of presentational devices it had discarded, such as interpolated verse, direct address, soliloquy, and aside. His use of the "alienation effect" was meant to keep the audience from being wholly caught up in the illusion of the reality of the enacted events on stage. It was intended to distance the audience and force it to think about those events and their implications in terms of the actual encompassing social reality. Brecht's aim was to create a "theatre for a scientific age," which would instruct as well as entertain and would present "a workable picture of the world" (1964:121,133). To accomplish this essentially "realist" end, he utilized, paradoxically, nonrealist, archaic, and therefore noticeable, means. These conventions strengthened and highlighted the boundaries between the play-world and the world of everyday reality, even as they also served to unite spectator and performer in a shared contemplation of the larger meaning of the dramatic action. Therefore, the double frames of the theatrical occasion were skewed in a new direction and the results were often hailed as a distinctively different form of stage poetry.

Brecht's work stands as a premier example of the genre known as epic theater. As a movement, epic theater arose in revolt against the naturalistic style. There is a certain historical irony here. Emile Zola had been the major proponent of naturalism in literature and drama. In 1873, he wrote a preface for his play *Thérèse Raquin* that came to be taken as a sort of manifesto for stage naturalism. In it, he insisted that the theater must be brought "into closer relation with the great movement toward truth and experimental science which has since the last century been on the increase in every manifestation of the human intellect" (1947:400). For Zola, it was naturalism that would create a theater for a scientific age, but only a half century later epic theater emerged with intent to destroy precisely that illusion of actuality which had been Zola's chief aim. An illusion now perceived to be created by stylized "unnatural" conventions (of speech, presentational mode, and scenic arrangement) cunningly contrived to suggest that the action on stage is not a play at all but real life.

The naturalistic style emphasized the convention of the "fourth wall," whereby the proscenium arch framed the dramatic action as tightly and rigidly as it had ever done, and became a symbolic fourth wall separating audience as witness and performers as actors. The epic theater meant to break down that wall and, therefore, to break through the shell of the particular in order to reveal wider implications. In doing so, it also fragmented the pattern of conventions associated with many earlier styles. It did it by employing masks, songs, addresses to the audience, asides, narratives, announcements, posters, tableaux, cut-down or symbolic settings, platform stages, simple curtains on wires, and multiple settings similar to the row of "mansions" used on the medieval stage. By combining and manipulating these elements, epic theater can create a rich compound of images but achieve a coherent impact at the same time. If at first its methods, as had happened with prior stylistic shifts, struck audiences as startling and even occasionally outrageous, by now this approach in its turn is seen as a "natural" and convincing form of theater. And more, perhaps, than any other antirealist movement of the early twentieth century, epic theater—through the vivid techniques it used to explode the tight compact structure of naturalism—has influenced all aspects of contemporary staging.

The emergence and development of epic theater also exemplify significant aspects of theatrical performance as a dynamic social and historical process. Epic theater arose in reaction to the realistic style in general and the naturalistic in particular. Naturalism had in its day spearheaded the revolt against the style established by the early nineteenth-century romantic movement. It, in turn, erupted after the French Revolution and as part of a backlash against the rigidities of neoclassicism and the constraints of rationalism. One could trace this pattern back and back. It seems evident that theatrical styles are intricately and intimately linked to evolving cultural consciousness although in no simple one-to-one manner.

To begin with, every audience is a contemporary audience. From the viewpoint of a phenomenological sociology of knowledge, every theatrical performance is grounded both in faith in the principle of the reciprocity of perspectives, and in a common stock of knowledge shared by performers and audience in the paramount world of everyday life. On this combination rests the necessary trust of the audience that the dramatic action is meaningful action and that that meaning (even if the play's theme is meaninglessness) can be deciphered (see Schutz, 1962). Thus, if communication is to take place, then both what is expressed and how it is expressed are necessarily dependent on the use and manipulation of deeply sedimented items in the common stock of knowledge. These items may be out of awareness because they are taken for granted and form the background preassumptions and frame of reference within which, through fresh insight expressed by innovation, new synthesis of meaning can emerge (see Berger and Luckmann, 1966). Without recognizable form, there is only the chaos of anomie, but without the insight of unique discovery and, therefore, the violation of some conventional understandings the constructed performance will result in dull and deadly theater. The performance must express and contain a tension between the familiar and the unexpected, the typical and the atypical, the old and the new; all of which demonstrates that theatrical art is always dynamic and, though structured, is always in process. At best, its rules, forms, and conventions serve at any given point only as a bridge between past and present, opening the way to the future. The structure, forms, and architecture of an established style stand as the archaeology of its history.

Hence, a new theatrical mode, a new style, may develop because it catches, articulates, embodies, and thus objectivates felt, but as yet unexternalized, subjective aspects of an emergent social reality. It makes the invisible visible and creates a new image of the human condition. In so doing, it functions as an act or orientation or re-orientation. It helps to re-define the objective social reality and serves as a crucial part of the self-illumination of society through symbols. As Shakespeare put it, "The purpose of playing, whose end, both at the first and now, was and is, to hold, as 'twere, the mirror up to nature; to show virtue her own feature, scorn her own image, and the very age and body of the time his form and pressure."

However, the new image, if it is to become an accepted image, will also become an established image and, finally, a conventionalized image. Symbol will become symbolic type, existential type, and finally stereotype. What was novel becomes incorporated as a familiar collective representation into the collective consciousness and the common stock of knowledge through rep petition and imitation, and in time, through continued repetition and imitation, becomes commonplace.

In becoming part of the common stock of knowledge, however, conventions and style open the foreground to further exploration and innovation. In a more or less stable society, or in a society with a more or less stable world view, elaboration and variations on established themes may suffice to keep an image alive, a device viable, and a style relevantly meaningful. But, in a time of rapid social change or shifting world view, the stage may be hard put to keep pace. The stage reality may become trapped by the drag of inertia produced by audiences reluctant to relinquish the comforting pleasures of a known and familiar stage idiom. It then stands in danger of falling further and further behind the actually changing social reality, becoming ever more distanced from it, until what was taken as convincing and authentic gradually begins to appear artificial and contrived. So the romantic revolt of the early nineteenth century—which demanded freedom from the dead forms of neo-classicism, extolled passion, imagination, and heroic and splendid spectacle, and took audiences by storm—was by the end of the century perceived as false, stagy and bombastic. In another few years, the realistic and naturalistic styles that replaced it were, in their turn, beginning to be written off by some as old hat. It is now realized that what is perceived as "natural" actually mirrors the nuances of the current paralinguistics and body language of everyday communication. As these subtly change, the basic style and conventional skeleton of the naturalistic expression of an earlier period stand revealed as passé. Today, Peter Brook reports:

> At Stratford . . . about five years, we agree, is the most a particular staging can live. It is not only the hairstyles, costumes and make-ups that look dated. All the different elements of staging—the shorthands of behavior that stand for certain emotions . . . —are all fluctuating on an invisible stock exchange all the time . . . In the theatre, every form is mortal; every form must be reconceived, and its new conception will bear the marks of all the influences that surround it [1968:15].

Thus productions today treat style not as "something added to a play as decoration" but as "the basic means of expression" and strive to achieve that style by selection: "the choice of certain conventions and techniques, the choice of certain qualities in the medium, and the limitation of the expression to those few qualities" (Kernodle, 1967:344). The methods of epic theater show that audiences can adjust to any convention or set of conventions provided these are relevant to the matters at hand and are used in a consistent way throughout the performance. So, for example, because Thorton Wilder intended the performers to break out of character and address the audience directly at the climax of the third act of *The Skin of Our Teeth*, he put similiar breaks in the first and second acts to establish a pattern.

Apropos of this concern with selectivity and internal, if not always external, unity, William James—in pondering the perception of reality and the question under what circumstances we think things are real—stressed the factors of selective attention, intimate involvement, and noncontradiction by what is otherwise known. In differentiating the several different "worlds" that attention and interest can make real for us, he argued that each possible subuniverse has "its own special and separate style of existence" and "each world, whilst it is attended to, is real after its own fashion; only the reality lapses with the attention" (1950: 291,293). To keep the audience's intimate involvement and attention from lapsing, the style of a performance should not, within its purview, contradict what is otherwise known (unless, of course, the playwright or director specifically intends, as did Brecht, to puncture the illusion of reality). Under all circumstances the audience expects a meaningful and/or significant eventfulness in performance. It may not be able to describe a style or know how it is achieved, but it will be aware of incongruity so that incongruity had better be deliberate and intentional.

Today style means uniting words, actions, movements, line, form, and colors in terms of the drama's structure and texture. Structure comprises the form of the play in time and is predicated upon the basic theme, plot, and characters. Texture involves what is directly and sensually experienced by the spectator: what the eye sees, the ear hears, and the felt mood (called "music" by Aristotle and created chiefly by the rhythm or rhythms of the play as expressed in movement, speech patterns, and today, often, by changes in the intensity of the lighting). Indeed, these fundamental dramatic values were all first analyzed by Aristotle, but the conventional understandings shared by actor and onlooker that enable their expression have evolved in many forms dependent upon what is or was conceived as "nature" and accepted as custom. This combination was nicely described by Samuel Johnson in 1751 as "that which is established because it is right . . . [and] that which is right only because it is established" (1966:36).

Aspects of the problem of social variability in defining nature and establishing custom have already been discussed, but not, however, precisely in relation to the three basic conditions of every dramatic performance. These conditions set time and space limits and thereby necessitate fundamental, though also varying, conventional arrangements, which deliberately depart from "nature" but enable the creation of a fictive "reality" within those limits. Thus, every performance takes place within a limited amount of social time and within a specific space as situated within the paramount world of everyday life. The performance, within the dramatic frame, responds to these limits. It does so first by condensation of action and dialogue to eventfully meaningful elements with little actual resemblence to the repetitious speech and insignificant happenings of mundane existence. Appearances to the contrary, the presented dramatic "reality" is always, in the Weberian sense, an ideal type construction. Second, movement and sound must always be adjusted to the requirements set by the theatrical architecture so that the audience can see and hear what is taking place. Third, the taken-for-granted everyday rules pertaining to "here" and "now" as opposed to "there," "then," and "will be," the cultural prescriptions that ordinarily define, stabilize, and, map the experiential flow, are temporarily suspended within the dramatic frame. Exactly how the conventional arrangements responding to these basic conditions are worked out also has a bearing on style. Keeping in mind the points previously discussed—the relationships between performers and audience, actor and witness, the double frames of the theatrical occasion, and the way these can be manipulated, how style and convention do or do not reflect social change— let us finally consider the ancient Greek theater, both in terms of the foregoing points and in terms of how it responded to the basic conditions of performance. With Greek drama, also, one can perceive the very invention of theater, as forms rooted in sacred ritual become secularized and humanized.

Ancient Greek drama was performed before an audience of thousands seated in a vast amphitheater in full daylight in the open air. Originally there had been only a dancing circle for a singing chanting chorus of celebrants, tamped out of hard earth, with an altar to Dionysus in the center. In time, as the ceremonies became more structured and the ritual more complex, the improvised dithyramb sung in honor of Dionysus expanded and crystallized into the goat song (from which the word "tragedy" derives), and the chorus acquired a leader. By the middle of the sixth century B.C., the Athens festivals had been moved to the southeastern slope of the Acropolis, a new dancing circle, or orchestra, had been created, and wooden seats for spectators had been set up against the hillside. Under Pisistratus, dramatic "contests" were inaugurated and, in 535 B.C., Thespis of Icaria introduced the first actor, as such, in addition to the chorus leader and won the first tragedy contest.

By the time Aeschylus had added a second actor and Sophocles a third, audiences of up to twenty thousand persons assembled to watch five days of ceremonies during which three poet–playwright–actor–managers would each competitively exhibit three tragedies and a satyr play; five comedies would be performed and dithyrambic hymns would be sung. Each day's ceremonies began at dawn with a purifying sacrifice and the offering of libations. Tiers of seats divided by aisles now rose up the terraced Acropolis slope and reached two-thirds of the way around the orchestra. Behind the orchestra stood the skene, a simple one-story building, with two wings (the paraskenia) thrusting forward toward the audience, and with doors opening onto the logeion, the speaking-place for the individual actors. There was no curtain, little by way of scenery, and a play's beginning was heralded by a trumpet. The three actors and the chorus were all male, masked, and costumed in richly colored, long, decorated robes. The actors had particularly elaborate costumes, and their masks permitted them to assume as many different roles as the plot required. The masks completely enclosed their heads, are believed to have concealed mechanisms for vocal amplification, and were painted to represent character, with the first conventional distinction being white for women and a dark hue for men. The painting of the masks was stylized and emphatic, and, although the masks obviously allowed no change of expression during a single episode, they could still give to each episode far more intense expression than any actual human face could. Spectators far up the slope could see and respond to the final blood-stained, blinded image of Oedipus.

Although the Greek theaters had superb acoustics and despite the possibility that the masks concealed vocal amplification devices, still the very size of the amphitheaters made the "right management" of the voice a basic requirement for effective acting. Most of the comments in Greek literature about acting or specific actions stressed the vocal characteristics of successful performance. Musical training of the voice and detailed study of enunciation, timing, and rhythm were required. Greek audiences were said to have been critical, exacting, suspicious of improbabilities in the sequence of incidents, sensitive to both expressions of impiety and false cadence, and swift to audibly reveal their pleasure or displeasure in the action or the actors. Both actors and chorus were expected to be proficient in three different kinds of vocal delivery: a mode of formal declaration, closest to the speech of the period but distinguished from it by a distinct emphasis on meter; a kind of chanting or recitative accompanied by a flute; and singing, again accompanied by flute. The singing took the form of solos, duets, trios, singing between the actor and the chorus, and, finally, the ode of the full chorus.

The chorus in the central orchestra was a key element in the structure and performance of Greek drama, being not only a visible link with that drama's origin in ritual but also, in its dramatic function, a reminder of the ritual form of the drama as a whole. When Thespis introduced the first actor, the chorus still remained the pivotal element of the drama with choral dance its essential feature. The acted portions of the play were then considered as interludes, the dance chants as the main design. Only gradually did the connected episodes take on significance as plot. In the course of his work, Aeschylus cut down the predominance of the chorus, but it was Sophocles who gave the compact acted–spoken drama first place. The descriptive dithyrambs were gradually transformed into dialogue and action, but during the episodes the chorus continued to comment on the events. As Kernodle (1967) describes it, this group response enlarged and reverberated "the emotions of the actors, sometimes protesting and opposing but in general serving

as the ideal spectators to stir and lead the emotions of the audience"(p. 164).
And, between the episodes, the chorus still took over. The odes:

> were accompanied by vigorous, sometimes even wild, dances and symbolic
> actions that filled an orchestra which in some cities was sixty to ninety feet
> in diameter. Sometimes the chorus expressed simple horror or lament.
> Sometimes it chanted and acted out in unison and in precise formation of
> rows and line, the acts of violence the characters were enacting
> offstage . . . Sometimes the chorus tells or enacts an incident of history or
> legend that throws light on the situation in the play. Sometimes the chorus
> puts into specific action what is a general intention in the mind of the main
> character [p.164f].

Thus, as the drama emerged out of ritual, it was the chorus that carried
the burden of establishing the rhythm and mood of the performance and of
conveying the full meaning of the action. Essentially it was the chorus that
defined the situation by linking the episodes, stating and restating the main
theme and supplying through stylized, conventionalized, and condensed
means—vocally, visually, and mimetically—that information the audience
needed to grasp the total theatrical composition. Moreover, the chorus also
came to be used to establish the scene of the action. In *Oedipus,* for example,
the chorus specifically repesented the Elders of Thebes. They were not assumed to be speaking directly for the Athenian audience. The setting is
supposed to be the Theban agora, not the theater of Dionysus. Hence, the
chorus as "ideal spectator" also foreshadows certain aspects of the play within
a play and symbolizes, within the dramatic frame, a particular communal
collective consciousness.

The masks combined with the group speech, song, dance, and miming
of action by the chorus resulted in dramas that were picturized on a grand
scale, as was required by and wholly in keeping with the dimensions of the
vast amphitheater.

So it was that the conventions and structure of Greek drama met the three
basic conditions of performance. Note also how that dramatic structure and
concomitant unique performance style subtly shifted as the thematic focus
and world view, exemplified in the works of Aeschylus, Sophocles, and
Euripides in turn, changed. Overall, the evolution of Greek drama should
be seen as a progressive secularization process and as a humanization of myth.
It also reflected a movement from the mechanical solidarity of the tribe to
the fragile organic solidarity of the city state. The ancient religious ceremony
became essentially civic ceremony. When the performers ran out of stories
about Dionysus and turned to other fields of myth for new material, the
original meaning of the ceremonial was lost. Although this development
apparently met some initial resistance on the grounds that tragedy "no longer
seemed to have any business with Dionysus" (Snell 1960:95), by the time of

Aeschylus the content of the dramas bore no trace of the original connection of drama with the worship of Dionysus. In the further process of change, the original sacred ritual forms became traditionalized, secularized, and finally conventionalized, and increasingly open to alteration. As the importance of the chorus diminished and the emphasis shifted to the interaction between the individual actors, the exalted lion-hearted titans, gods, and primeval kings of Aeschylus gave way to the noble heroes of Sophocles. They were still stately and high-born but more human in character, caught in opposition to the world around them, even, as in *Antigone*, caught in the clash between an older tribal morality and an emergent civic morality. Finally, with Euripides, "the first modern," the process of human detachment from hieratic ensemble of the old order was complete. Man became the measure and audiences began to praise a "more natural and human acting style" (Cole and Chinoy, 1949:5). Painted scenery began to appear and costume grew more "realistic."

In 406 B.C., only a year after the death of Euripides, Aristophanes presented *The Frogs*. In it, he dramatized and satirized the change that had taken place, which he utterly deplored. As far as he was concerned, tragedy was dead, and Euripides and Socrates had killed it. For Aristophanes, tragedy meant "noble deeds" and "heroical souls" concerned with "valor, honor and right." Primarily it meant the works of Aeschylus, with whom, however, he had to admit contemporary Athenians "somehow did not hit it off." Nonetheless, in *The Frogs*, in the heated exchanges between the shades of Aeschylus and Euripides competing for the chair of tragedy in Hades, the shift in content and style becomes obvious. Thus, the character representing Euripides claims with "clearcut phrases and wit refined . . . in my democratic way" to have slimmed and neatened the "bloated" art of Aeschylus "swollen with . . . turgid gasconading words . . . great wild-bull words, fierce bugaboos, with bristling crests and shaggy eyebrows too, which not a soul could understand." In return, Aeschylus calls Euripides "an enemy of gods and men . . . foisting tales of incest on the stage . . . scandalous scenes" peopled with "bawds and panders" (Aristophanes, 1943:700–710). He argues as follows:

> Alas, poor witling, and can't you see
> That for mighty thoughts and heroic aims
> The words themselves must appropriate be?
> And grander belike on the ear should strike
> The speech of heroes and godlike powers
> Since even the robes that invest their limbs
> Are statelier grander robes than ours.
> Such was *my* plan: but when *you* began,
> You spoilt and degraded it all . . .
> Your kings in tatters and rags you dressed

> And brought them on, a beggardly show,
> To move, forsooth, our pity and ruth. [Ibid.:709.]

Aristophanes had been accurate, actually, in seeing that the great literary age of Attic tragedy was over. In the fourth century, B.C., great actors replaced the poets in importance, but it was the "chattery-babble collector" and "pauper-creating, rags-and-patches-stitcher," Euripides, who was honored as the classic exponent of drama in all forms, while the "bombastiliquent" Aeschylus was nearly forgotten (ibid.:700). It was Euripides whose influence would continue to be felt throughout Roman times and, in the West, since the Renaissance. It would be left to much later theorists of German romanticism, such as Schlegal and Nietzsche, to revive Aristophanes' argument, to indict Euripides on the same charges of realism, rationalism, and immorality, to dismiss him as the voice of "bourgeois mediocrity," and to assert that the domain of tragedy properly belonged to mythic kings and Dionysian demigods. We have almost come full circle except that, as stated earlier, the romantic revolt in theater in the nineteenth century was again followed by a shift to realism.

The development of the Greek theater serves to illustrate the various social components of performance and performance style, which have been explored in this chapter and which, mutatis mutandis, are always present. It demonstrates the social origins of dramatic structure and the process and pattern of stylistic change, which have occurred again and again in theatrical history. The conditions of performance in time and space always set certain limits and they do not spring ex nihilo. The time limits are established within a larger social time frame, and the architecture and spatial arrangements have a social history. The theatrical conventions that enable meaning to be conveyed are shaped by the conditions of performance, depend upon a mutual understanding between performers and audience, and are by no means fixed for all time. The contemporary world view or world views help to shape the theme and content of the enacted events within the dramatic frame in terms of plot, character, and the modes of embodied performance. The combination of these elements in distinct, coherent, and hence recognizable ways creates a certain style. But that which is wholly recognizable and familiar loses interest for the spectator. It becomes stale. Therefore, in theater there must always be both structure and change, and, if tradition has grown too rigid, revolt.

References

Aristophanes. 1943. *The Frogs*. In *Fifteen Greek Plays*, trans. Benjamin Bickley Rogers. New York: Oxford Univ. Press, pp. 670–724.

Barba, Eugenio. 1963. "Theatre Laboratory 13 Rzedow." *Tulane Drama Review*, 3:162.

Berger, Peter, and Luckmann, Thomas. 1966. *The Social Construction of Reality*. Garden City, N.Y.: Doubleday.

Brecht, Bertolt. 1964. *Brecht on Brecht*. New York: Hill & Wang.

Brook, Peter. 1968. *The Empty Space*. New York: Avon Books.

Cole, Toby, and Helen Krich Chinoy. 1949. *Actors on Acting*. New York: Crown.

Goffman, Erving. 1974. *Frame Analysis*. New York: Harper Colophon Books.

Grotowski, Jerzy. 1968. *Towards a Poor Theatre*. New York: Simon & Schuster.

James, William. 1950. *Principles of Psychology*, vol. 2. New York: Dover.

Johnson, Samuel. 1966. Cited in Karl S. Guthke, *Modern Tragicomedy*. New York: Random House, p. 36.

Kernodle, George R. 1967. *Invitation of the Theatre*. New York: Harcourt, Brace, & World.

Kirby, Michael. 1969. "Environmental Theatre." In *Total Theater*, ed. E. T. Kirby. New York: E. P. Dutton.

Piscator, Erwin. 1949. "Objective Acting." In *Actors on Acting*, ed. Toby Cole and Helen Krich Chinoy. New York: Crown, pp. 285–91.

Planché, J. R. 1959. Quoted in A. M. Nagler, *A Source Book in Theatrical History*. New York: Dover, p. 462.

Schutz, Alfred. 1962. *Collected Papers*, vol. 1. The Hague: Martinus Nijhoff.

Snell, Bruno. 1960. *The Discovery of the Mind*. New York: Harper & Row.

Tiryakian, Edward. 1962. *Existentialism and Sociologism*. Englewood Cliffs, N.J.: Prentice–Hall.

Zola, Emile. 1947. "Preface to Therese Raquin" (trans.). In *European Theories of the Drama*, ed. Barrett H. Clark. New York: Crown, pp. 400–401.

9

The Early History and Development of the Solo Vocalist: Social Stress in Singing

JUNE RIESS GOLDNER

In this chapter, I will examine the emergence of the role of the virtuoso singer from the earliest appearances of solo vocalists until their establishment as a central and prominent role within the organization of opera. I will analyze the creation and early development of the singer's role, describing how it came into existence and how it began to evolve in its definition and articulation as an artistic occupational role. Moreover, in this chapter I attempt to explain how women attained such positions in the occupational world of men.

Although the concept of role has been fundamental to the field of sociology, work in this area has consisted mainly of the theoretical development, elaboration, and refinement of a technical role language. Few studies have said anything about how roles are created.[1] Although there are many studies in the occupational literature on work roles, these mostly deal with socialization of new members into existing roles.

Studying the emergence of the role of the virtuoso singer involves first looking at the early history of the singing tradition in the West, examining how singers came to their positions and then how their expectations, attitudes, values, abilities, backgrounds, and personalities contributed to the way in which this new role came to be organized and defined and the various types of strains involved in its development. We must also ask what the expectations   151

were that developed in singers' relationships with relevant role partners—
notably composers, sponsors, other singers, and the audience—which further
delineated the role.[2]

In tracing the beginnings of this artistic role, we are concerned furthermore
with the various social, political, economic, and musical determinants that
influenced its creation and growth and the social position and function of
the singer in society. Barnett (1959:210) suggests that this can be accomplished
by "conceiving of art as a process in which the artist, the work of art, and
the art public are interacting elements." Our work in this sense becomes a
social history, exploring the impact of structural and institutional factors on
the role of these performers and the styles in which they performed.

This study thus begins to investigate the dynamics of the emergence of an
aesthetic role through the history of its occupants and their position and
relationships in the organization of music in society. Again, it will be central
to this chapter to note the position—or nonposition—of women as singers.

Any history of vocal art is difficult. Examples of the musical composition
of songs only became plentiful around 1500, when advances were made in
musical printing. In addition, there are, of course, no sources of actual
singing and singing styles through most of this art's long development—not
until very recently, with the invention of sound recording in the late nineteenth century. We are, therefore, dependent upon deductions made from
the fragments of musical compositions sung and upon the hearsay of con-
temporaries for descriptions of the voices of the past. In order to piece together
the major developments and changes in singing and singing style, including
characteristics of singers, expectations surrounding singers, their social relationships, and the social position of this specialized role as it developed into
an occupation, we will rely on histories of singing, histories of song, and
comprehensive histories of Western music in general and more specific studies
on singers as well as personal journals and memoirs and various musical
documents.

Although detailed progress in the art of song is poorly documented prior
to the advent of opera around 1600 and although only a few names of singers
before that time have come down to us, we know that singing has been part
of human society since its beginning. Talking of the considerable army of
singers already equipped with a brilliant technique available around the time
of the birth of opera, Henderson (1921:64) asks what we might ask at almost
any time during the progress of vocal art: "Whence came these artists? Whence
came their art? . . . The subject has been dismissed curtly in musical histories . . . [W]ho were the masters of voice?"

Rushmore (1971:3–4), discussing "hearsay voices," states that though we
have no knowledge of when human beings first evolved the ability to sing or
of how primitive people actually sang, there are indications of the subject

matter of their songs. Magical–religious, heroic, and tragic songs, songs of humankind and nature, these serve the purposes which others contend have always existed—music expressing individual emotion or ceremonial in character.

Rushmore (1971:6) states that anthropologists have found that the female maintained an equality with the male in most tribes in fulfilling these functions of song. He refers to a feminist writer, Sophie Drinker, who suggests that women were superior to men, who couldn't sing as readily while out chasing and killing the day's rations. A woman's more routinized domestic duties allowed for a greater cultivation of the art (Rushmore, 1971:5). Wallaschek (1970), who along with Bowra (1962) attempts to speculate about the nature and function of primitive song and primitive singers through the analysis of anthropological studies on primitive peoples in the modern world, finds that in these cultures women generally take a prominent part in musical activities.

The first songs seem to have been mainly communal rather than individual. And singers and other musicians in nonliterate primitive societies were not at first specialists. As singing evolved, however, ". . . it was natural that certain individuals among the group should be discovered to have superior voices and musical talent" (Rushmore, 1971:6). Such individuals were either called upon or took their "'rightful' place, in musical situations. . . . Here we begin to approach professionalism, which is usually defined in terms of whether the musician is paid for and supported economically by his skill" (Merriam, 1964:124). Payment might range from occasional gifts for specific acts to complete economic support.[3]

Power was attributed to use of the voice to communicate thoughts and feelings and to record facts and events. Singers were held in awe, but at the same time were often feared: "In the minds of superstitious primitive people the magical effect of the singing voice seemed to be linked in some way with the terrifying spirits themselves" (Rushmore, 1971:6–7). Highly rewarded singers, musicians, and wandering minstrels—necessary to village life—were nevertheless considered disreputable and deviant. We also find that art practiced for economic purposes was often despised, while the artists were honored (out of fear, awe, or necessity), and the condemned economic motivation was encouraged by contributions. The ambivalent attitude toward this role— "of low status and high importance coupled with deviant behavior allowed by the society and capitalized upon by the musician" (Merriam, 1964:137)— is perhaps a characteristic of behavior common to the musician's role and of entertainers and artists in general. Jazz musicians are the most obvious modern example.

With the changes from communal to solo singing we note in the scant literature on such solo vocalists much less discussion about women as musicians. As this specialized role becomes economically rewarded and gains in status in at least some ways, we find it increasingly occupied by men.

Before proceeding chronologically, it will be important to pursue briefly one further line of thought—the desirable height of the voice among primitive singers—as this is critical to tracing the position of women as singers over time. It is often noted that male singers sang unusually high for their normal range. It is possible that the male voice was formerly higher than now. Other reasons for voices being pitched so high go back to the origins of music—nature's instruments, like "the cleft in the rock, the hole in the cabin, the distant trickling water, or the wind blowing into a reed" (Deacon, 1910:364) and nature's bird and other animal vocalists—which the human voice imitated. Falsetto[4] voices are also frequently noted as common to both sexes. Holding his hand before his mouth, a blind singer in East Africa "produced a quite pleasing tone which could be heard at a great distance, and everyone was delighted, especially with the peculiar shrill falsetto notes" (Wallaschek, 1970:68). The piercing quality and the carrying ability of the high voice added to its desirability.

In the legends, epics, and myths of the ancient world, the supernatural origins of music and the magical quality of singing reappear. Orpheus, the first great solo singer, sang to his lyre: ". . . there was every kind of bird brought under the spell of the singing, and all beasts of the mountains . . . ., and a horse stood entranced, held in control, not by a bridle, but by the music . . ." (Quoted in Rushmore, 1971:8). In the tales of the Homeric Greek era, outstanding vocal skill was most highly regarded and rewarded. Vocal virtuosity had begun.

Music became a chief element in the education of Greek youth of the Golden Age. For the most part, this education was of boys.[5] The primary function of music was pedagogical, to build up character and morals. Its practice was, therefore, public and communal. As with athletic ability, skill in music became competitive, and musical accomplishments were presented at the agones—contests in athletics, chariot and horse racing, music, literature, drama, poetry recitation, etc. The Greeks, as Lang (1941:2) describes them, had, however, a second soul in their breast besides the one striving for clarity, temperance, and moderation. The other supposedly drove them toward the fantastic and orgiastic, the cult of Dionysus. In moderation, controlled, and for specific purposes (those of the state), music was good; unleashed and emotional, it was frowned upon. Out of fear of their susceptibility to the Dionysiac tendency, the Greeks preached control and moderation with great fervor. Therefore, it seems probable that in ancient Greece the singing voice and its art—the attractions of which it has to be admitted come down fully on the side of Dionysus—never approached the range and power of the other performing arts . . . " (Rushmore, 1971:7–8).

Although in Plato's system music occupied the leading position among the arts, he nonetheless complained of the deterioration of music in the hands of professional musicians because of their "disorderly tastes," which catered to the prevailing vulgarities of the multitude (Duey, 1951:25). Aristotle's complaints about the undesirable effects of elaborate performance technique indicate the existence, nevertheless, of a high degree of virtuosity. Implied in his comments is also the debasement of the individual for his use of the art for lucrative, practical, or personal purposes—"'mercenary musicians' to entertain dinner guests" (Henderson, 1921:21)—that is also found among some primitive groups. Though we know little about the Greek public's attitude toward and tastes in music, we might assume that the more passionate, unrestricted, and perhaps embellished voice in song (Plato warned about the warblings and blandishments of song [Jander, 1980:339]) had, despite attacks upon it, great public appeal. Pincherle, in *The World of the Virtuoso* (1956:27), finds it understandable "that in all times the exaggerations and divagations of virtuosity have made it susceptible to violent hatreds . . ." He explains such severity by the disproportion existing between the quality of the art of popular virtuosos and the adulation they aroused, "an adulation blind, without nuances . . ."

In conclusion, the Greeks conceived of music as, and only as, moral force, controlled and subservient to the idea.[6] In such a moral climate, Rushmore (1971:8) claims, the art of singing was not likely to develop.

In contrast to the Greek moral spirit of control and restraint, the Roman ideal was pleasure and surrender to the senses. Greek music, as adopted by Romans, quickened and gained rhythm and was influenced by elaborate Oriental music brought back to Rome from the Egyptian campaigns (Rushmore, 1971:9). This increase in grandiosity was aided by the institution of slavery, which permitted the training of musicians and professional entertainers on a large scale. The Roman public "exercised critical scrutiny over artists and gave vent to its disapproval if the singer or player made mistakes" (Lang, 1941:33). Such audiences could discern distinctions among singers and therefore created stars.

There were those singers who accompanied themselves on the cithara, dramatic singers performing in costume and mask, and lyrical singers of hymns and short songs—advanced virtuosi about whom we know more than any previously. The scholar Dionysius of Halicarnassus mentioned the high degree of skill demanded of professionals and the great variety of intervals used, and stated that music necessitated that the words should be subordinated to the tune, and not the tune to the words (Duey, 1951:28). This performer-biased approach is in direct contradiction to our earlier comments on Plato's philosophy and again foretells the battle that will be fought throughout vocal history. Dionysius' treatise discusses the necessity of long training to achieve mastery and to be able to produce effects with the utmost ease from sheer force of habit and warns that no rules can suffice to make experts of those who are determined to dispense with study and practice (Duey, 1951:28). These are observations we find repeated to the present day. They indicate that at that time a highly specialized technique must already have existed, which would have required arduous training for its mastery. There are no accounts, however, of the quality of these voices, their range, or the vocalizations they performed. In addition to practicing scales and exercises and avoiding straining the voice, singers were expected to live healthy, temperate, and well-regulated lives, for the good of the voice. Quintilian relates how they protected their throats by holding handkerchiefs before their mouths when speaking, writes Lang (1941:33), and how they avoided the sun, fog, and wind. Many of these virtuosi sang their own compositions. They undertook concert tours and demanded princely earnings. ". . . [C]ommunities which were the scenes of their triumphs erected statues in their honor and gave them honorary citizenship" (Lang, 1941:34). Lang attributes the "supercilious and temperamental" attitudes of these artists to the adulation and often scandalous worship they enjoyed. For example, Tigellius, capricious and temperamental, was quite capable of refusing to sing even when the emperor commanded him, if the mood was not upon him; equally, he might perform whether bidden or not (Rushmore, 1971:10).

Jealousy among musical artists resulted at least partially from agone competitions and the Capitoline games, where poets, musicians, and singers from the empire and far countries competed every fourth year. "Owing to the presence of the emperor and the select audience of nobles, these games lent considerable dignity and fame to the competing artists, and a winner was considered the foremost artist in his domain, his fame spreading even beyond the limits of the empire" (Lang, 1941:33). In their jealousies and rivalries, singers often resorted to claques and even bribery. In these ancient singing specimens are found glimpses of the characteristics that persisted in this role. These were professional virtuosi, lauded by the public, disciplined in their art but often not in their personalities, who engaged in battle with other singers for fame and fortune.

As in most time periods, antivirtuosity forces were also prevalent in Rome. Plutarch in his *De Musica* wrote that music had undergone a notable regression, and he complained bitterly of its degeneration from its once high and noble state: ". . . [O]ur men of art . . . have brought into the theatres a sort of effeminate musical tattling, mere sound without substance . . . most depraved with diversity of notes and baneful innovations" (quoted in Duey, 1951:29).

Our discussion so far has shown the practice of singing limited to men. Its vogue among Roman women is seen in the writings of Lucian, who praised the singing and cithara playing both of aristocratic women and of courtesans (Lang, 1941:35). Amateur musicians flourished during the empire, and it appears that female singers were confined to this position. In most of antiquity, professional female singers and musicians were generally held in ill repute.

By the fourth century A.D. a force had grown in the world that was to have the greatest possible effect on singers and their songs. Although the ancients sang in the home and in their temples and theaters, "our own art is the child of the Catholic Church" asserts Henderson (1921:2). He states that its history can be traced in greater detail when that church became a single organization (324 A.D., with the unification of the Roman Empire, and consequently the Roman Church, under Constantine), "its functions centralized under the dominion of one monarch, and its musical style informed by a well defined purpose."

The church realized the power of music to stimulate belief, attract converts, and conquer souls. St. Basil saw the virtue in singing's power "to unite the people in the symphony of a single choir" (quoted in Jander, 1980:339). The congregation was encouraged in singing psalms and hymns to the glory of God, and by the third century it had become customary to hear men of the congregation singing out a verse of the psalm, women and children replying with another, and both joining in the refrain (Rushmore, 1971:12). The participation of women in the liturgical chant met with mixed feelings. Although Paul's rule, "Let the women be silent in the holy assemblies" (1 Cor. 14:34), was in strict conformity with the practices of the synagogue and the rabbinic warning that "the voice of woman leads to licentiousness" (quoted in Werner, 1963:324), it was not unanimously accepted in the Christian church. Numerous authorities championed the psalm singing of women in the services.[7] Compromises were sought and occasionally attempted. An example is the Syrian *Testament of the Lord* (fifth century), which would tolerate a female response, if the psalm itself was intoned by a male singer (Werner, 1963:324).

The elementary form of syllabic chant—usually Jewish, using one or at most two notes to a syllable—was the form in which the simple communications of the liturgy were set forth. But, "even at the outset, when the fathers of the church had no thought of vocal or musical art, the art principle was present, unrecognized by them. . . . Soon after the singing of several notes to a syllable became permissible the purely musical expressiveness and decorative quality of that style became patent . . ." (Henderson, 1921:6–7). This mode was reserved for the expression of the higher emotions. The congregation sang florid phrases in their responses within the antiphonal services, while the plain chant was displayed in the liturgical utterances of the priests.

It was soon realized, however, that besides raising religious exaltation, singing also brought out other emotions and impulses in direct contradiction to Christian teachings. ". . . The warm, sensuous tones of the singing voice, particularly of a woman, evoked all too powerfully the earthiness of man's nature" (Rushmore, 1971:12). The author's description of this situation is reminiscent of the Greek controversy over singing: "Within an orthodoxy of obedience and self-denial, the free, exhilarating expression of singing sat most uncomfortably" (Rushmore, 1971:12). St. Augustine wrote: ". . . When it happpens to me to be more moved by the singing than by what is sung, I confess myself to have sinned criminally, and then I would rather not have heard the singing" (quoted in Grout, 1973:26). Concerned over the perils of vocal pleasure, the church in 318 moved first against the disturbing power of the female voice, forbidding the voluptuous song of women to be heard in church. Soon neither men nor women of the congregation were permitted to lift their voices in praise of God. Response singing and other parts of the service were designated to specially trained choirs of canons, or singing men, by the Council of Laodicea around 350. The council forbade active partic11ipation by the congregation, defending "rightful singers against the encroachment of undesirable people" (Lang, 1941:52).

Pope Sylvester reportedly had founded a school of chant in Rome early in the fourth century, which would have made possible the transfer of the musical service to the choir. Henderson (1921:17) suggests that, in the beginning, the purpose of such schools was for learning the chants themselves (committing them to memory was one of the most difficult and lengthy tasks of the church singer). But since unity in delivery had to be attained—the Rules of St. Paul and St. Stephen required that psalmody be executed by the choir "as if it were one voice; none of the singers should sing faster or louder than the others" (quoted in Lang, 1941:53)— schools of chant had to address themselves to stylistic rudiments as well:

> . . . [F]rom the endeavor to form a style of delivery for the church chant must have come the discovery of the fundamental elements of vocal technic. . . .
>   . . . All that remained to be added was a moderate amount of facility in the florid passages, a facility which was destined to develop into unexpected and amazing brilliancy. [Henderson, 1921:17–18.]

Whether this virtuosity developed or not is not agreed upon in the literature.

Duey (1951:30), on the one hand, claims that the medieval centuries—an era in which the church made the subservience of the performer to the music philosopher complete—did not offer much evidence of vocal virtuosity. "Any art ruled over by such a dictum must wither. . . . Nearly a thousand years passed before the singing artist regained his position of importance. For at least half this time nothing worthy of the name of virtuosity is evident" (Duey, 1951:30). How seriously these philosophies were taken and how completely the church controlled the performer is questionable. Perhaps the controversy resides in the definition of a "performer." Would Duey have included the canons in this class? Was church singing a performance? Our sources expound on vocal music within the church but hardly mention other manifestations of vocal art. Nevertheless, there evidently existed a considerable vogue of profane music and entertainment, as evidenced in a passage Lang (1941:53) quotes from St. Basil: "There are towns where one can enjoy all sorts of histrionic spectacles from morning to night. And, we must admit, the more people hear lascivious and pernicious songs, which raise in their souls impure and voluptuous desires, the more they want to hear." The church attempted to keep the people away from such professional singers with threats, such as, ". . . Those who delight their eyes and ears on such spectacles commit adultery" (Lang, 1941:53). They also aimed their warnings at the singers. Forbidding such a popular means of expression was naturally unrealistic, however. Secular singing, though suppressed, continued, though we know little about it. Perhaps this is the reason for Duey's claim that vocal virtuosity was absent during these years.

Contrary to such assertions, Henderson (1921:20) contends that, almost in its inception, the chant was touched by the luxurious taste of professional singers and decorated with the flowers of song called in Italian *fiorituri*. He outlines three major influences that quickly obliterated its original simplicity: (1) the employment of professional singers in the church; (2) the existence of a considerable store of vocal technique dating from antiquity and ready to be adapted; and (3) the development and preservation of vocal skill by the schools of chant *(scholae cantorum)*. Chants, the author thus demonstrates, were not dull and monotonous but filled with richness and variety by trained singers. These were solo chanters who, Henderson (1921:20) emphasizes, assumed the right to "give freedom to their fancies" and introduced into their singing the ornaments that had existed since antiquity. They quickly acquired "the self glory that has clung to singers" (Henderson, 1921:22) and swelled with vanity, even showing a fondness for certain personal adornments.

Singing schools, having deteriorated during the overthrow of Rome and the fall of the empire (476), were reorganized during the early Middle Ages, culminating soon after Gregory became pope with his founding of the Schola Cantorum in 590. This school for singers established the authoritative delivery of the musical liturgy and provided singers for the Sistine Chapel Papel Choir. Standards of style were set and singers' careers controlled in the church's attempts at procuring a monopoly on musical life. "For the next seven or eight hundred years the Church held the curious position of building and maintaining a technical and aesthetic standard of singing by presenting to the public, so to speak, fine professional vocalists, while at the same time trying to prevent the public from singing themselves" (Rushmore, 1971:14).

Two buildings were set aside, one housing the singers and clergy of the papal church, the other an orphanage to undertake training and educating future members of the choir. Pupils with good voices were selected from the various church-directed scholae and obtained pensions during their nine years of studies.

Based on the scrupulous care in selection and the rigorous and lengthy training that was involved, Henderson (1921:33–34) concludes that these voices must have possessed the power and flexibility that have long been associated with the best Italian singing, the supreme test of vocal progress in the epoch-making school being the ability to sing solo music of a type elegantly florid. Embroideries were sometimes longer than the chants themselves. Many writers, Henderson (1921:41) states, complained of the prominence accorded to this kind of vocal fantasia, and Grout (1973:63) mentions the occasional appearance in manuscripts of admonitions to singers against self-display. Finally, Henderson (1921:38–39) points to modern discoveries in the music itself as proof of the level of cultivation reached in the art of singing. Such evidence is in sharp contrast to a notion of great disregard for the performer's or interpreter's role during this age.[8]

Though we have no actual descriptions of how these men sounded, a preference for the high voice—particularly the high voice that is flexible and capable of the elegant delivery of melismatic lines—is evident in the repertory of ecclesiastical chant. Isadore of Seville, writing in the seventh century, listed numerous types of voices (most of which he considered offensive), comparing their characteristics. Of these, "The perfect voice is high, sweet and clear; it is high so as to be adequate in the upper range; it is clear so as to fill the ears amply; it is sweet so as to delight the spirits of the listeners" (quoted in Duey, 1951:32). This preference, demonstrated in much early vocal composition, seems to have been a universal opinion and one that persisted. Women, the archetypal possessors of such voices, were, however, restrained from using them in religious song for about a century.

Before continuing with the history of the virtuoso singer in the church, we must turn to the secular side of vocal art, which was finally making serious advances. Itinerant singers of popular song were recording the life of the time: of the peasant, lover, warrior, and noble. Bauer and Peyser (1932:89) contend that they came from every rank, "gay scions who had spent their wherewithal, impoverished craftsmen, and even monks, tired of the discipline of the monastery . . ." However, the memories and traditions they reflected were those of the pagan past. And, though increasingly considered indispensible as secular entertainers, these itinerant musicians (often called minstrels) were not socially acceptable and were generally regarded as vagabonds and notoriously immoral persons. The church saw "in the minstrel's instinctive and genuine love of life and its pleasures the gravest threat to the spiritual welfare of the people" (Lang, 1941:109). Regardless of the contempt in which these secular musicians were held by the church, it is noted (Bauer and Peyser, 1932:90) that they were welcomed everywhere without "benefit of clergy." Again we see that desired artists and entertainers were obtained despite the objections of the dominant institution, the church.

Of the various types of wandering musicians and singers that existed during the eleventh century, the jongleur—the French example of the tough, bawdy, traveling entertainer of his day, a one-man vaudeville show with his songs, dances, funny stories, and tricks (Rushmore, 1971:15)—was a master at his craft and a sound musician. In the isolated, fortified settlements, wandering entertainers provided a diversion from medieval battle. They were rewarded by both rich and poor in proportion to their musical skill and power of pleasing and can be viewed as somewhat independent singer–entertainers.

With the constant danger of war, "the man of God had to step into the background and cede precedence to the man of arms . . . knighthood came into being" (Pahlen, 1949:33). In the twelfth- and thirteenth-century ideology of the knight, worldly matters were coming to the fore: "friendship, warlike adventures, experiences in far-off lands, and, especially, love . . . they sang of them, and wanted to be told of them as they sat round the campfire or in the lofty halls of their castles . . ."(Pahlen, 1949:34). It was from the upper classes that artists were produced who would improvise the songs of the heroic and the amorous. Noble poet–composer–singers, the troubadours of Provençe and the later trouvères of northern France were among the earliest, if not the first, trained secular musicians, having been educated in abbeys where their courses of instruction included ecclesiastical song. Their creations thus embodied a marriage of sacred and profane music united by the language of the people (Henderson, 1921:49–50).

The troubadours (four hundred of whose names are known) and trouvères (two hundred of whose names have come down to us) held a higher and unequivocal rank compared to the jongleur. They "exercised their art for art's sake" (Lang, 1941:102), receiving no remuneration, but were treated with great respect at the courts of munificent royal patrons. Among them were numerous kings and, Bauer and Peyser (1932:93) claim, seventeen women. (This, however, is the only mention of such women.) Because of their rank and their relationship to court life, the ethical code of the knightly artists forbade their being subjected to unnecessary contact with the populace (Lang, 1941:108). They therefore became more exclusively poets and composers (for which they had received the literary and technical training), or frequently just poets, and left the vocal and instrumental performance of the verses of their lays or ballads to jongleurs (generally more skilled in these areas) whom they employed. This composer–performer relationship originated in the Middle Ages a new sort of antagonism—"that which opposed the creator to the interpreter, the composer to the singer" (Pincherle, 1956:28)—which has persisted through all ages.

The troubadour movement spread, but, as feudalism waned, people flocked to walled towns for refuge against robbers. "Warring nobles had espoused conquest to the neglect of music. The common people were hungry for it . . ."(Bauer and Peyser, 1932:95). Although the minstrel singer's association with the troubadour had lent legitimacy and prestige to his secular craft, he still embodied a somewhat ambivalent popularity reminiscent of the primitive minstrels discussed previously: " . . .[P]eople flocked to hear him and loved him for his fantastic nature and dexterity. Yet they feared him because of his multiple abilities, which seemed sinister . . ."(Lang, 1941:110). Despite this questionable aspect of the minstrel's occupation (or sometimes because of it), he was able to obtain from nobles, burghers, and peasants what he wanted and lived in relative comfort and plentitude. Itinerant musicians— necessary at balls and other festive functions, to serenade, and for theatrical performances—required board and lodging and soon demanded to be paid. Several permanently employed artists could be depended upon and would be cheaper in the end. Other musicians entered the service of lords, seeking protection, employment, and security in the European seats of power. By the fourteenth century, no court was without its musicians and no noble without his singers.

A major change had occurred during the Middle Ages in the role of the professional musician. "Though the church remained the great school for musicians, it now was possible to be a musician and a composer of secular music" (Hughes, 1970:97). By the fourteenth century secular singing was a legitimate and fairly prestigious occupation. This marks the starting point of the Renaissance musician's role.

During the late Middle Ages, technical aspects of music underwent critical changes, brought about by the introduction of polyphonic music.[9] Reasons for the advance from monophony to polyphony are offered by Pahlen (1949:42–44):

> The Gregorian chant could be, had to be, homophonic, for it expressed a collective ideal: precisely the same for everybody. The new town life became more complicated. . . .
> . . . No longer did a solitary person tell of heroic deeds to the accompaniment of a lyre, while the others listened breathlessly. . . . If they had all sung the same thing like the monks in the Gregorian chant, it would hardly have satisfied their individualistic tendencies. And so they invented a number of vocal lines running a parallel course and assigning to each executant an individual and interesting task.

This new music (called *ars nova*) first developed where the currents of intellectual and political activities met (Pahlen, 1949:45)—first Paris and then

Flanders. It soon spread throughout Europe and reached it apex in Italy. Flemish singers and composers, many of whom were both, came into great demand, and "for the first time singers of one nationality were sought after to perform for audiences in another country" (Jander, 1980:341).

At the same time, this secular musical culture had a parallel growth in sacred music, where polyphony was being reconciled with the practice of Gregorian church art. Because of the availability of large and well-trained choirs, its greatest potential existed here. While on the one hand the powerful body of the clergy endeavored to preserve intact in public worship the chant's simple expression of the congregational spirit, "[o]n the other hand were the composers and descantors . . . becoming by degrees more and more preoccupied by the artistic problem, and employing more and more in their enrichments of the service material essentially different in character from plain song" (Duey, 1951:35).

Duey (1951:34) lists continuous ecclesiastical complaints about the corrupt practices of singers, from the tenth century onward: overdone suaveness, the introduction of extraneous elements or elaborations, and wanton voices eager for ostentation. Ecumenical councils attempted to proscribe many of these malpractices. A papal pronouncement of Pope John XXII in 1324 described singers as preferring to devise methods of their own rather than to continue singing in the old way and consequently ". . . their voices are incessantly running to and fro, intoxicating the ear, not soothing it . . ." (p. 36). They were ordered to desist or undergo penalties, but such circumscriptions were apparently short-lived. Writing around 1362, Ambros said, "The singer could not better display his art than, when asked to improvise a descant to a tenor at sight, to render it as richly and as expensively as he was able" (quoted in ibid.).

In the masterpieces of Palestrina, polyphonic music reached its summit, but its decline was imminent. Technical details had grown to gigantic proportions. From three-voice motets, masses with double choirs of twenty or more voices became nothing out of the ordinary. "Polyphony had grown to be less of an art than a mechanical ability and had become so complicated that the people turned away from it more and more. . . . [R]eaction set in and carried to victory the very opposite principle" (Pahlen, 1949:59). With the coming of the Renaissance and the age of humanism, the individual emerged as such. "Until then they had mainly been as members of a unit, as were their voices [whether a common vocal unit as in plain chant or a differentiated one as in polyphonic song]. . . " (Rushmore, 1971:17). An ideology that relied on the individual instead of the dominating institution of the church supported a new emphasis and increased appreciation of the solo virtuoso performer.

In Italy the new songs were *madrigale*, in France *chansons*, and in Germany

Lieder. These represented "the perfection of polyphonic music in its secular aspect" (Nef, 1964:113–14)—chamber compositions for several voices, but with one voice leading, that revealed a relationship to the music of the troubadours and a broadly popular foundation. " . . .[C]omposers allotted to the soprano the sustained melody, written in a simple fluent cantilena . . ." (quoted in Henderson, 1921: 79). Such melodic high parts were most likely composed for dilettante singers who did not possess the brilliant qualities of professionally trained artists. Women joined with men in singing these polyphonic secular frottole and strambotti songs. Henderson (1921:60) maintains, "Unless we are willing to believe that boys or male sopranos were to be found in every chorus and household, we must conclude that women sang in the polyphonic works of the time." Jander concurs. "Probably a large number of female singers and instrumentalists in European courts, until well into the 16th century, were of courtesan status, which is probably one reason why it is difficult to trace their presence through financial records and other scholarly documentation" (1980:341).

The discovery of the female treble voice in secular music created "an exciting new sound which the Counter-Reformation Church could not do without" (ibid.: 341–42). In the early sacred polyphony, falsetto singing had played an important part, and the use of boys' voices for high parts is also noted. However, the elaborate polyphonic style, which flourished by the middle of the fifteenth century, "necessitated a much wider range of voices and a higher degree of virtuosity than anything that had gone before" (Heriot, 1975:10). Choir boys and falsettists became impractical and inadequate in the florid upper ranges, and castrati[10] began to appear in church choirs in great numbers in the sixteenth century. "With women barred from participation in church music, only the castrato could provide the sound required, and so moral qualms regarding castration were set aside" (Jander, 1980:342).

Although the new secular style's strong element of virtuosity involved all singers, basses as well as high voices, "the most significant development in the history of singing during the second half of the 16th century was the emergence of the female voice (especially the soprano) as both an important participant in performance and an influential factor in composition" (Jander, 1980:341). Noble women (ladies of the Este court at Ferrara and the Gonzaga court at Mantua, for example) were accomplished musicians themselves and avid patrons of the arts. Although in the generation of Isabella d'Este, a notable example, all secular music used vocal ranges comfortable for male voices (according to Jander, 1980:341), madrigals of the ensuing decades reflect the discovery of the soprano voice. This development occurred in various courts of northern Italy, reaching its peak in Ferrara during the reign of Alfonso II d'Este in the late 1500s. He brought together first a ladies ensemble of female courtier singers and then acquired trained sopranos to

form his famous *concerto delle donne*. These women were daughters of prominent artists and merchants. "The first group was made up of courtiers who
happened to sing, the second of singers who, because of their musical ability,
were made courtiers" (Newcomb, 1980:7). They were probably the first professional women singers. Their new sound, an ensemble of high voices, became
the vogue and was imitated elsewhere. Names of castrati can also be found
in the court records but generally as members of the larger choirs (*capella
di musica*) which existed along with the smaller *musica secreta* chamber
ensembles.

Although early secular song embodied human feeling, as distinguished
from religious abstraction or devotion (Henderson, 1921:88–89), it is the
dawn of opera that finally brings a more dramatic element, a drive for expression, and an attempt at the tragic. Zacconi (quoted in Duey, 1951:43) describes what was expected of the sophisticated art of the skilled singer at the
end of the sixteenth century: "Music has always been, and still more with
every hour is, embellished by the diligence and effort of singers. It is made
new, or changed, not by means of figures which are always the same but
with graces and accents it is made to seem more beautiful." History's "recurring screeds against vocal ornamentation" tend only to show that
" . . . audiences over the centuries have been persistently receptive to the
delights of well-performed vocal *fioritura*" (Jander, 1980:339). Two varieties
of such exponents of singing existed at the turn of the century. In the churches
were thoroughly trained male singers—the best now castrati—the culmination
of an "unbroken line of descent of the art of song" (Henderson, 1921:70)
from the earliest church singing schools to this period immediately preceding
the birth of Italian opera. Excellent female singers were available in the
courts. However, the church forbade the appearance of women on the Roman
stage, and female theatrical performers were generally disapproved of and
were associated with prostitution and licentiousness, as had been the case
since antiquity. The castrato voice was quickly discovered by opera composers
"who made better use of its special qualities than did the composers of the
Catholic church music" (Jander, 1980:342). And so the castrati stepped out
of the churches toward a stage offering greater glory, glamor, and fortune,
and where they were "at greater liberty to indulge themselves in what they
were most adept at—virtuosic embellishments and interpolations of highly
elaborate cadenzas . . ." (Rushmore, 1971:19). This challenging voice, determined and destined to steal the praises of the opera public, became the
major contender to women singers and reigned in opera throughout the next
century, forcing women again to take a back seat in the new art form.

> . . . [T]he castrati were very important figures in opera almost from its
> inception until 1800 and even a little later, and were absolutely pre-eminent
> during a large part of that time; . . . audiences of succeeding generations

> have preferred these half-men with voices as high as women's, both to
> women themselves and to natural men . . . [Heriot, 1975:23].

The history of singing is a history of stress—of competing musical preferences and philosophical orientations, of competing organizations and institutions, of competing social categories of singers and voice types. The
development of the singer's role involves all kinds of social stress: solo versus
group performance, simplicity versus complexity or virtuosity, high versus
low status, the high versus the low voice and the female versus the male, the
vocalist versus the composer, discipline versus freedom. We have only begun
to pursue these.

Vocal history is, at the same time, a history of the continual and increasing
emphasis on the high virtuosic voice as the medium of vocal beauty and
technical display. "Throughout the slow advance toward the Italian opera we
can without difficulty trace a steady movement toward the elevation of a
single-voiced melody to the throne of vocal art and the crowning of the high
voice as the royalty of singing" (Henderson, 1921:78). Although such female
voices had excelled in the secular vocal music of the latter sixteenth century,
they were scant competition for the masses of castrated male singers, whose
thorough vocal training in the churches and whose unnaturally produced
high tones equipped them also for the role of the star soprano in opera that
might otherwise have gone to the "rightful" occupants of such roles—women.
In addition, it is in the institution of the opera that the occupational role of
the singing star crystallized. In opera's beginnings, the castrati were the pre-
dominant occupants of this role—the "primo uomo"—and it is through them
that this would occur.

Notes

1. Among the few exceptions are Carr-Saunders and Wilson (1962) and Goldner
(1967). Other work on the development of artistic occupational roles includes Couch
(1979), Kamerman (1979), Martorella (1979), and Ridgeway (1975).

2. Levinson (1957:293–94) maintains that "individual role-conception and role-
performance do not emanate fully formed from the depths of personality. Nor are
they simply mirror images of a mold established by social structure."

3. "Occupations" may be defined as "that specific activity with a market value
which an individual continually pursues for the purpose of obtaining a steady flow
of income" (Salz, 1962:58).

4. An artificially produced singing voice (weaker and somewhat nasal) used, generally by males, to obtain notes above the normal range of the full voice.

5. A society that cherished the heroic ideal, ancient Greece was essentially masculine in character. Man was the one perceived to make the utmost of his body and mind, and women did not generally receive formal education.

6. The argument as to which had precedence, which was superior, which was more important—the music or the idea (or music or the words of the text)—was one that permeated opera also. The direction of subservience is essential to an understanding of the singer's role, his prestige and power, and his relationships with others involved in making music.

7. It must be noted that this is only the first instance we will note in which the church overlooked Christian dictates in order to procure the voices it desired.

8. In *The History of Music in Performance*, Dorian (1942:23) examines the art of musical interpretation: "Between a musical work and the world stands the interpreter who brings the score to life by his performance . . . This situation in music, as compared to the other arts, is unique."

9. Music is said to be polyphonic if it is composed of two or more voice parts (or several melodic lines) developed in a parallel manner and producing a harmony. The highest voice in part music, descant is a somewhat florid melody sung by a few high voices as a decorative addition in hymn singing. The art of descant (or discant), as distinguished from the practice of singing from the written polyphony of composer, is the kind of florid improvisation (ornamentation, coloration, embellishment) that singers provided themselves.

10. The castrato (also called evirato, musico) was an emasculated male who at a young age (before puberty) had been subjected to an operation that halted the development of the vocal chords. He therefore retained the height and agility of a boy's voice, which, at adulthood, would reside in the body (and thus possess the lung power) of a man, or, as some have described it, a female voice in a male body.

References

Barnett, James H. 1959. "The Sociology of Art." In *Sociology Today*, ed. Robert K. Merton, Leonard Broom, and Leonard S. Cottrell. New York: Basic Books, pp. 197–214.

Bauer, Marion, and Ethel R. Peyser. 1932. *Music through the Ages*. London: Putnam's.

Bowra, Cecil M. 1962. *Primitive Song*. New York: World.

Carr-Saunders, A. M., and P. A. Wilson. 1962. "The Emergence of Professions." In *Man, Work and Society*, ed. Sigmund Nosow and William H. Form. New York: Basic Books, pp. 199–206.

Couch, Stephen R. 1979. "The Orchestra as Factory." Paper presented at the American Sociological Association Annual Meetings, Boston, August 28.

Deacon, Harry Collins. 1910. "Singing." In *The Standard Musical Encyclopedia*, vol. 2., ed. John H. Clifford. New York: University Society, pp. 363–67.

Dorian, Frederick. 1942. *The History of Music in Performance*. New York: Norton.

Duey, Philip A. 1951. *Bel Canto in Its Golden Age*. New York: Columbia.

Goldner, Fred H. 1967. "Role Emergence and the Ethics of Ambiguity." In *Ethics, Politics, and Social Research*, ed. Gideon Sjoberg. Cambridge, Mass.: Schenkman, pp. 245–66.

Grout, Donald Jay. 1973. *A History of Western Music* (1960). New York: Norton.

Henderson, William J. 1921. *Early History of Singing*. New York: Longmans, Green.

Heriot, Angus. 1975. *The Castrati in Opera* (1927). New York: Da Capo.

Hughes, Charles W. 1970. *The Human Side of Music* (1948). New York: Da Capo.

Jander, Owen. 1980. "Singing." In *The New Grove Dictionary of Music and Musicians*, 6th ed., vol. 17, ed. Stanley Sadie. London: Macmillan, pp. 338–46.

Kamerman, Jack B. 1979. "The Symphony Orchestra Conductor: A Study of the Career of an Occupation." Ph.D. diss., New York University, New York, N.Y.

Lang, Paul Henry. 1941. *Music in Western Civilization*. New York: Norton.

Levinson, Daniel J. 1957. "Role, Personality, and Social Structure." In *Sociological Theory*, ed. Lewis A. Coser and Bernard Rosenberg. New York: Macmillan, pp. 284–97.

Martorella, Rosanne. 1979. "Occupational Specialization and Aesthetic Change in Opera: Some Historical Inquiries." *International Review of the Aesthetics and Sociology of Music*, 10:89–98.

Merriam, Alan P. 1964. *The Anthropology of Music*. Evanston, Ill.: Northwestern Univ. Press.

Nef, Karl. 1964. *An Outline of the History of Music* (1935), trans. Carl F. Pfatteicher. New York: Columbia.

Newcomb, Anthony. 1980. *The Madrigal at Ferrara*, vol. 1. Princeton, N.J.: Princeton Univ. Press.

Pahlen, Kurt. 1949. *Music of the World*, trans. James A. Galston. New York: Crown.

Pincherle, Marc. 1956. *The World of the Virtuoso*, trans. Hubert E. M. Russell. New York: Norton.

Ridgeway, Sally. 1975. "When Object Becomes Idea: The Social History of an Avant Garde Art Movement." Ph.D. diss., City University of New York Graduate Center, New York, N.Y.

Rushmore, Robert. 1971. *The Singing Voice*. New York: Dodd, Mead.

Salz, Arthur. 1962. "Occupations in Their Historical Perspective." In *Man, Work, and Society*, ed. Sigmund Nosow and William H. Form. New York: Basic Books, pp. 58–63.

Wallaschek, Richard. 1970. *Primitive Music* (1893). New York: Da Capo.

Werner, Eric. 1963. *The Sacred Bridge* (1959). New York: Columbia.

10

The Rationalization of Symphony Orchestra Conductors' Interpretive Styles

JACK KAMERMAN

Introduction

This chapter deals with one aspect (increasing rationalization) of the career of an occupation,[1] the symphony orchestra conductor, in one setting, the United States. This theme will be focused by attempting to explain the shift in interpretive style among conductors from the romantic or subjective approach, which dominated conducting in the last half of the nineteenth century and early in the twentieth century, to the neoclassic or objective approach, which came into ascendancy in the 1930s and 1940s and continues as the dominant mode even today.[2] I will argue that the career of conductor, from its emergence in the mid-nineteenth century to the present day, is characterized by increasing rationalization and that this rationalization and its roots underlie the shift in interpretive style from romantic to neoclassic. This rationalization is evidenced in: (1) the standardization of interpretations, i.e., their reduction to "formulas"; (2) the rising importance of technique; and (3) the conceptualization of conductor as technician and historian and the increasing importance of "objectivity," i.e., emphasis on the "objective" document (the printed score) rather than the subjective intuition and emotions of the interpreter.

It will further be argued that this process of rationalization is influenced 169 by the following factors, related as the numbering indicates to the evidences of rationalization mentioned above: (1)(a) unionization of musicians, (b) tenure of conductors with U.S. orchestras, (c) influence of style leaders; (2)(a) technical improvements in the manufacture of instruments, (b) technical advances in the reproduction of music, e.g., phonographs, radio, and television, (c) professionalization of musicians, (d) changes in the training of conductors; and (3)(a) the change in repertory from a preponderance of contemporary music (in the eighteenth and nineteenth centuries) to music of the past (in the twentieth century), (b) enlargement of the division of labor in music to include nonartistic technical positions.[3]

The Two Styles of Interpretation Defined

It is obvious that all interpretation of musical scores is in a sense "subjective."[4] Although composers have increasingly elaborated and refined the system of musical notation, to some extent performing a score relies on the interpretation of the composer's intentions. As the musicologist Frederick Dorian has written:

> Obviously one cannot expect to set an inflexible, mathematical standard in art; if ideas of composers are subjective and their directions relative (in spite of such mechanical aids as the metronome), the interpreter's knowledge is likewise subjective, and therefore his ways of performance are subjective too [1942:30].

In addition, the older the score, the more difficult becomes the problem of deciphering a composer's intentions. Early scores, for one thing, contained no markings for the main tempo of a composition (ibid.:28). Also, there is no way of telling whether what *is* contained in the score was put there by the composer. Charles O'Connell, writing of the reputed king of twentieth-century literalists, Arturo Toscanini, succinctly made this point:

> He [Toscanini] worships a Beethoven score as if it had come with the ink still wet from the hand of the great man: ignoring the fact that there is probably no Beethoven score published that hasn't been tampered with, in which dynamic and metronomic marks haven't been inserted by some obscure hack in the employ of Breitkopf or Härtel or other publishers [1947:133].

Finally, composers often altered their own scores several times. For example, there exists a recording of one of Chopin's nocturnes (op. 9, no. 2, in E-flat major), which was played from Chopin's own score. The score contained several variants never included in the performances of current "literal" interpreters of Chopin. "Those who heard Chopin agree that he rarely played the same piece in the same way. Varying his playing with his mood, he gave full scope to his imagination and fantasy. In fact he tried to preserve a certain improvisatory quality which was impossible to notate. Indeed, he often played pieces with variants from his published text . . ." (Blickstein, 1967).[5] Also, Anton Bruckner's symphonies went through several editions as he was persuaded by one "friend" after another to streamline his scores.

Is the distinction between objective and subjective interpretation spurious? Not if the terms are taken as statements of position vis-à-vis a score, i.e., adhering to the composer's intentions held as a desideratum rather than as accomplished fact. Again, Dorian (1942) has neatly parsed the question:

> Richard Wagner's poetic and powerful interpretation of the opening of the Fifth [Beethoven's Symphony in C minor, op. 67] cannot be tested by objective standards, that is to say, by musical clues provided in Beethoven's score. No matter how fascinating we find his explanation, it must be classified as subjective, as it brings to the fore Wagner's views on Beethoven rather than the actual interpretive criteria for the music as we understand them from reading of the script. In any case, the *subjective* approach reflects the interpreter's individuality more than it does the world of the masterwork—not only in details like those that have just been demonstrated, but also in the delineation of the composition as a whole.
>
> In opposition to such a subjective reading stands the *objective* treatment, where the interpreter's principal attitude is that of unconditional loyalty to the script. Setting aside his personal opinion and detaching himself from his individual feelings, the objective interpreter has but one goal in mind: to interpret the music in the way the author conceived it. Logically, the objective interpreter of the Fifth will perform the opening measures according to the metronomic and other objective determinations, as indicated by the score and not by his personal feelings [pp. 26–27].[6]

There are then two interpretive approaches on which most conductors can be divided: the objectivist or neoclassic approach and the subjective or romantic approach.

The Standardization of Interpretation

Interpretations in the romantic tradition were highly personalized. They were developed in long rehearsals (an innovation of the latter half of the nineteenth century). The romantic style utilized techniques that had to be carefully worked through with an orchestra.

Mendelssohn, Bülow, Wagner and Liszt soon made another advance in that they succeeded in compelling adequate rehearsal in advance of public performance. To impose upon the orchestra or chorus one's private interpretation by means of a grueling series of rehearsals would have seemed impudent to all but a few aggressive musical authoritarians. But conditions were ripening for such an eventuality. The orchestral personnel was becoming more numerous, entrance cues less routine, and tonal balance more difficult to maintain. Rubato and other earmarks of romanticism were being developed, which . . . made coordination more and more difficult . . . [Mueller, 1951:316–17.]

In addition to adequate rehearsals, adequate tenure of a conductor with an orchestra was necessary to impose these highly personalized interpretations. Yet it is precisely these two requisites of a highly individualistic performance that have declined during the twentieth century.

Unionization of musicians began in the United States with the formation and charter of musicians' union in New York in 1864.[7] Unions eventually succeeded in limiting the importation of foreign musicians, improving wages, and—most important for present purposes—limiting rehearsal hours. In addition to the effects of unionization, there has been a steady increase in the number of concerts symphony musicians play during a season, due both to the increasing frequency of concerts and to the lengthening of symphony seasons.

The tenure of conductors with orchestras in the United States has also decreased during this century. The figures in Table 4 clearly demonstrate this. In Table 4, the breakdown into birthdates of pre- and post-1900 is somewhat arbitrary. However, conductors born in 1900 would have assumed

Table 4. Tenure of Permanent Conductors of Major American Orchestras (in Percentages)

	Born before 1900 (N = 40)	Born 1900 or Later (N = 11)
Average Tenure	9.3 years	6.8 years
	Pre-1900	1900 or Later
Under 5 Years	32	45
5–10 Years	40	45
Over 10 Years	28	10

SOURCES: Blom, 1954; Sabin, 1964; Sadie, 1980; Wooldridge, 1970:344–45.
NOTE: Figures are given for six orchestras: Boston Symphony, New York Philharmonic, Minnesota Orchestra (formerly the Minneapolis Symphony), and Chicago, Cleveland, and Philadelphia orchestras.

their major posts in the 1930s and 1940s, the period of the neoclassic revival. Also, conductors whose positions are current were not included, since their tenure is not over.

Jet travel has made globe hopping possible; consequently, conductors can divide their time between permanent leaderships of several orchestras. The music critic Alan Rich (1972:56) pointed to a growing similarity in the "sounds" of many orchestras and attributed this to their lack of a "permanent" conductor. In a piece entitled "Bigamy on the Orchestral Front" he wrote:

> When his new contract becomes effective, Ozawa will be in effect the principal conductor of two major American orchestras 3,000 miles apart, the Boston and San Francisco. The same situation obtains for a great many other conductors today: Boulez in New York and with the BBC in London; Maazel in Cleveland, London, and Berlin; Zubi-bubi [Zubin Mehta] in Los Angeles and Israel; Solti in Chicago and Paris; etc. . . .[Y]ou can buy the most adept orchestral players in the world, put them together on a stage in a house with the most beautiful acoustical conditions in all the world . . . and you still won't have a symphony orchestra—not, that is, until a single dominant personality is put on the podium, to work with the musicians week after week, studying the strengths and weaknesses of the individual players, and gradually molding a sound that comes to represent the uniqueness of that orchestra . . . One of the things that has disturbed me a great deal lately is the impression that most of the world's symphony orchestras are beginning to sound alike. You begin to suspect this after a few weeks at Carnegie Hall's excellent Visiting Orchestra series; even though every conductor carries his own ideas about orchestral sound and balance, there is developing a world-wide all-purpose tone. The only orchestra I have heard lately of which this isn't true is, in fact, the Philadelphia under Ormandy. I don't much like the sound of the orchestra, or the uses to which it is often put, but there's one thing, for damn sure: you *know* it's the Philadelphia Orchestra, even with your eyes shut. That is because Ormandy stays put.

Harold Schonberg (1967:358) made much the same point when he predicted the decline of national schools of conducting:

> . . . [I]t is hard to tell the difference between a young American and a young English or Hungarian conductor, just as it is getting harder and harder to distinguish national styles in piano playing or composition. Even symphony orchestras are beginning to sound alike, no matter where their point of origin.

Another aspect of the standardization of interpretation is the attempt to reduce performance to calculable rules.[8] Toscanini represented the epitome of this movement toward calculability:

> He [Toscanini] marks the meter so clearly that every downbeat takes on a slight stress—not a pulsation or lilt, as in Viennese waltzes, but a tiny, tiny,

dry accent, like the click of a well-running machine. This mechanical purring both gives to his readings a great rhythmic clarity and assures the listener that all is under control. It is also, nevertheless, a little bit lulling. One gets hypnotized by the smooth-working mechanics of the execution and forgets to listen to the music as a human communication. . . .

Excitement is of the essence in Toscanini's concept of musical performance. But his is not the kind of excitement that has been the specialty of the more emotional conductors of the past fifty years. Theirs was a personal projection, a transformation through each conductor's own mind of what the conductor considered to be the composer's meaning. At its best this supposed a marriage of historical and literary with musical culture . . . For musicians of this tradition *every piece is a different piece, every author and epoch another case for stylistic differentiation and for special understanding.* . . .

He [Toscanini] quite shamelessly whips up the tempo . . . just making the music, like his baton, go round and round, if he finds his audience's attention tending to waver. *No piece has to mean anything specific.* . . .

The radical simplification of interpretive problems that all this entails has changed orchestral conducting from a matter of culture and its personal projection into something more like *engineering.* Young conductors don't bother much anymore to feel music or to make their musicians feel it. They *analyze* it, concentrate in rehearsals on the essentials of its rhetoric, and let the expressive details fall where they may, counting on each man's skill and everybody's instinctive musicianship to take care of these eventually. [Thomson, 1968:54–55, 60–62; emphases mine.]

Charles O'Connell (1947:134–35) also notes Toscanini's attempt to reduce matters of dynamics to simple general rules:

His dynamics, though, are absolute and untempered, I think. A *fortissimo* is always "all out" and a *pianissimo* is always at the threshold of hearing. He himself has said that one should play an "*ff*" so strongly that he can't hear his partner and a "*pp*" so softly that his partner can't hear him. Here is a masterpiece of clear and practical definition. It is likewise wrong. Must "*ff*" always and inevitably signify the limit of one's capacity to generate tone or "*pp*" the limit of one's ability to suppress it? I do not think so, and I do not think that it is this concept of dynamic contrast that makes Toscanini's music so sharply black and white . . . Even this kind of playing has its uses, and if I were in a position to do so I should recommend to all conductors that they study Toscanini's records as virtually perfect representations of music that sounds precisely as written, and I should further recommend that they should go on from there and interject some element of humanity and warmth.

That a Toscanini should have arisen is a tribute to his peculiar genius (i.e., lies in biographical details); that he should have become the symbol of the wave of the future is attributable both to public-relations men at RCA and, in a larger sense, to the circumstances outlined above, which created the climate in which a Toscanini and all the little "Toscaninis" could flourish and prevail.[9]

The Rise of Technique

Along with the standardization of interpretation, the rise of technique also marked the rationalization of conducting in this century. Orchestral playing until the mid-nineteenth century was poor by present-day standards.

> At a time when the tempo of a Beethoven *scherzo* depended on the technical competency of the lackadaisical habits of an underpaid musician, when first chairs were gained by seniority, and violists were recruited from superannuated and decrepit violinists, the greatest needs felt by a conductor and composer like Berlioz were discipline, accuracy, ability, and determination to "stick to the notes." [Mueller, 1951:325.]

The technical improvement of instruments themselves, e.g., the invention of a new key mechanism for woodwinds early in the nineteenth century, also allowed more accurate playing. While technical excellence was developed further during the romantic era, it became the earmark of conductors of the neoclassic bent. Where the script becomes central, emphasis on playing the notes precisely (the antithesis of Pablo Casals's caution to "play the music not the notes") seems inevitable. The qualities that are admired in these conductors—e.g., Toscanini, Szell, and Weingartner—are clarity and precision.

One hypothesis to explain this focus on technique was offered by the late Lester Salomon (1972) in an editorial column in *Allegro* (the official publication of Local 802 of the American Federation of Musicians). He argued that many conductors demand an unrealistic level of technical excellence from orchestral players because they themselves have never played an orchestral instrument. Rather, they are pianist conductors.

> The Pianist-Conductor Syndrome is caused by a combination of things. It's easy to produce a pitch on the piano—anyone with or without talent or ability can do it—compared to the complexities faced by woodwind, brass, string, percussion and harp players. A pianist doesn't have to concern himself with intonation: either the piano is in tune—more or less—or it isn't . . . Another causative is that the piano is obviously a percussion instrument and the ordinary pianist-conductor usually can't get it through his skull that an orchestra doesn't respond with percussive attacks all the time. The pianist doesn't have to face the problem of creating a pitch on each and every note.

The fact that fewer and fewer conductors come from the ranks of the orchestra or from careers as instrumental soloists (other than pianists) becomes important, consequently, as a partial explanation for the focus on technique (see Table 5).

The phonograph and radio broadcast have contributed to raising the expectations of audiences for technical excellence in two ways. First, huge audiences are exposed to the best orchestral playing in the world, creating a sophistication through exposure such as few people could claim before. Second, technical adulteration of performances can create, in Virgil Thomson's phrase, "process music," a perfection where none existed in the original performance. Master tapes can be spliced and respliced, deleting single wrong notes until a technically "perfect" performance is achieved. The interpretive continuity may consequently be sacrificed for a measure of technical perfection. To a listener, however, this flawless facade will be taken as the level of technical perfection an artist is capable of. "Live" performances may be something of a letdown afterward.

The Conductor as Historian and Technician and the Score as Document

As the repertoire of orchestras is removed further and further from the present, the conductor, of necessity, becomes a kind of interpretive historian. His interpretations are less and less informed by conversations with composers, by experiences as a player in orchestras led by composers, by personal experiences as a concertgoer to performances led by composers, or by sharing a common world. His lineage as a student is now four, five, or more generations removed from the composers of the eighteenth and nineteenth centuries whose works comprise the bulk of the current orchestral repertory.

Table 5.   Conductors with Backgrounds as Instrumentalists (in Percentages)

	Born before 1900 (N = 35)	Born 1900 or Later (N = 13)
Trained as Instrumentalists other than Pianists	46	35
Trained as Pianists	23	27
Other*	31	38

SOURCES: Blom, 1954; Sabin, 1964; Sadie, 1980; Wooldridge, 1970:344–45.

*Includes conductors trained as conductors only and conductors for whom no information was available.

The reliance on the score as a kind of definitive account is further evidence of the rationalization of conducting. The score is seen as an "objective" account of the composer's intentions; performances are renditions of some "objective" truth, not personal and affective statements of the conductor. Again Toscanini offers a particularly pointed example. In discussing the romantic conductor Willem Mengelberg, he said, "Once he came to me and told me at great length the proper German way to conduct the *Coriolanus Overture*. He had got it, he said, from a conductor who supposedly had got it straight from Beethoven. Bah! I told him I got it straight from Beethoven himself, from the score" (Schonberg, 1967: 254).[10] That scores (as was pointed out earlier) do not in fact have this essential quality is not as important as the fact that they are perceived as having it.

Specialists (i.e., musicologists) are called upon to authenticate scores and instrumentation.[11] The conductor is no longer the singular definitive authority he was in the romantic era because the performance is no longer taken as an expression of his personality; rather, it is a rendition of the letter of the score. So crucial does the objective document become that composers' own tamperings with their own scores during performances are disregarded as though the truth contained in the score transcended even the individuality of the composer (Mueller, 1951:323–28).[12]

In addition to the mediation of the musicologist, the work of the conductor is encroached upon by radio and audio engineers and technicians, so that, to some extent, performances are modified on purely technical considerations. Commenting on the role of the radio engineer, Frank Black (1946), a conductor associated with radio station WNBC, wrote:

> If your crescendo threatens to upset the equilibrium of that needle [on the control panel]—well, it's too bad for your crescendo. It simply never reaches its intended climax. On the other hand, the engineer can achieve a "fake" crescendo from his control panel that would make Rossini green with envy. Yes, he is a very important person [pp. 68–69].

And on the role of the program director:

> You need to have confidence in the director. You may interpret Beethoven, but the director (with the help of the engineer at the controls) interprets your interpretation of Beethoven. Your ear tells you what goes on in the studio, but the director's ear is also at work in the control booth and, as the name indicates, he *controls* what goes on the air [ibid.].[13]

The conductor must to some extent become a recording technician, experimenting with different seatings to produce effects, especially for recordings. Quadraphonic sound, which was hailed as the final step in replicating the concert-hall listening experience, has mainly been used to create effects specific to quadraphonic record listening (unless orchestras begin hanging various of their choirs from platforms at different points in the auditorium).

Conclusion

In this chapter I have examined some of the determinants of conductors' interpretive styles. I have attempted to point to developments in conducting that are confluent with rationalization in other areas of society, which embody, in Schiller's oft-quoted phrase, "the disenchantment of the world," and which make less and less *comprehensible* a critic's characterization of a Furtwängler performance of the Franck Symphony in D, "he burns incense at a mystic shrine."

Notes

1. ". . .*the career of an occupation* consists in changes of its internal organization and its place in the division of labor of which society itself consists" (Hughes, 1958:9).

2. There were signs of a romantic revival in the 1970s, but it is still too early to call it a trend.

3. These factors overlap to some extent, e.g., a style leader such as Toscanini had an unparalleled exposure because of the advent of the radio concert and mass-media hard sell.

4. This was not as salient a problem before the nineteenth century because much music was written for specific occasions with little thought given to posterity. And the performances of that music were often supervised by the composer; consequently, the matter of *interpretation*, i.e., a subjective vs. an objective approach to the score, rarely arose.

5. Electronic music may solve this problem by eliminating the interpreter altogether.

6. Another clear statement of the distinction is contained in the essay, "About Conducting," by the eminent conductor Felix Weingartner (1969:110), an objectivist. He criticized the followers of Hans von Bülow (the major subjectivist or romantic conductor of the last half of the nineteenth century):

> . . .it was in the end regrettable that by the behavior, artistic and personal, of some "new-modish Bülows" so much attention was directed to the person of the conductor that the audience even came to regard the composers as the creatures, as it were, of their interpreters, and in conjunction with the name of a conductor people spoke of "his" Beethoven, "his" Brahms, or "his" Wagner.

Or later in the same essay (p. 116), "The conductor must before all things be sincere towards the work he is to produce, towards himself, and towards the public. He must not think, when he takes the score in hand, 'What can I make out of this work?' but, 'What has the composer wanted to say in it?' "

7. For the source of much of this information and a history of the American musicians' unions in general, see Leiter (1953).

> 8.   The "objective" discharge of business primarily means a discharge of busi-
>   ness according to calculable rules and "without regard for persons." Its
>   [bureaucracy's] specific nature. . . develops the more the bureaucracy is
>   "dehumanized" the more completely it succeeds in eliminating from of-
>   ficial business love, hatred, and all purely personal, irrational, and emo-
>   tional elements which escape calculation [Weber, 1958a:215–16].

"This drive to reduce artistic creativity to the form of a calculable procedure based on comprehensive principles appears to all in music." Don Martindale and Johannes Riedel in their introduction to Weber's *The Rational and Social Foundations of Music* (Weber, 1958b:xxii).

From the same introduction (p. xii):

> In the dynamics of Western musical development lie many tensions be-
> tween rational and affective motives. The value of musical rationalization
> is the transformation of the process of musical production into a calculable
> affair operating with known means, effective instruments, and understand-
> able rules. Constantly running counter to this is the drive for expressive
> flexibility.

9. Another source of standardization may be the availability of "canned" inter-pretations for imitation, i.e., the recorded performances of famous conductors, that short-cut knowledge acquired through studying or playing the score on a piano. (Dorian, 1942:342–43.)

Irving Kolodin coined the phrase "the phonographic memory" to describe the same situation. In a review of the conducting prodigy Ferruccio Burco, he wrote (1958:53–55):

> It is far simpler and more direct to hear the music so often from a recording
> that *its sound becomes a mere device for recalling the arrangement of symbols
> involved* [emphasis mine]. . . It cannot be a mere coincidence that such
> prodigies have emerged in a time when mechanical reproduction of or-
> chestral music has been accessible as never before. . . Did any of this
> make Burco a conductor? Does driving a car make one a mechanic? His
> performance suggested a new kind of musical phenomenon—a backseat
> driver, rather than a leader or conductor. Given an orchestra in good
> order, with ample artistic gas and technical oil to expend, he could drive
> along with it comfortably, perhaps even sense when the speed limits were
> being exceeded and call for a little caution. Should it stall, however, or,
> what is more to the point, stop functioning altogether, he would no more
> be able to get it going than you or I on the highway.

I find his metaphor interesting in itself.

10. As Schonberg (1967:173) has commented, "In romanticism the ego was all-

important, the performer on the level of the creator, and one's aspirations were much more important than any such vague thing as scholarship or fidelity to the printed note. Nobody in the nineteenth century thought about 'fidelity'; he thought about self-expression."

11. "Musicology, one of the newest of the scholarly disciplines, has been conditioning all performers and critics to a greater or lesser degree since World War II. For the past fifty years, musicologists have been attempting to *codify* musical thought and performance practice of the past [emphasis mine] and in the last twenty years a tremendous amount of material has been published" (Schonberg, 1967:365).

12. Mueller (1951:324) has called the score "at best an awkward and incomplete symbolization of the creator's intention. . . Indeed there is some evidence that Beethoven, himself, was not a calm interpreter, but rather indulged in exaggerated extremes of emotional expression and rubato style while performing before the Viennese nobility." Also, recall the case of the Chopin *Nocturne* cited earlier.

13. This view was supported by an officer of the Arturo Toscanini Society in a conversation I had with him a few years ago. I commented on the dry, thin sound Toscanini's orchestra had in the recordings I had heard. He said that this was attributable to the acoustics of the recording studio RCA used and, more importantly, to the engineer who happened to be on duty. To illustrate his point he played a rehearsal recording made during the same period as one of the commercial recordings I had heard, but with a different engineer. Although the orchestral sound was not exactly opulent, it was considerably richer than the sound accorded by the other engineer.

References

Black, Frank J. 1946. "Conducting for Radio." In *Music in Radio Broadcasting*, ed. Gilbert Chase. New York: McGraw–Hill.

Blickstein, Edward. 1967. "The Lost Art of Chopin Interpretation." Reprinted on the jacket of the recording, "The Great Chopin Interpreters" (VM–115). New York: Veritas Records, Inc.

Blom, Eric (ed.). 1954. *Grove's Dictionary of Music and Musicians*, 5th ed. New York: St. Martin's Press.

Canby, Edward Tatnall. 1972. "Canby Looks at Timeless Recordings." *Audio*, October, pp. 82, 84.

Carse, Adam. 1929. *Orchestral Conducting*. London: Augener.

1940 *The Orchestra in the 18th Century*. Cambridge: W. Heffer & Sons.

1948 *The Orchestra from Beethoven to Berlioz*. Cambridge: W. Heffer & Sons.

Dorian, Frederick. 1942. *The History of Music in Performance: The Art of Musical Interpretation from the Renaissance to Our Day*. New York: W. W. Norton.

Hughes, Everett Cherrington. 1958. *Men and Their Work*. Glencoe, Ill.: Free Press.

Kolodin, Irving. 1958. *The Musical Life*. New York: Alfred A. Knopf.

Leiter, Robert D. 1953. *The Musicians and Petrillo*. New York: Bookman Associates.

Mueller, John H. 1951. *The American Symphony Orchestra: A Social History of Musical Taste.* Bloomington: Indiana Univ. Press.

O'Connell, Charles. 1947. *The Other Side of the Record.* New York: Alfred A. Knopf.

Rich, Alan. 1972. "Bigamy on the Orchestral Front." *New York,* February 28, p. 56.

Sabin, Robert (ed.). 1964. *International Cyclopedia of Music and Musicians,* 9th ed. New York: Dodd, Mead.

Sadie, Stanley (ed.). 1980. *New Grove's Dictionary of Music and Musicians.* Washington, D.C.: Grove's Dictionaries of Music.

Salomon, Lester. 1972. "The Pianist–Conductor Syndrome." *Allegro,* October, pp. 3, 11.

Schonberg, Harold C. 1967. *The Great Conductors.* New York: Simon & Schuster.

Thomson, Virgil. 1968. *The Musical Scene* (1945). New York: Greenwood Press.

Weber, Max. 1958a. *From Max Weber: Essays in Sociology,* ed. H. H. Gerth and C. Wright Mills. New York: Oxford Univ. Press.

1958b. *The Rational and Social Foundations of Music,* trans. Don Martindale et al. Carbondale: Southern Illinois Univ. Press.

Weingartner, Felix. 1969. *Weingartner on Music and Conducting.* New York: Dover.

11

Politics and Artistic Interpretation

DMITRI SHOSTAKOVICH

. . . .

I remember how they stopped a rehearsal of *Hamlet* at the Moscow Art Theater. It was, if you can put it that way, Stalin's "favorite" theater. More precisely, it was the only theater that the leader approved fully and entirely. For the actor playing Hamlet, the banning of the play become a real tragedy. Hamlet had been his dream, everyone around him understood that this would have been a fantastic Hamlet. But Stalin's word was law, and the leader and teacher didn't even have to give a written order. There was no order, just a wish. Why forbid? You might go down in history with a less than noble image. It's better to merely ask, as Stalin did, "Why is this necessary—playing *Hamlet* in the Art Theater, eh?" That was all, that was enough. The play was removed and the actor drank himself to death.

And for many long years *Hamlet* was not seen on the Soviet stage. Everyone knew about Stalin's question directed at the Art Theater and no one wanted to risk it. Everyone was afraid.

And *King Lear?* Everyone knows that our best Lear was Mikhoels in the Jewish Theater and everyone knows his fate.* A terrible fate. And what about the fate of our best translator of Shakespeare—Pasternak?

Almost every name bears a tragedy, more tragic than anything in Shake-

---

*Solomon Mikhailovich Mikhoels (Vovsi; 1890–1948), Jewish actor and director. He was brutally murdered on Stalin's orders and the murder was said to be an attack by hooligans. In 1943, when Mikhoels was chairman of the Jewish Anti-Fascist Committee (later disbanded by Stalin), he came to America on Albert Einstein's invitation. In New York he appeared with Mayor La Guardia in the Polo Grounds before a crowd of 50,000.

speare. No, it's better not to become involved with Shakespeare. Only careless people would take on such a losing proposition. That Shakespeare is highly explosive.

But back then, in my youth, I gave in to Akimov's exhortations. He was a unique director, a siren with a cabbage head. Akimov was always elegantly dressed and extremely polite, but it was better not to be the butt of his wit or his pen. Akimov was a mean artist. His caricatures were lethal. I think I got off lightly.

Akimov obtained provisional permission for a production of *Hamlet*. This was a major victory. The problem was that the previous Moscow production of the play was deemed totally inadmissible by the censors. The legendary Mikhail Chekhov played Hamlet. He, as you know, was an anthroposophist, and he imbued his theater with anthroposophy. *Hamlet* was staged that way. Mikhail Chekhov set the play in Purgatory. Literally. That is, Chekhov thought that Shakespeare had written a purely symbolic play, that everyone was actually dead. The courtiers were the souls of the dead and the protagonists were anthroposophic symbols.

Probably Mikhail Chekhov sincerely believed that Shakespeare really was an anthroposophist, and that's how he played Hamlet. The atmosphere was otherworldly. The actors were brilliant, after all, and Chekhov was simply a genius. The audience came away from this strange *Hamlet* with the feeling that it had just come from the other world. You see what mysterious ideas artistic people can have. You might call them delirious. Officials saw the play and, horrified, banned *Hamlet* immediately as a reactionary, pessimistic, and mystical play.

Akimov, as I said, was a mean man, but a jolly one. He saw Mikhail Chekhov's interpretation of Hamlet and was outraged. He told me, "I look at the stage and think, Could the author of this morose delirium really be Shakespeare?" Akimov developed a passionate desire to stage his own *Hamlet*. That often happens: inspiration from the contrary, so to speak. For example, Meyerhold conceived his version of *The Queen of Spades* under the influence of a terrible production he had seen. He later told me that he would have been ready to strangle the tenor who sang Gherman if he had run into him in a dark alley.

Akimov suffered mightily during Chekhov's *Hamlet* and it was the final straw that led to his own conception of the play. The concept was, I must say, revolutionary. Akimov decided to stage it as a comedy. A comedy of struggle for power. Akimov gave the part to a rather famous comic actor. The actor was stocky and fat, a man who loved food and drink. I might note that this corresponds to the text of the play, which mentions Hamlet's corpulence. But the audience is completely unused to it. It's used to exalted Hamlets, to sexless Hamlets, I would say. Or rather, to androgynous ones in black, thigh-hugging tights. Women have played Hamlet—Asta Nilsen, I think. And Zinaida Raikh planned to play it. With *her* body. I think it's the only male role in world literature that women have attempted. And now suddenly a fat Hamlet. With a loud voice, full of vitality.

When Akimov informed the theater authorities of his project, they were also surprised. There didn't seem to be anything to forbid here. And in any case, this concept didn't reek of reactionary mysticism. On the contrary, it gave off the healthy smell of alcohol. For Hamlet, according to Akimov, was a merry, cheerful, and hard-working man who enjoyed his drink. Actually, there wasn't anyone who didn't in this unique version. Gertrude, Claudius, Polonius, even Ophelia, drank. In Akimov's version, Ophelia drowns because she's drunk. In the language of a medical examiner's report: "an autopsy revealed traces of heavy alcoholic intoxication." The gravediggers spoke thus: "To drink or not to drink—that is the question." The doubter was set straight: "What question? Of course, to drink." The dialogue was written specially for this scene.

Now about the struggle for power. This struggle became the central theme of *Hamlet* for Akimov. The struggle for the crown. And none of the traditional pangs of guilt, the doubts, and so on. I'm sick of that struggle for power, the eternal theme of art. You can't get away from it. Particularly in our times. So. Hamlet pretends to be mad the better to trick Claudius. Akimov calculated that in the play Hamlet feigns madness seventeen times. Akimov's Hamlet wages a persistent and clever fight for the throne. There is no Ghost, as I said. Hamlet himself impersonates the Ghost. He does that to frighten and terrorize the courtiers. Hamlet wants to present an important witness for his side, from the other world, to have the witness confirm that Claudius is on the throne illegally. And so the scene of the Ghost's appearance was staged as pure comedy.

As for "To be or not to be," Hamlet spoke the lines weighing the crown in his hands. He tried it on, twirled it every which way. His relations with Ophelia, a bitch and a spy, were unambiguous. Hamlet was screwing her. And Ophelia, pregnant, got drunk and drowned herself.

Polonius was marvelous. This was perhaps the acting triumph of Akimov's production (another of his paradoxes). The famous Boris Shchukin played the role. Later Shchukin became even more famous as the first actor to portray Lenin on the screen. Or rather, as the first professional actor upon whom such a historic mission was bestowed.

Shchukin, like Akimov, was a very nasty man. He tried various approaches to the role of Polonius. But nothing seemed to work at first. I later got to know Shchukin better, when he was putting on a Balzac play in his theater and asked me to write the music. It was then that Shchukin revealed a small secret of his success in *Hamlet*.

I think the story is interesting and quite educational for actors. A small lesson in the art of acting. I laughed heartily when I heard it. Shchukin wanted to get away from the clichés. Polonius's part isn't very clear. He seems clever and at the same time rather stupid. He can be a "noble father," that's how he behaved with his son. But in relation to his daughter he's a panderer. Usually Polonius's appearances are boring for the audience. But the audience is used to it and bears it. The feeling is that if it's a classic, you have to bear certain things. You must have respect for the classics.

This was Shchukin's method. He found traits and characteristics in his friends that would help him create a role, and that's what he did with Polonius. He took something from one friend and something else from another. And then at a rehearsal Shchukin tried reading Polonius's monologue as though he was Stanislavsky.

And suddenly the role began taking shape. Everything fell into place. Even the most difficult parts of the role, when spoken in the manner and from the persona of Stanislavsky, suddenly sounded convincing. Shchukin copied Stanislavsky impeccably. You could cry laughing. The result was something majestic and slightly stupid. The man lives comfortably, very well, yet he prattles on with this nonsense. That's how Shchukin portrayed Stanislavsky.

. . . .

12

Interview:
John Bishop

The Playwright's Effect on Acting

J.K. *Do you ever write a play with particular actors in mind?*

J.B. *Yes, a lot, but not stars. I'm with a company called Circle Repertory Company, which is an off-Broadway theater. We have a permanent company, so we tend to write for particular actors in the company. Some of them happen to be stars—Bill Hurt. . . Judd Hirsch. I don't write with an actor like a star in mind, if that was your question.*

J.K. *I mean, do you ever tailor what you write with a particular actor in mind, knowing what their strengths are, their weaknesses. . .*

J.B. *Their rhythms. I call them rhythms. Yes.*

J.K. *What is your relationship to the actors and the director? If you're with a company, presumably you get to be at rehearsals. . .*

J.B. *How do I relate to it? It becomes very political. At first I'm very active, and then I stay away from rehearsal until it's set, which would mean a period of a couple of weeks. And then I come back—and I only do that for my own political reasons: I don't want the director to turn around and say, "I haven't got it right yet." I want to be able to say, "They have it right and I don't like it," or, "I do like it," or, "I would like to see you change this." Normally, everything should go through the director to the actor. It ought to. It usually does, but I would say that 25 percent of the time, the director is not conveying it, or I get impatient. Then, it's just a question of saying to the actor, in terms of the lines so I don't*

John Bishop is a resident playwright at the Circle Repertory Company in New York. He has written a number of plays, including *The Trip Back Down*, which was produced on Broadway in 1977. He was interviewed by Jack Kamerman at his home in New York City in March 1982.

step in the other guy's territory, "Is that a directorial thing you're doing?" It's very political. You see, I am a director, so I sort of know how to do that a little bit, but it gets tricky. A good actor will turn and say, "Well, gee, John, Marshall [Mason, artistic director of the Circle Repertory Company] told me to do something else." And I'll go back to Marshall. But very often, if it's about the word, if it's about the way the word should be said, they'll listen to the playwright first because he really knows what he wants.

J.K.: How do you feel when you see actors in your plays where you haven't had any input?

J.B. It's terrible. I've never seen a revival of my plays done by some other theater that I was happy with. Never. I must say that other playwrights I've talked to used to say, "Don't go to see someone else do the play." It's seldom a very good experience. One or two good performances, but they generally don't come out good.

J.K. Do you ever articulate your displeasure?

J.B. Yes, I have. Recently, as a matter of fact, there was a revival of a play of mine done by a professional acting teachers' group here in New York, and I went to see it. I said, "It looks like **Little House on the Prairie** and it's about people you wouldn't want in your living room." And that's about all I said. I wasn't pleased with it.

J.K. Do you write any acting directions into your plays?

J.B. Oh, yes.

J.K. How specific?

J.B. I try not to be too specific. One of the things that makes me angry is when a director ignores stage directions. I must say that at Circle Repertory they're very good about not doing that. But speaking about going to see other productions, that's what happens. They ignore stage directions and they get themselves in terrible trouble. I try to limit it. I try not to put in anything that's extraneous, but I do try to let the actor know sometimes in which way a line is being said. Maybe he just says, "Okay," and you might want to say that that's [to be said] "dryly." I find I use the word "dryly" a lot because there are many things we say in dry humor that could be interpreted in two or three different ways. Or "with amusement." I'll say, "with humor." Whereas if the scene is going one way, and it looks as though the actor could be angry, and I choose to make him amused by it, then I really have to tell the actor what's happening.

J.K. How much room is there in your plays, compared to other playwrights' work, for interpretation?

J.B. I'll tell you. My answer to that is that one of these actors I just saw do the revival of my play said, "I understand you and I have a disagreement.

There are many ways of playing a part." I said, "There are many ways of playing a part, but there's only one right way." There's not a lot of room, I feel, for any psychological reinterpretation. I think that my characters are psychologically centered. I don't leave them much room. I don't think most good playwrights do leave much room for interpretation. I used to think that. When I was in school, we used to talk about the room for interpretation, but if it's a good playwright and you get into the character as an actor—and I've been an actor—you're going to find what he's after. There's certainly room for at what point the character may feel something, and I certainly will rewrite for actors when I see them go in a certain direction. I've rewritten whole scenes, because I've seen, oh, he wants to go a different way. . . and he's right.

The Bases of Performing Styles

J.K.   *What do you think influences performing styles?*

J.B.   *The director. The times also. In a specific play, the director and the playwright, the tone of the play. However, the acting styles, as you know, change over the years. If we watch a thirties movie and we see the way men walk, it's quite amazing to see what was a manly walk in those days. The amount of projection is different. The acting now is much more, I guess, what you'd call naturalistic, real. The camera has had a lot to do with that.*

J.K.   *Why do you think that's taken place?*

J.B.   *The reality, you mean? That's an enormous question. I did notice acting styles begin to change in the fifties. Marlon Brando and Montgomery Clift and James Dean were really beginning a new style of acting. It is less flamboyant, it is realer. Now the question is, is it any realer than it was in 1930? Probably not, so it's how we perceive reality on the stage or on the screen. Why do we need more reality or what seems to be more honesty? (Then I have to ask myself, is it really more honesty, because I remember my father as a young man and his friends, and they seemed to be a little more, what's the word I want to use, external. So the acting is just reflecting the time we're in.) I've noticed that since the sixties men and women [have been] talking faster, less inflection, quieter. You could say it was drugs that helped bring that on. I'm not sure it was. I personally think we're moving toward a less verbal style of communication, and I don't like to see that happening. I think that probably television or film has a lot to do with it. **Cinema verité**, documentaries, we begin to see more and more reality in terms of people on the street . . . I'm just reminded of something. When I was directing—I've only* been writing for about six years—I remember a period when I was astounded and intrigued with live news coverage. I would say that was in the late fifties and early sixties. . . intrigued by people on the street being caught saying something. . . intrigued by the honesty of the emotion, the honesty of the moment. . . fascinated by it. Even commercials were doing it. The kind of commercials that were very popular then were sort of, "Well, I like it, and I think we'll buy three of them." They were very real and I believe that as reality began to pervade, the writers certainly tuned into it, writers like David Story and Pinter began to go for, instead of heightened reality, almost a lessened reality, if there is such a word. It's like really going under, it's playing what is underneath everything. And I think that just watching the way actors work today and on film, that that's sort of what's happening to it. And I think it's television.

It's seeing reality. How can you watch the news at seven-thirty and hear some father say his son has disappeared, he doesn't know where he is, and eight o'clock watch a program purporting to be a realistic portrayal of an American event and see some actor over-acting it. He can't do that. He's got to be the reality we saw on the news. I guess that answers the question, for me, anyhow.

J.K. You're saying that when you could make a separation between reality and play acting, that's a different situation from if reality appears in places where you know it's real, and yet it's a television program. . .

J.B. Yeah. There's a melting together of the two, and the responsible actor can't do, he won't be accepted doing, what he wants to with histrionics. He has to imitate life more, which is what I think he should be doing anyhow.

J.K. Do you think that any part of it could be that people change the way they see themselves, that people now see themselves in a more subtle way? They try to get behind what someone's saying. They don't take what people say at face value.

J.B. Oh, certainly, absolutely, that's happening. Body language: what does he really mean by that?

J.K. Are you, as a playwright, tuned into changes in acting styles?

J.B. Oh, yes.

J.K. Do you take them into account when you write?

J.B. No, because I think that we both change at the same time, the actor and the playwright. I think the acting style is really a reflection of the kind of reality that the public wants to see. So the playwright is probably going along in the same direction. I don't think there are different kinds of acting styles except what the play requires. Restoration, Elizabethan, Greek—whatever the play requires, that's what the acting style is.

J.K. *But then, in the fifties, would playwrights have written with the knowledge that method acting was in the ascendancy?*

J.B. *Yeah, probably, but I think it's sort of back and forth. It's which came first, the chicken or the egg. It would really be hard to say whether Odets was before the method or the method was before Odets. Or whether Williams was before the method. They almost came together; those things happen together and we recognize it happening. But the minds are both going the same way, like some universal track we all hook on. I don't believe that one watches the other and says, "Oh, I guess we better do this." I think it just sort of evolves out of society.*

The Playwright on Playwriting

J.K. *One final question: Since you write for a specific company, then you not only have a knowledge of the strengths and the limitations of the actors, but you also have a knowledge of the financial limitations of the company. And you play in a particular theater, so you have a sense of what's possible in that theater. Do you think it's ever the other way around, as in music when Berlioz said, "I'm going to write this thing and I don't care if I can't assemble six hundred musicians. I'm going to write it for six hundred musicians."*

J.B. *Yes, absolutely. The play that's going on next week [**The Great Grandson of Jedediah Kohler**] has sixteen characters, and we normally operate in a two-hundred-seat house, and we've been very successful there. For this we've moved to a five-hundred-seat house and put it in repertory with **Richard II** because it's the only way we could pay all those actors. It frustrates me to think that I have to write a three-character, one-set play.*

Writing for a theater is very important to me and I sometimes think that some things I write shouldn't be done anywhere but in a living room.

J.K. *Chamber theater.*

J.B. *Just for myself I can say, I do think of the space. I do think of the financial limitations. I know the next play that I write will be a very small play. But gosh, if you want to write with a kind of sweep and panorama, you just have to do it and say, the hell with the cost. There's always somebody who will do it. Generally some regional theater will do it. My first play [**The Trip Back Down**], which went from off-Broadway to Broadway, had fourteen characters in it. It was hard to keep it open for more than about three months. But also it's seldom done anywhere else because of the size of the cast, except in regional theater* *occasionally, where they have a big group, or some colleges. So I suppose you think of it when you sit down. You say, oh my God, keep it to six people, eight people. I think as an audience member I get very tired of opening a program and seeing three characters listed. God, I can remember when intermission would come and there were still four more characters to enter.*

J.K. *Do you think anyone in a regional theater or a college theater sits down and says, "All right, we have such-and-such a budget, so we can only afford a four-actor play, with one set. And it has to be three chairs. . ."?*

J.B. *Three chairs, that's Broadway. What did we really decide the other night? Three of us were sitting down, Milan Stitt, he wrote **The Runner Stumbles**, Lanford [Wilson], who wrote **Fifth of July**, **Tally's Folly**, we decided to parody what you would need to write a play that would run forever outside of New York. Milan decided you must have a part for a woman in her mid-forties to early fifties because she usually runs the community theater. It shouldn't be a big role. I wish I'd written down everything else we decided, because we came up with the perfect play that would run forever.*

SECTION FIVE

AUDIENCES AND CRITICS: RESPONSES TO PERFORMANCE

I am sitting in the smallest room of my house. I have your review before me. In a moment it will be behind me.

Max Reger

Although critics and audiences are quite distinct entities today, they function interdependently. Throughout history some profession or institution has always existed whose role it is to acclaim, assess, and/or reject performers and their presentations. However, the full-time occupation of critic grew as a result of the middle class's ever-expanding attendance at live performances.

During the eighteenth century, Germany experienced a climate of dilettantism, creating knowledgeable and active concertgoers. The critic (at first, a musician composer) became specialized within literary circles and assumed the role of mediator between composer and audience. He first acted as interpreter of a musical composition, but as printing expanded to include publication of daily newspapers, professional criticism became more widespread, its tasks more diverse and specialized. The critical function came to be viewed as an essential part of the artistic community, and of the production process. As critics evidenced their power by reviews, audiences expressed their power by their willingness to purchase tickets at the box office.

In looking at the past, it appears certain that critics had to wait for the establishment of a daily press before aesthetic criticism was acknowledged as an art form. Some form of art criticism appeared in Greece and Rome. At that time, however, criticism was developed within a literary elite, and took the form of a philosophical treatise on theory and composition of a piece. Ancient critics also sought to relate specific art forms to other cultural and symbolic systems of the time.

Historically, we designate early-eighteenth-century England as the beginning of criticism; in particular, Addison's analyses of Italian opera in *The Spectator* of 1711 (Blom, 1959:523). Shortly thereafter, a number of highly intellectual and theoretical periodicals were published. However, the emerging middle class of northern Europe, who regularly attended established concert series in Hamburg (1722) and Paris (1725), increasingly influenced the journalistic styles of periodicals. In the rest of Europe and throughout the eighteenth century, amateur musicians, writers, and philosophers continued to give some attention to music in their general writings. The widespread popularization of musical life created the demand for a mediator between audience and composer, and the first musical writer to fill this capacity was Friedrich Rochlitz (1769–1842), who had no other occupation but that of musical writer.

The romanticism of the eighteenth century influenced musical criticism in German, French, and English periodicals. At this time, composers themselves took up writing, and many composer critics defended themselves against the highly subjective professional critics of the time. Edward Hanslick (1855–1904) became an important critic especially because of his controversial criticisms of the Liszt–Wagner school. In the midst of this heated discussion, Hanslick attempted to lay the foundation for the role of music critic with regard to delineating prerequisites of technique and aesthetics. The latter part of the nineteenth century produced a flood of critics, including the prolific and astute Bernard Shaw.

By the beginning of the twentieth century, periodicals and daily newspapers had expanded, along with the desire of management and impresarios to advertise their performances. Although European countries varied in their publication of critical writings, generally a dichotomy resulted between the critic, who was more learned and intellectually aligned with the composer or playwright, and the "journalist–critic," who wrote for the readers of the daily press.

Throughout his development, the critic has established a line of communication between the creative artist and the audience. Today, he is viewed as a professional analyst and interpreter, of either a work of art or a live performance. The more successful have developed individualized styles of writing, which in and of themselves are entertaining, but few would deny the power of critics, regardless of the attractiveness of their style.

This brief historical review highlights the changing functions of the critic's role as determined by the market in which he worked. Consequently, the aesthetic questions whether criticism should be subjective or objective, interpretation or review, arose as a result of the expanded and diverse market for the arts, and the demands of audiences.

This section attempts to analyze the contemporary audience in terms of its composition, reasons for attendance, influence on the development of repertoire trends, and preferences for particular stars. Some comparisons among dance, theater, music, and opera are made, and it is shown how preferences for a particular art form reflect differences in the audiences' gender, age, and ethnic, religious, and class backgrounds.

Such an approach is referred to as the demographic, in which socioeconomic characteristics are used to explain why people attend one type of performing art over another. The motivating factors behind consumer choices in attendance or nonattendance may also be explained by the life-style approach, in which social researchers develop a profile of audiences and establish relationships between attitudes and the tendency to perform specific actions (e.g., attend a performance). What is revealed is the diversity in tastes, mediated by the composition of arts audience. After all, within a single performance, the audience may include the casual goer, the regular attender, the patron, the ardent fan, and the critic. Hence, its community is diverse, reaching a broad spectrum of tastes and interests—which may not all be, e.g., musical. Readers should keep this point in mind while reading these chapters, realizing how the composition of the audience reflects a general life-style, which has predisposed the audience to particular consumer choices.

Paul DiMaggio and Michael Useem draw upon 268 studies of visitors to museums and audiences of live performing arts in the United States, and illustrate the relevance of social class to frequent attendance at arts events. They conclude by raising the issue of the social role of elite art within a democracy.

The study "Audience Development," conducted by the Research Division of the National Endowment for the Arts, contains data which may be applied by arts managers. In analyzing the composition of audiences for symphony and theater, it delineates predictors for arts attendance and develops strategies that could affect future attendance. Effective marketing techniques and changes in ticket prices and repertoire, for example, are relevant factors in encouraging attendance.

In summation, this section examines how audiences and critics have evolved as significant roles within the total production process, affecting decisions with regard to casting and repertoire.

Reference

Blom, Eric. 1959. *Grove's Dictionary of Music and Musicians*, 5th Ed., vol. 2 (C–E). New York: St. Martin's Press.

13

Cultural Democracy in a Period of Cultural Expansion: The Social Composition of Arts Audiences in the United States

PAUL DIMAGGIO/MICHAEL USEEM

The nature of the public for the arts in the United States has been a source of speculation and controversy for much of this country's history. Alexis de Tocqueville, the liberal French aristocrat who studied American democracy during the 1830s, noted then that America's puritan simplicity and unbounded resources were more conducive to commerce than to culture. Nonetheless, he suggested, as the frontier closed and the puritan legacy weakened, the natural tendencies of democracy might bring in unprecedented public involvement in the arts.

> Not only will the number of those who take an interest in the production of mind be greater, but the taste for intellectual enjoyment will descend, step by step, even to those who, in aristocratic societies, seem to have neither time nor ability to indulge in them. [Tocqueville, 1956:162.]

Tocqueville predicted the democratization of both the production and appreciation of art as the United States became more mature, but a half century later Thorstein Veblen (1899) could not see it. Having witnessed the rise of great fortunes that Tocqueville had not foreseen, Veblen feared that the arts (as well as most aspects of culture, learning, and manners) had become the playthings of the rich—baubles and badges of social standing less respected for their beauty or intrinsic merit than for their rarity and expense. High culture, thought Veblen, would remain the preserve of the wealthy because only they had the leisure to attend to it and the power to define what, in fact, would be considered "art."

The opposing viewpoints of Tocqueville and Veblen have reappeared in debates throughout this century. In recent years, for instance, some writers have discerned a cultural "boom," asserting that the arts, while previously the monopoly of an elite, have become central to the lives of much of the American public. Alvin Toffler, perhaps the most optimistic spokesperson for this position, cites the rise of a massive middle-class constituency for the arts and contends that "millions of Americans have been attracted to the arts, changing the composition of the audience profoundly." While not all Americans are part of the culture boom, he argues, "a major step toward democratization has, indeed, been taken." As a result, the "rise of a mass public for the arts can, in its way, be compared with the rise of mass literacy in the eighteenth century in England" (Toffler, 1965:34; also see *Ms. Magazine*, 1977).

Others see just the opposite. For instance, Herbert Gans maintains that high culture remains the preserve of a small circle of *aficionados* and a diverse "user-oriented" public that includes art patrons, collectors, highly educated professionals, and business executives. High culture continues to serve "a small public that prides itself on exclusiveness" (Gans, 1974:77). Similarly, Baumol and Bowen, in their major study of audiences for the performing arts in the mid-1960s, concluded that:

> if there has been a significant rise in the size of audiences in recent years, it has certainly not yet encompassed the general public. . . . Attempts to reach a wider and more representative audience, to interest the less educated or the less affluent, have so far had limited effects (1966:96).

The debate has gone on, in part, because of the lack of definitive evidence on the composition of arts audiences, and is only likely to intensify as more and more public money is put into the arts. Since 1966, the annual budget of the National Endowment for the Arts, the federal government's primary funding agency, has risen from $2.5 million to over $149 million. State contributions to the arts have grown from $1.7 million to over $55 million annually. State art agencies have increased from 18 to 55, and community arts councils from about one hundred to over twelve hundred (*Cultural Post*, 1976:16; National Committee for Cultural Resources, 1975:11; Netzer, 1978; National Endowment for the Arts, 1978). There has also been rapid expansion in the scale of arts activities. Between 1965 and 1975, the number of major professional dance companies rose from 10 to 51; resident, nonprofit professional theaters from 25 to 101; professional opera companies from 23 to 45;

professional orchestras from 58 to 105; and touring dance companies from 27 to 86 (*Cultural Post*, 1976:16). The vast increase in the level of public support for the arts has, naturally, stimulated concern about the social composition of the expanding arts public (DiMaggio and Useem, 1978b). Policy makers and interest groups increasingly ask if government programs are underwriting an activity enjoyed by a large cross-section of the American public; or are they backing an activity that remains the special preserve of an exclusive social elite? Good baseline figures on audience social composition are clearly prerequisites if such policy questions are to be answered.

Comprehensive audience indicators are also important if we are to learn the extent to which cultural resources are inequitably distributed in the United States. Evidence suggests that the highly unequal distribution of cultural resources can be an important factor in maintaining class boundaries and in perpetuating social immobility from generation to generation. Exclusive social events surrounding the consumption of high culture provide valuable ritual occasions for the reaffirmation of elite solidarity. Familiarity with cultural matters and the possession of cultural credentials—initially bestowed by elite family socialization and later reinforced by involvement in cultural affairs—are important assets for ascent in the class hierarchy (Bourdieu, 1973; DiMaggio and Useem, 1978a). The extent to which cultural resources play a role in social class maintenance and reproduction depends on the degree of inequality in rates of cultural consumption. Thus, arts audience composition information is also important for understanding the extent to which the arts may help perpetuate class hierarchy.

Unfortunately, a comprehensive portrait of the American arts audience has not been available for resolution of these policy and analytic issues. Our primary purpose in this paper is to present major elements of such a portrait: our evidence will indicate the extent to which the major visual and performing arts are consumed by a cross-section of the public. A second purpose is to see if there has been any discernable trend toward broadening the arts audience over the past decade. The number of performing and visual arts organizations has expanded tremendously in recent years, the infusion of public money has been massive, but has there been a democratization of arts consumption, as some analysts claim? Our main efforts here will be devoted to establishing baseline data necessary if analytic efforts and policy debates are to go forward effectively, rather than to entering such analyses and debates more directly.

Until recently there were not enough studies of American arts audiences to make the present effort possible, but work in the past ten years has been sufficient to permit tentative identification of the extent of elite dominance of the arts audience and changes in audience social composition over time.[1] Although few have been published, many studies have been conducted, primarily of audiences for single art organizations. A single study provides little generalizable information, but the set of studies can provide a reasonably reliable and comprehensive portrait of the U.S. art audience. We have tried to assemble as many as possible of the arts-audience studies conducted since 1960 and to derive from them both overall compositional indicators and trends in composition during recent years.

The Audience Studies

Although audience surveys have been conducted for years, few have been published and many lost or buried in the organizations that conducted them. To obtain as complete as possible a set of audience studies, we first conducted an extensive bibliographic search to create a complete list of published studies conducted since 1960. A review of thirty-five standard indexes and bibliographic sources yielded approximately forty-five useful references. Twelve institutional libraries (e.g., those of the Massachusetts Council for the Arts and the Center for Arts Information in New York City) were consulted for additional references.

Next, it was necessary to approach those organizations that might have conducted the many unpublished studies. We compiled a list of more than twelve hundred arts organizations: museums, performing-arts organizations, regional, state and local arts councils, support organizations for specific art forms, and foundations involved in arts funding. Museums and performing-arts organizations were selected from *The Art Museum Directory* and the *National Directory of Civic Centers and Performing Arts Organizations* on the basis of size, on the assumption that larger organizations are more apt to be able to conduct audience research. Included were all instrumental-music and theatrical organizations reporting budgets of over $100,000 annually, all other performing-arts organizations with budgets of over $50,000, and all museums reporting 100,000 or more visitors annually. (For comparative purposes, one hundred randomly selected smaller museums and performing-arts organizations were added to this list.) A brief form was addressed to the director or manager of each organization, inquiring whether the organization had ever conducted, commissioned or participated in an audience survey. If such a study had been conducted, we requested the name and address of the study's director and either a copy of the final report or information on how to obtain a copy. Respondents were also asked if they knew of any other organizations that had conducted audience studies. The response rate to this inquiry rose to slightly over 50 percent after one follow-up letter. In addition to the bibliographic search and mail survey, further efforts were made to acquire unpublished studies by contacting individuals known to be knowledgeable about arts research, and by placing queries in

eight arts-related periodicals and newsletters (e.g., American Symphony Orchestra League *Newsletter, Musical America, New York Times Sunday Book
Review*).

Materials were collected on 268 audience studies:[2] 74 of theater audiences;
44 of art-museum visitors; 32 of visitors to natural history, general, anthropology, and related museums and exhibits; 19 of science-museum or science-
exhibit visitors; 16 of classical-music audiences; 14 of audiences for two or
more kinds of art institutions; 12 of history-museum visitors; 11 of art-center
visitors; 7 of opera audiences; and 6 of ballet and dance audiences. (Thirty-
three were of population cross-sections, which included both arts consumers
and nonconsumers.) Of the studies, more than 80 percent dated from 1972
or later and almost none were earlier than 1966.

The studies included surveys of visitors and audiences for institutions that
cover the full range in size and function. Nonetheless, there is some bias in
the data: nothing is known about the universe of all studies conducted; nor
do we know about the representativeness of organizations that conduct audience studies in comparison to all museums or live performing-arts institutions. We cannot be sure how much our summary statistics might deviate
from the actual composition of American audiences for museums and live
performing arts. Although most of the studies eventually received were from
medium and small-sized organizations, our inquiries had been mostly to large
and medium-sized organizations. Thus the larger organizations are overrepresented in our data, in comparison to their number among all arts organizations, if not in comparison to the proportion of all annual visits and
attendance for which they account. There is some reason to assume that the
larger organizations in the larger cities draw a somewhat more affluent and
well-educated public than do smaller or community-based organizations. On
the other hand, since the technical quality of the studies was extremely
uneven, since response rates and total numbers of respondents varied so
greatly, and since some necessary data were not available, there was neither
a powerful rationale for, nor the possibility of, weighting organizations by
total attendance, size or location, prior to calculating overall audience-com-
position figures. The effect of granting data from small organizations equal
weight with data from major organizations may countervail the tendency for
the overrepresentation of major organizations' studies to inflate the audience
percentages in high-status categories.

The audiences from which data have been drawn may be unrepresentative
in several other ways. We do not know if audiences studied are systematically
different from those not studied. Out of the universe of all audience studies
that have been conducted, we would speculate that we gathered a larger
percentage of the published than of the unpublished studies, of recent than
of less recent studies, of studies for which reports were written than of studies

yielding no formal reports, of major in-house or academic studies than of proprietary studies, and of studies of organizations with relatively low staff turnover than of studies of organizations with relatively greater staff turnover. Given the number and diversity of the studies from which our conclusions are drawn, we believe such factors do not decisively bias the findings one way or the other. Nonetheless, our statistics must be seen as *estimates* rather than as rigorous descriptions of the public for museums and the live performing arts; they do represent the best figures obtainable from data available now or in the near future.

The Composition of Arts Audiences

Of the many characteristics of audiences included in the studies we reviewed, we decided to concentrate on only six of the most central social features for which data were available in a number of studies: gender, age, education, occupation, income and race. Since many of the 268 studies assembled did not acquire information on all six, our summary statistics must be based on subsets of the studies. In some cases a specific study surveyed several distinct audiences, and these are counted as separate audiences in obtaining the overall compositional estimates. The estimates are generally presented for museums and the performing arts separately and, when possible, for specific types of each: art, science and history museums; ballet and dance, theater, orchestra and opera in the performing arts. There were too few studies of other art forms to allow estimates of their audience composition.

Gender

Art, in this country, has been associated with femininity, and it has often been suggested that women are disproportionately represented in arts audiences. One theater trade association report complained that theater-going "repudiates for many people the all-American, red-blooded image of what is supposed to be 'all-right' for a man to do and still be considered 'all-man' " (Theater Communications Group, 1967:31). An early study of a symphonic-music audience attributed the predominance of women to the fact that "women have greater esthetic appreciation for music, as they do for art and literature, than men, who place greater emphasis on theoretical, economic, political, and practical-success values" (Beldo, 1956:15).

Our analysis of 72 studies of 112 audiences for which gender of respondents was reported indicates, however, that women are only slightly overrepresented among arts attenders and that variation among audiences is enormous (see Table 6). The percentage of men in the United States population is 49; the median percentage of men reported among museum visitors is 46, and in performing-arts audiences 43. Sex composition varied among the art forms.

Audiences for ballet and dance were most heavily female (a median 60 percent) while, among the performing arts, opera audiences drew the largest proportion of males (46 percent). Art museums drew large female percentages (median 57 percent); history and science museums were slightly favored by men (52 percent). Composition varied extensively among audiences within an art form, with male percentages ranging from 30 to 71 percent in museums and from 31 to 58 percent for the performing arts. Men outnumbered women in a quarter of the performing-arts audiences and two-fifths of the museum visitors.

We should warn that response bias may significantly skew the observed proportions from the true population proportions. Baumol and Bowen (1966) suggest that husbands tend to fill out survey forms when the cooperation of only one spouse is requested. Book and Globerman (1975), in contrast, contend that men delegate the responsibility to women, creating a female bias. In two museum studies, men were found slightly more likely to volunteer if one person in a group was interviewed (Abbey and Cameron, 1960; New York State Education Department and Janus Museum Consultants, 1968). The extent and nature of gender bias thus depends upon the specific research design of a study and for this set of studies the overall effect cannot be estimated.

Finally, we should note that a substantial fraction of the wide variation observed from study to study may stem from factors such as survey time, performance or exhibit content and geographic variation. Since labor-force participation is greater among men than among women, more women are likely to attend on weekdays (Johnson, 1969; National Research Center of the Arts, 1976a; 1976b; 1977). Sex ratios among ballet audiences and museum visitors are known to be affected by the particular program (Leo Burnett, U.S.A., 1975; National Research Center of the Arts, 1976c). Female arts-audience percentages vary from 51 percent in New York City to 62 percent in Washington State (National Research Center of the Arts, 1976a; 1976b).

Age

Most of the studies with age data showed what percentage of the audience was in particular age categories. The categories were so varied that we computed the median age for each audience (Table 7). Eighty-two studies had age data on 145 distinct audiences: the median age for performing-arts audiences was 35, that for museum-visitor populations was 31. Both figures are between the median age of the entire U.S. population (28) and the median age for the population sixteen and over (40). But extensive age variation was apparent both within and between art forms: the medians for performing-arts audiences ranged from 21 to 49; for museum-visitor populations, from 19 to 51. Typical arts audiences, then, had age profiles similar to that of the

Table 6. Men in Audience Studies, by Art Form

Art Form	Median Percentage	Percentage Range	\multicolumn{8}{c}{Number of Studies within Percentage Range}	Total No. of Studies
			27–32	32–37	37–42	42–47	47–52	52–57	57–62	62–72	
All Museums	46.0	30–71	2	3	8	13	10	5	4	4	45
Art Museums	43.0	30–59	2	3	8	10	6		1		30
History Museums	48.5	44–53				2	1	1			4
Science Museums	52.0	43–71				1	3	4	3		11
All Performing Arts	42.5	31–58	1	15	14	21	6	8	2		67
Ballet and Dance	40.0	31–50	1	5	3	2	2				13
Theater	42.5	32–58		8	7	11	3	3	1		33
Orchestra	44.5	33–54		2	3	4	1	2			12
Opera	46.1	41–58			1	4	1	3			9

Table 7. Median Age of Audiences, by Art Form

Art Form	Median of Medians	Range of Medians	\multicolumn{8}{c}{Number of Studies within Age Range}	Total No. of Studies
			19–22	23–26	27–30	31–34	35–38	39–42	43–46	47–50	
All Museums	31	19–51	2	2	16	11	3	4	1	1	40
Art Museums	31	26–51		1	6	6	2	2	1	1	19
History Museums	33	28–42			2	1	1	1			5
Science Museums	29	19–40	2	1	8	4	1	1			16
All Performing Arts	35	21–49	5	7	14	23	22	21	8	5	105
Ballet and Dance	33	30–38			1	11	3				15
Theater	34	21–48	5	6	12	9	13	10	3	2	60
Orchestra	40	24–49		1	1	2	3	8	3	2	20
Opera	41	33–40				1	3	3	2	1	10

entire U.S. population, but specific audiences frequently diverged considerably from this central tendency.

Ballet and theater attracted the youngest audiences of the performing arts, with medians of 33 and 34 respectively, while opera and symphony drew the oldest, with median ages of 41 and 40. The median age for science-museum visitor populations was two years lower than that for art-museum visitors (median age of 31) and four years lower than for history-museum visitors (median age of 33).

Most of the surveys analyzed had studied only people over a certain age. Surprisingly, however, there were no systematic differences between the findings of studies that restricted their sample populations and those that did not. We suspect that many studies either formally or in practice excluded young respondents without reporting that they did so. Furthermore, it would appear that, except for science and history museums, individuals under the age of sixteen usually represent a negligible percentage of arts audiences.

Age composition appears to vary systematically by season, with younger visitors and attenders attracted during the summer, although this variation is not universal (National Research Center of the Arts, 1976b; O'Hare, 1974). Age composition may also vary by performance time: median ages for weekend evening performances were consistently lower than for matinees or weekday evenings (National Research Center of the Arts, 1976a; 1976b; 1976c). Finally, the type of program also appears to have an impact on audience age (Moore, 1968; National Research Center of the Arts, 1976c).

Education

The studies used categories so different that we could not always calculate medians, so it is necessary to describe audience educational composition by reporting percentages of audiences in five categories of educational attainment. Findings for each category are based on somewhat different sets of audiences.

Seventy-one studies reporting findings for 108 audiences and visitor groups indicate that the well educated are overrepresented with striking consistency in arts audiences, relative to their share of the U.S. population (Table 8). The proportion of college graduates reported for arts audiences exceeded the proportion of the adult population with college diplomas in all but one of ninety-seven audiences studied; the percentage of individuals who had not completed high school was below the national level in all but one of seventy-two audiences studied. (Both exceptions are attributable to sampling of large numbers of high-school students.) In seventy-eight of eighty-three audiences

Table 8.   Formal Education of Audiences, by Art Form

Art Form	Some Post-BA Training			Education Level: At Least College Graduate**			At Least Some College††			High School Graduate or Less			Less than High School Graduate		
	M	R	(N)	M	R	(N)	M	R	(N)	M	R	(N)	M	R	(N)
All Museums	17.5	6–35	(13)	41.1	10–66	(23)	72.3	30–93	(18)	27.6	8–69	(18)	9.0	4–57	(23)
Art Museums	22.0	18–35	(5)	48.0	41–66	(9)	83.5	75–90	(6)	17.0	10–25	(6)	5.5	4–16	(8)
Other Museums*	13.5	6–20	(8)	34.4	10–53	(14)	59.6	30–93	(12)	40.4	8–69	(12)	13.1	7–57	(14)
All Performing Arts	32.0	9–66	(42)	61.8	23–87	(53)	83.0	62–95	(44)	17.0	5–38	(45)	4.0	1–19	(45)
Theater†	32.7	20–50	(24)	58.0	23–80	(27)	82.7	56–93	(25)	17.1	8–44	(26)	4.0	1–15	(21)
Classical Music	37.5	21–66	(8)	63.0	46–87	(9)	83.4	63–95	(8)	14.6	5–37	(8)	1.7	1–19	(8)
Ballet and Dance‡	45.5	20–50	(5)	65.0	55–73	(10)	87.1	77–92	(5)	12.9	8–23	(5)	3.0	1–5	(10)
Opera	37.3	29–49	(5)	61.8	49–75	(7)	83.0	67–94	(6)	18.8	7–33	(6)	4.1	2–7	(6)
Museums and Performing Arts¶	30.0	6–66	(73)	54.0	10–87	(97)	78.0	30–95	(83)	22.0	5–69	(84)	5.0	1–57	(72)
U.S. Population over 24 Years of Age, 1975	n.a.			13.9			26.3			73.7			37.5		

NOTE: M = median percentage; R = range of percentages; N = number of studies.
*Includes science, history, natural history, anthropology, and general museums.
†Excludes audiences of outdoor dramas.
‡Dance audience percentages available only for two educational levels—at least college graduate and less than high school graduate.
¶Number of studies exceeds sum of other categories due to inclusion of regional studies reporting attendance of all, undifferentiated art forms.
**Includes those with post-B.A. training.
***Includes those who had post-B.A. training.
††Includes those who were college graduates and those who had post-B.A. training.

for which findings are available, the proportion of attenders with at least some college training was twice that for the general public.

Thirty percent of the typical audience had some graduate training; a median 54 percent had acquired at least a bachelor's degree, compared to 14 percent of the national adult population. Only 22 percent of the median audience had not attended any college, compared to 74 percent of the public as a whole, and only 5 percent were not high-school graduates, in contrast to 38 percent of the adult public. Educational attainment of performing-arts audiences was found to be somewhat higher than that of museum visitors. The median percentage reported for individuals with graduate training was 31 for the performing arts and 18 for museums. The median percentage of college graduates was similarly higher in the performing arts, 56 to 41. Museums also attracted more visitors with relatively little education than did the performing arts. The median percentage of non-high-school graduates was 9 for museums and 5 for the performing arts; for individuals with no schooling past high school the median percentages were 28 for museum-visitor populations and 21 for performing-arts audiences. Some, but not all, of the discrepancy is attributable to the greater representation of young people among museum visitors.

Among the performing arts, ballet and dance audiences included even larger proportions of well-educated attenders than did other forms; theater audiences included slightly lower proportions of the well educated. Among museums, art museums attracted a more well-educated public than did history, science, and other museums, though still not so well educated as audiences for the performing arts.

It is evident, then, that visitors to museums and audiences for the live performing arts are considerably more well educated than is the public at large. Within the arts, museums appear to serve a somewhat broader public than do the performing arts; nonetheless, in educational attainment, museum visitors and performing-arts audiences are far more similiar to one another than is either group to the general public.

There are several reasons why the arts audience has a very high proportion of the college-educated. First, understanding most works of art requires a certain amount of familiarity and background information to undertake the decoding that leads to appreciation. As Pierre Bourdieu notes, a work of art "only exists as such for a person who has the means to appropriate it" (Bourdieu, 1968:594). Higher education provides access to an environment where the means for appropriation can be readily acquired. Second, because higher education also offers exposure to an environment where the arts are valued, a college graduate has often experienced, at least for a period, peer pressure to attend arts events. Finally, a disproportionate number of men and women who acquire a higher education have parents who are also well educated.

Children of the well educated are more likely than others to have been exposed to the arts when they were young, and this early socialization persists into adulthood (Andreasen and Belk, 1978; Cober, 1977).

Occupation

As with educational attainment, occupational categories used in the studies varied widely and were often vague. We thus designed categories to be compatible with as many study findings as possible, and comparable to the classifications used by the U.S. Census. In some cases, categories were merged to fit our classificatory system; where study results could not be reliably altered to fit our system, they were omitted. Our findings for each occupational category, then, are based on somewhat different sets of audiences. Finally, because many studies reported occupation by percentages of total respondents, it was necessary to recompute the distributions and use employed respondents only.

Analysis of data from fifty-nine studies of ninety-six audiences indicates that arts audiences are dominated by individuals in high-status occupations. Professionals, who constituted 15 percent of the employed civilian labor force in 1975, composed a median 55 percent of employed persons in the arts audiences (Table 9). Conversely, blue-collar workers were conspicuous by their absence, a mere 4 percent of employed respondents in the arts audiences, as compared to 34 percent of the employed civilian labor force as a whole.

The marked overrepresentation of professionals was strikingly consistent throughout the studies. Professionals were present in percentages greater than their share of the population in every one of sixty-five arts audiences for which appropriate data were reported: in all but four of these, their share was twice their percentage of the work force; in 46 of 65, it was three times the national figure; and in more than a quarter of the audiences, they were overrepresented by a factor of four. (It is even possible that professionals, as defined by the United States Census, may have been underreported, since many studies provided residual "white-collar" categories in which some lower-status professionals may have included themselves rather than within the "professional" category itself.)

Proportions of professionals were significantly higher in audiences for performing arts than in attendance at museums (59 to 42 percent), primarily because of the relatively low medians of professionals attending non-art museums (Table 10). In six art-museum studies the median attendance by professionals was 59 percent, the same as for the performing arts, while in eleven studies of other museums the median attendance by professionals was 42

Table 9. Occupational Distribution of Audiences

Occupation	Percentage of Employed Labor Force (1975)*	Median Percentage of Employed Respondents in Arts Audience	
		%	(N)†
Professionals	15.0	55.9	(65)
Teachers	4.1	22.1	(22)
Artists, Writers, Entertainers	1.0	8.2	(8)
Managerial	10.5	14.9	(51)
Clerical, Sales	24.2	14.6	(41)
Service	14.1	3.7	(13)
Blue-Collar	33.6	3.7	(71)

	Percentage of U.S. Population Aged 16 or Over*	Median Percentage of All Respondents in Arts Audience	
		%	(N)
Homemakers	23.1	14.0	(78)
Students	5.5	18.0	(80)
Retired, Unemployed	11.2	4.5	(65)

NOTE: U.S. Census categories and audience categories are only approximately comparable due to varying classification schemes used in arts audience studies.
*SOURCES: U.S. Bureau of the Census (1976); U.S. Bureau of Labor Statistics (1976). Figures for U.S. population aged 16 or over exclude military personnel.
†Number of audience studies reporting information for this category.

percent. Aside from the non-art-museum category, findings were remarkably uniform among art forms, ranging from 56 percent for theater to 61 percent for classical music audiences.

One group of professionals—teachers, including college and university faculty—constituted 21 percent of the twenty-two arts audiences for which findings were available, with a median 18 percent for performing arts and 23 percent for museums. This latter figure is more than five times the percentage of teachers in the employed civilian work force (4 percent).

Managers—defined to include respondents in "business" and "executive" categories used in some studies—composed 15 percent of employed respondents in the median of fifty-one audiences for which percentages were reported. In contrast, managers make up 11 percent of the employed work force. The median proportion of managers among performing-arts audiences (16) was higher than their representation among museum visitors (9 and 10 percent for art and other museums, respectively). The finding that managers are overrepresented in arts audiences to a far lesser degree than are professionals points toward the applicability in the United States of Bourdieu's thesis,

Table 10.   Occupational Distribution of Audiences, by Art Form

Art Form	Professional/ Managerial			Professional Only			Occupation — Teachers			Managerial Only			Clerical & Sales		
	M	R	(N)	M	R	(N)	M	R	(N)	M	R	(N)	M	R	(N)
All Museums	65.3	27–96	(32)	42.2	12–73	(17)	23.1	15–33	(6)	9.6	4–27	(14)	14.3	5–28	(23)
Art Museums	77.1	56–96	(16)	59.2	31–74	(6)	23.1	15–33	(5)	9.0	4–27	(6)	14.3	4–22	(14)
Other Museums	53.2	27–72	(16)	41.9	12–50	(11)				10.2	6–22	(8)	16.0	5–28	(9)
All Performing Arts	70.9	49–95	(42)	59.1	24–80	(44)	17.9	6–33	(16)	15.6	4–27	(33)	18.0	8–33	(15)
Ballet and Dance	74.6	61–88	(9)	59.6	55–73	(8)				15.2	7–22	(7)			
Theater	69.5	49–95	(23)	56.3	23–70	(25)	17.9	6–33	(7)	16.0	4–27	(20)			
Orchestra	75.5	64–87	(5)	61.1	50–80	(6)							19.7	8–29	(10)
Opera				58.3	50–70	(5)									

Art Form	Blue-Collar			Homemakers			Students			Retired & Unemployed		
	M	R	(N)	M	R	(N)	M	R	(N)	M	R	(N)
All Museums	8.5	0–45	(35)	14.5	6–26	(24)	22.0	0–57	(25)	5.0	1–21	(21)
Art Museums	3.1	0–12	(16)	13.0	7–22	(9)	22.5	0–40	(10)	8.0	3–21	(9)
Other Museums	16.7	4–45	(19)	15.8	6–26	(15)	20.0	10–57	(15)	3.3	1–9	(12)
All Performing Arts	2.8	0–27	(34)	14.0	5–52	(51)	17.1	5–63	(51)	3.9	0–16	(40)
Ballet and Dance	2.7	1–7	(10)	11.1	6–32	(10)	15.0	9–34	(10)	3.0	1–5	(9)
Theater	2.9	0–27	(15)	14.0	5–52	(27)	18.9	5–63	(27)	4.2	0–16	(24)
Orchestra				19.0	5–26	(7)	18.0	7–31	(7)			
Opera	2.8	1–13	(5)	16.2	8–40	(6)	10.7	7–23	(6)			

NOTE: The "professional/managerial" and "professional only" categories include teachers. The percentages for "homemakers," "students," and "retired/unemployed" are based on all respondents; the percentages for the other categories are based on employed respondents only. Percentages are not reported when fewer than five studies are available.

developed with French data, that "cultural capital" (educational credentials and familiarity with elite culture) is of special value for the upward mobility strategies of professional groups (Bourdieu, 1973; Bourdieu et al., 1974).

Since a number of research reports included professionals and managers in a single category, we also merged these categories in the other studies we assembled, to provide a more consistent, if rough, index of the representation of individuals in elite occupations among the audiences surveyed. Among employed respondents, the median percentage of professionals and managers in seventy-seven arts audiences for which data were available was 71 percent, more than two and a half times this group's share of the employed work force as a whole (26 percent). Their median percentages among audiences for the performing arts ranged from 70 percent for theater to 76 percent for classical music. The median managerial/professional percentage for art museums was 77 percent, higher than for any of the performing arts; the percentage for other museums was 53 percent, lower than for any of the performing arts.

If managers and professionals were present in numbers modestly higher than their share of the U.S. population, clerical and sales personnel composed a somewhat smaller percentage of audiences than their share of the work force. The median representation of clerks and salespeople among employed respondents in the forty-one audiences for which data were available was 15 percent, while they constitute 24 percent of the employed civilian work force. Their median for attending the performing arts (18 percent) was higher than for visiting museums (14 percent).

As striking as the overrepresentation of professionals was the virtual absence of blue-collar workers from the audiences surveyed. In the seventy-one audiences for which data were available, blue-collar workers comprised a median 4 percent. That the median is even this high is due to the inclusion of nineteen studies of visitors to museums other than art museums, which reported a much higher median blue-collar participation of 17 percent. The median blue-collar share of performing-arts audiences was only 2.8 percent and blue-collar representation among art-museum visitors was a median 3.1 percent. Excluding visitors to non-art museums, the proportion of blue-collar workers in thirty-four of fifty-two arts audiences for which percentages were reported was *less than one tenth* of their share of the employed civilian work force. In only nine audiences was it as high as two fifths. Among art forms, blue-collar percentages were remarkably consistent: 2.7 percent for ballet and dance; 2.8 percent for opera; 2.9 percent for theater; and 3.1 percent for art museums.

The presence of three other groups—students, "homemakers," and retired and unemployed persons—was also analyzed. Homemakers constituted a median 14 percent of the seventy-eight audiences for which data were available, although they made up 23 percent of the over-sixteen civilian population in 1975. Students were sharply overrepresented: only 6 percent of the over-sixteen civilian population as a whole were students, but students constituted 18 percent of the median of eighty audiences with available data. Attendance of both groups varied greatly from audience to audience. Finally, the median percentage of retired and unemployed persons (usually reported as a single category) in sixty-five audiences for which appropriate data were available, was 5 percent, as compared to their 11 percent of the civilian over-sixteen population in 1975.

Occupations with the highest rates of attendance were also those with the highest educational attainment. Occupation may have a special influence on attendance because there are occupational and professional status-cultures in which familiarity with the arts is valued and encouraged (Parkin, 1974). That the relationship between occupation and attendance would be even more striking if finer occupational categories were available is indicated both by the findings for teachers in this study and by the work of Wilensky (1964), who found systematic differences in cultural taste between independent lawyers and those employed by law firms.

Income

Income data were available for eighty-eight audiences for museums and the performing arts. It proved possible to compare the various studies if we transformed categorical reports of audience percentages in different income ranges into median incomes for each audience, then used the consumer price index to transform all medians into constant mid-1976 dollars.

The median income for seventy performing-arts audiences was $18,983, approximately $4,500 above that of the public as a whole (Table 11). When audiences for eighteen outdoor dramas with patriotic and religious themes were omitted, the median income for the performing-arts audiences rose to $20,250. Among the performing arts, median incomes were lowest for theater audiences ($16,819 including outdoor dramas; $19,342 excluding them) and highest for opera audiences ($21,024). Excluding the eighteen outdoor-drama surveys, only three of fifty-three performing-arts audiences reported an income median below that of the general public.

The median income for museum visitors was $17,158, and ranged from $16,757 for history museums to $18,148 for art museums. Visitors to museums, then, appear to be significantly more affluent than the general public and significantly less affluent than performing-arts attenders. Among the many factors responsible for this finding, which was drawn from a small set of reports, are the generally lower admissions charged by museums and their

Table 11. Median Income of Audiences, by Art Form

Art Form	Median of Medians	Range of Median	(N)
All Museums	17,158	13,394–30,618	(18)
Art Museums	18,148	14,016–30,618	(10)
History Museums	16,757	13,394–29,005	(3)
Science Museums	17,269	14,765–20,851	(5)
All Performing Arts	18,903	9,466–28,027	(70)
Ballet and Dance	20,082	16,452–22,404	(10)
Theater			
Excluding Outdoor Drama	19,342	9,469–25,784	(27)
Including Outdoor Drama	16,819	9,466–25,784	(45)
Orchestra	20,825	18,221–28,027	(11)
Opera	21,024	19,017–27,245	(5)

NOTE: Median family income, U.S. population: 1960, $10,778; 1970, $14,431; 1975, $14,476.
*In constant mid-1976 dollars.

greater appeal to students and young people, particularly parents with young children.

Racial and Ethnic Minorities

That there are usually few blacks and other racial and ethnic minorities in arts audiences has been commented on frequently and, indeed, has been a matter of some concern to the arts community. In 1972, the American Association of Museums called attention to the problem of making museums relevant and hospitable to inner-city and minority people, noting that the movement of many segments of the middle class to the suburbs and of lower-class blacks, Mexican-Americans and Puerto Ricans to the core city "have left the museum, an urban institution, to some extent a beached whale" (American Association of Museums, 1972:6). Museums have not been alone in recognizing this dilemma. Recently, the Kennedy Center for the Performing Arts formed a special committee to find out why so few of Washington's many black residents attend the center's events.

Minorities were, indeed, underrepresented in most of the relatively few audiences for which data on race were acquired in the studies we reviewed. Although blacks constituted 12.3 percent of the total urban population in 1970, they represented a median 3 percent of the fifteen arts audiences for which data were available. Minorities—blacks, Orientals, and persons of

Spanish origin—accounted for a median 7 percent of the 35 audiences for which figures were reported, although they are over 20 percent of the population as a whole. In a number of studies outside the West Coast and Southwest, individuals of Spanish origin were not separated from the white population, thus depressing the minority total. We surmise, however, from the few studies in these areas doing separate counts, that Hispanic people generally account for a very small percentage of the audience and that their exclusion depresses the minority median by no more than 1 percent.

The median minority percentage for thirteen audiences for the performing arts was 7, and for eleven sets of art-museum visitors it was also 7. As with other socioeconomic dimensions, visitor populations of museums other than art museums included a broader cross-section of the public; for eleven sets of visitors to such museums the median minority percentage is 11.

Such overall figures should be interpreted cautiously because of the small number of audiences studied, variation in the definition of minority and, above all, the large variation in the proportion of members of different minority groups in different locales. The set of studies reviewed here, for example, contains data from the Washington, D.C. area (where blacks composed 24.6 percent of the metropolitan population in 1970) and from Washington State (where only just over one in fifty persons was black). Similarly, persons of Spanish origin represent a substantial portion of the populations of Los Angeles and New York City (15.0 and 11.1 percent, respectively), but are a much less significant presence in such places as Boston or Montgomery, Alabama. For this reason, a selected comparison can be useful. For instance, in thirteen of the fourteen audiences for which there were data on black attenders and comparable census data, black were underrepresented relative to their numbers in the local population by ratios of up to eighteen-to-one. In five studies of museums in the San Francisco area, where blacks composed 10.6 percent of the metropolitan population in 1970, the highest black proportion was only 3 percent (Schwartz, 1971; Colvin, 1976; McElroy and Bellow, 1975; deYoung Memorial Museum, n.d.a; n.d.b). In two New York City audiences, blacks represented 3 and 4 percent of attenders, in contrast to over 16 percent of the metropolitan population (National Research Center of the Arts, 1976c; 1977).

Although the existing data do not permit a definitive assessment—for example, no surveys of museums or performing-arts companies appealing predominantly to minority-group members were available—it seems likely that blacks and other minorities are generally sharply underrepresented in performing-arts audiences and among museum visitors, relative to their share of the population. This is not in itself surprising, since a higher percentage of minorities than whites are very young, poor, without college educations, and/or employed in blue-collar or service occupations—all categories with disproportionately low participation in arts audiences. Although existing data do not permit an assessment, it is likely that poverty and lack of education, rather than cultural factors or minority exclusion, are largely responsible for the low level of minority arts attendance.

Audience Structure

Available evidence suggests that the arts audience has a core group who frequently attend a variety of events, and various peripheral groups who occasionally sample only a single art form. Those near the center constitute active arts social circles; friendships and acquaintanceships are formed around a shared interest in the arts, cultural events are central topics of informal discussion and exchange, and there is a strong expectation of high attendance at, and knowledge of, the arts. Several studies report that frequent attenders are more likely than infrequent visitors to hear about arts events through their social networks, to count cultural consumers among their friends and to indicate that arts attendance is fashionable in their social milieu (Beldo, 1956; David, 1977; National Research Center of the Arts, 1975a; 1975b; 1975c).

Those most often among the arts audience are also usually those with more education. Sixteen audiences studies in our possession examined the relationship between frequency of attendance and education, and all sixteen found that regular visitors are more highly educated than irregular visitors for both museums and the performing arts. A cross-sectional study of California residents, for instance, found that of those who had not visited a museum during the past year, 7 percent held a college degree or more; of the infrequent museum visitors (one to five times), 18 percent were college educated; and of the frequent visitors (more than five times), 31 percent held college degrees. The corresponding figures for the performing arts are 7, 18 and 43 percent, respectively (National Research Center of the Arts, 1975b).

Those at the center of the arts audience also tend to have higher incomes than those at the periphery, though the evidence here is less clearcut than for education. Thirteen of seventeen studies with relevant data report higher incomes for frequent attenders than for infrequent attenders, but one study revealed no difference and three indicated the reverse (the three latter audiences were for ballet or dance).

It is not clear whether frequency of attendance is associated with gender and age. Four studies reported that frequent attenders had a higher proportion of men, six a lower proportion of men, and two studies found no difference. Similarly, six studies concluded that frequent attenders were older than infrequent visitors, three found the opposite, and two reported no age difference.

To summarize the unambiguous trends: the social composition of the arts audience is far more elite than the general public, and the center of the audience is more elite than its periphery. Education and, to a lesser degree, income are good predictors not only of who consumes the arts but of the intensity of their consumption.

Trends toward Democratization

Our overall findings clearly indicate that in this country the public for the visual and live performing arts is distinctly elite in level of education, occupation, income, and in race. The statistics we were able to summarize from the many studies reviewed show little indication of cultural democracy. But it seemed at least possible that the aggregation of all the studies might be disguising a trend toward greater involvement of poorly represented groups, as the "cultural boom" has continued in recent years. To see if such a trend is present, we have evaluated audience composition data at several different time periods between 1960 and 1976. Since relatively few of our studies were conducted during the 1960s, studies have been grouped into several-year spans so that each period includes at least six audience studies (with the exception of one period for the data on education). Few museum studies were available for some periods, so analysis is limited to the performing arts. It should be cautioned that the pre-1965 studies included a number conducted by Baumol and Bowen (1966). These studies yielded social profiles significantly more elite than those of other audience surveys undertaken at that time. Since relatively few other early studies are available, the Baumol and Bowen surveys (between eight and thirteen, depending on the social characteristic) dominate the mid- and early-1960s audience composition figures.

Gender

The proportion of men in the performing-arts audience evidences little change over time, though there is a slight drop in recent years (Table 12). Excluding the earliest period examined (pre-1966), the median percentages of men in the five successive periods between 1966 and 1976 are 46, 42, 45, 37, and 39. However, in all periods except one (1974–1975) the percentage of men varies from the low 30s to the low 50s, indicating that there is far more variation in gender composition from event to event than between time periods.

Age

There is no indication of any trend toward younger audiences. The median ages of audiences in six successive periods since 1967 are 36, 41, 30, 36, 38,

Table 12.   Time Trends in the Composition of Performing Arts Audiences

Social Character and Time Period	Median of Medians	Range of Median	(N)
Gender: Percent Men			
1960–65	56	45–58	(10)
1966–69	46	32–54	(7)
1970–71	42	36–51	(11)
1972–73	45	33–54	(11)
1974–75	37	35–43	(9)
1976	39	34–54	(13)
Age: Median Age			
1960–67	37	33–45	(9)
1968–70	36	24–46	(6)
1971–72	41	34–42	(8)
1973	30	21–35	(11)
1974	36	22–43	(8)
1975	38	29–48	(12)
1976	33	21–45	(18)
Education: Percent with			
College Degree or More			
1960–66	72	61–86	(14)
1967–72	47	21–66	(15)
1973	63	55–65	(6)
1974	67	54–74	(4)
1975	57	48–65	(7)
1976	65	34–76	(13)
Occupation:			
Percent Professional/Technical			
1960–69	65	48–80	(11)
1970–74	57	50–63	(10)
1975–76	59	24–73	(20)
Percent Blue-Collar Worker			
1960–69	2.4	1–5	(8)
1970–74	2.8	0–5	(14)
1975–76	3.0	1–7	(11)
Income: 1976 Dollars			
1960–67	23,407	19,342–28,027	(11)
1967–70	19,017	16,819–25,229	(10)
1971–73	19,684	9,466–27,245	(12)
1974–75	18,983	15,292–23,202	(7)
1976	20,004	14,003–21,004	(11)

and 33. Within the time periods, the median ages differed from study to study by 8 to 24 years.

Education

The proportion of the performing arts audience with at least a college education did not decline over time. The fourteen studies in the earliest time period (1960–1966) report a median figure of 72 percent for the college educated; the fifteen studies of the following period (1967–1972) indicate a median percentage of 47; and the surveys conducted in the next four one-year periods report median percentages of 63, 67, 57, and 65. While the education level appears to fluctuate considerably between the first three time periods, much if not most of the change reflects special features of the studies conducted during these periods. Thirteen of fourteen pre-1967 studies were executed by Baumol and Bowen, while seven of fifteen studies during the 1967–1972 period were conducted on audiences of university productions. (None of the post-1972 studies were of campus audiences.)

Occupation

Using two indices of the occupational composition of performing arts audiences—the percentages of professional/technical workers and blue-collar workers—it is evident that little change has occurred over the past seventeen years. Professionals and technicians constituted 65 percent of the audience in the 1960s, 57 percent during the 1970–1974 period, and 59 percent in 1975–1976; the blue-collar shares of the audience were 2.4, 2.8, and 3.0 percent, respectively.

Income

Income trends mirror those reported for other social indicators. The median of the median audience income for the 1967–1970 period was $19,017 (in constant mid-1976 dollars). For the three following periods the median income stood at $19,684, $18,983, and $20,004, respectively. The average income for 1960–1967 was recorded at $23,407, but again this is almost entirely based on the Baumol and Bowen surveys of prominent performing-arts audiences. It is again notable that the median incomes reported for audience studies within a time period vary far more than do the averages between the periods.

Our data, then, do not reveal any striking changes in the composition of the audience over the past one and one-half decades. It should be cautioned, however, that the heterogeneity of the audience studies evaluated here may have concealed various subtler trends. For example, if audiences for one art form were becoming increasingly male while audiences for another were including greater percentages of women, such a change would not be discernable in our data. Similarly, if theater audiences in major cities were becoming more diverse, while theater audiences in smaller cities and suburbs were becoming less so, no change would be observed. Also, if pre-1960 data had been available, they might have revealed that, although the past one and one-half decades have seen little change, longer-range changes in audience composition have occurred. Finally, it should be remembered that while the overall composition appears static in recent years, important short-range trends could exist in other elements of audience structure. An increase in arts activity outside of major cities and the more frequent touring of arts organizations in outlying areas may mean, for instance, that the upper-middle and upper class in nonmetropolitan areas now have more access to the arts than ever before.

Barriers to Democratization

The studies reviewed here consistently indicated that the audiences for the visual and live performing arts are more well educated, of higher occupational standing, and more affluent than the general populace. The strong relationship between education and attendance, the extreme overrepresentation of professionals and managers, and the virtual absence of blue-collar workers were particularly striking. Moreover, cultural democratization (if defined as increasing representation of nonelites among visitors to museums and performing arts events) does not seem to be occurring, despite arguments to the contrary, outreach efforts of some arts administrators, and a degree of pressure from those responsible for public funding of the arts (see DiMaggio and Useem, 1978b). The absence of discernable democratization suggests that there may be formidable barriers to any effort to open up the arts.

Although we cannot analyze these barriers here, we can suggest that they are related both to elite resistance to democratization and to entry problems facing nonelites. Elite resistance exists because, as Veblen perceived, arts events, aside from their aesthetic value, provide opportunities for reaffirmation of elite social and cultural cohesion. Participation in the world of the arts may be particularly crucial for the upper-middle class, the group whose status is most marginal to the elite, in that arts consumption provides this group with opportunity for symbolic identification with the upper class and may even yield socially useful contacts. Moreover, as Bourdieu has argued, cultural capital, both in formal education and in refined aesthetic taste, can serve as a useful medium for the transmission of elite position from generation to generation. By instilling cultivated aesthetic tastes and providing support for advanced university training, elite families endow their offspring with cultural capital that can be converted into social standing and economic position in later life (Bourdieu, 1973; Bourdieu et al., 1974; Bourdieu and Boltanski, 1977; DiMaggio and Useem, 1978a). Thus, it is not surprising that some elites resist efforts to democratize the arts, for diversifying the audience can only undermine the social value of the arts for elite standing and cohesion.

At the same time, those outside the upper and upper-middle classes face important impediments to attendance, whatever the degree of opposition to their involvement by elites. These barriers include: lack of information about arts events and motivation to attend; relative lack of the training needed to ensure appreciation of and familiarity with the arts; relative unfamiliarity and often discomfort with the social conventions of the contexts in which the arts are presented; and lack of access to cultural brokers—artists, dealers, and critics—who define changes in artistic taste and standards (DiMaggio and Useem, 1978a).

Whatever their precise forms, a topic itself deserving careful inquiry, the result of the existence of such barriers is that the cultural resources considered here are very inequitably distributed; and there is no clear evidence that they are becoming less so, despite the expansion of large-scale public support for cultural activities. For those concerned with the nature of the constituency served by arts organizations increasingly supported by public money, our findings imply that a highly unrepresentative constituency has been, and continues to be, the primary beneficiary. There are no signs that the democratization of arts funding is bringing a democratization of arts consumption. It is possible, of course, that more aggressive "outreach" programs, the allocation of additional monies to community-based and participatory-oriented arts activities, and greater attention to the arts in school programs may ultimately help broaden the arts public.

For those concerned with the broader role the arts may play in American society, dominance of arts audiences by members of the upper-middle and upper classes, evident in the overall portrait we were able to sketch here, clearly suggests that the arts play a significant role in defining class boundaries. Whatever the particular social barriers and differences in aesthetic taste involved in elite dominance may be, their existence (and persistence) also suggest that, like the education system, the arts are important in preserving class standing in the local community from generation to generation. Presently available evidence at least suggests that Veblen's predictions about the most probable relationship between art and democracy are still more accurate than those of Tocqueville.

Notes

1. "Elite" is used here to refer to the upper class and upper-middle class. The upper class comprises those who own or manage large business firms, as well as families with substantial wealth. The upper-middle class primarily consists of those who are highly educated and whose work involves the manipulation of knowledge and information (e.g., lawyers, physicians, journalists, teachers, scientists). The concept of "cultural democracy" has also been ascribed a specific and somewhat limited meaning in this chapter. It refers here only to the social composition of those who visit museums and attend performing arts events. Issues involving control over the production of culture and the management of arts organizations, as well as the consumption of culture transmitted in other forms, are beyond the scope of the present chapter.

2. A complete bibliography of the studies can be found in DiMaggio et al., 1978.

References

Abbey, D. S., and Duncan F. Cameron. 1960. *The Museum Visitor: II—Survey Results*. Toronto: Royal Ontario Museum.

American Association of Museums. 1972. *Museums: Their New Audience*. Washington, D.C.

Andreasen, Alan R., and Russell W. Belk. 1978. "Consumer Response to Arts Offerings: A Study of Theater and Symphony in Four Southern Cities." In *Research in the Arts*, ed. David Cwi. Baltimore: Walters Art Gallery.

Baumol, William, and William Bowen. 1966. *The Performing Arts: The Economic Dilemma*. Cambridge: M.I.T. Press.

Beldo, Les. 1956. *A Report of Three Surveys: A State-Wide Survey Conducted by the Minnesota Poll, Minneapolis Star and Tribune; An In-Concert Survey and a Personal Interview Survey Both Conducted by Mid-Continent Surveys, Minneapolis, Minnesota*. Minneapolis: Campbell-Mithun.

Book, S. H., and S. Globerman. 1975. *The Audience for the Performing Arts: A Study of Attendance Patterns in Ontario*. Toronto: Ontario Arts Council.

Bourdieu, Pierre. 1968. "Outline of a Sociological Theory of Art Perception." *International Social Science Journal*, 20 (4):589–612.

1973 "Cultural Reproduction and Social Reproduction." *Knowledge, Education, and Cultural Change*, ed Richard Brown. London: Tavistock.

Bourdieu, Pierre, and Luc Boltanski. 1977. "Changes in Social Structure and Changes in the Demand for Education." Unpublished manuscript.

Bourdieu, Pierre, Luc Boltanski, and Monique de Saint Martin. 1974. "Les Strategies de Reconversion." *Social Science Information*, 12(5):61–113.

Brustein, Robert. 1977. "Whither the Arts and Humanities Endowments?" *New York Times*, December 19.

Cober, Rodney, L. 1977. "A Psychographic Life Style Analysis of Intergenerational Continuity in Development of the Rural Theatre Audience." Master's thesis, Pennsylvania State University, State College, Pa.

Colvin, Clair. 1976. *A Membership Study of the Fine Arts Museums of San Francisco and the Asian Art Museum*. San Francisco: Fine Arts Museums of San Francisco.

Cultural Post. 1976. "Estimated Growth in Selected Cultural Fields: 1965–1975." May/June: 16.

David, Deborah S. 1977. "The Ballet Audience: One Group or Three?" Unpublished manuscript.

deYoung, M. H., Memorial Museum. n.d.a. *Acoustiguide Survey Final Talley*. San Francisco.

n.d.b. *American Art: An Exhibition from the Collection of Mr. and Mrs. John D. Rockefeller 3rd*. San Francisco.

DiMaggio, Paul, and Michael Useem. 1978a. "Social Class and Arts Consumption: The Origins and Consequences of Class Differences in Exposure to the Arts in America." *Theory and Society*, 5(March):141–61.

1978b "Cultural Property and Public Policy: Emerging Tensions in Government Support for the Arts." *Social Research*, 45(Summer):356–89.

DiMaggio, Paul, Michael Useem, and Paula Brown. 1978. *Audience Studies of the Performing Arts and Museums: A Critical Review*. Washington, D.C.: Research Division, National Endowment for the Arts.

Gans, Herbert. 1974. *Popular Culture and High Culture: An Analysis and Evaluation of Taste*. New York: Basic Books.

Johnson, David A. 1969. "Museum Attendance in the New York Metropolitan Region." *Curator*, 12(3):201–30.

Leo Burnett U.S.A. 1975. *The Art Institute Survey*. Chicago: Research Department, Leo Burnett U.S.A., November 5.

McElroy, Guy, and Cleveland Bellow. 1975. *Museum Audience Survey, 1974–75*. San Francisco: M. H. deYoung Memorial Museum.

Moore, Thomas Gale. 1968. *The Economics of the American Theater*. Durham, N.C.: Duke University Press.

Ms. Magazine. 1977. "How the Arts Boom Will Affect You." November.

National Committee for Cultural Resources. 1975. *National Report on the Arts*. New York.

National Endowment for the Arts. 1978. *The State Arts Agencies in 1974: All Present and Accounted for*. Washington, D.C.: Research Division, National Endowment for the Arts.

National Research Center of the Arts. 1975a. *Americans and the Arts: A Survey of Public Opinion.* New York: Associated Councils of the Arts.

1975b *Californians and the Arts: A Survey of Public Attitudes toward and Participation in the Arts and Culture in the State of California.* New York.

1975c *Anchorage, Alaska: Public Perspective on the Arts and Culture; Report on a Survey Conducted for Anchorage Arts Council.* New York.

1976a *A Study of Washingtonians' Attendance at Performing Arts Events and Museums.* New York.

1976b *The New York Cultural Consumer.* New York: New York Foundation for the Arts.

1976c *The Joffrey Ballet Audience: A Survey of the Spring 1976 Season at the City Center Theater.* New York.

1977 *A Profile of Consumer Use and Evaluation: The American Museum of Natural History; Based on a Survey of Attendance July 1974–July 1975.* New York: American Museum of Natural History.

Netzer, Dick. 1978. *The Subsidized Muse: Public Support for the Arts in the U.S.* New York: Cambridge University Press.

New York State Education Department and Janus Museums Consultants, Ltd. 1968. *The 1966 Audience of the New York State Museum: An Evaluation of the Museum's Visitors Program.* Albany: University of the State of New York, State Education Department, Division of Evaluation.

O'Hare, Michael. 1974. "The Audience of the Museum of Fine Arts." *Curator,* 17(2):126–59.

Parkin, Frank. 1974. "Strategies of Social Closure in Class Formation." In *The Social Analysis of Class Structure,* ed. Frank Parkin. London: Tavistock.

Schwartz, Steve. 1971. *Results of Survey of Oakland Museum Visitors.* Oakland: Oakland Museum.

Theatre Communications Group. 1967. *Toward a New Audience: A Report on a Continuing Workshop in Audience Development.* New York.

Tocqueville, Alexis de. 1956. *Democracy in America.* New York: New American Library.

Toffler, Alvin. 1965. *The Culture Consumers.* Baltimore: Penguin Books.

U.S. Bureau of the Census. 1976. *Statistical Abstracts, 1976.* Washington, D.C.: U.S. Government Printing Office.

U.S. Bureau of Labor Statistics. 1976. *Handbook of Labor Statistics, 1976.* Washington, D.C.: U.S. Government Printing Office.

Veblen, Thorstein. 1899. *The Theory of the Leisure Class: An Economic Study in the Evaluation of Institutions.* New York: Macmillan.

Wilensky, Harold L. 1964. "Mass Society and Mass Culture: Interdependence or Independence?" *American Sociological Review,* 29(2):173–97.

14

Audience Development in Four Southern Cities

RESEARCH DIVISION
NATIONAL ENDOWMENT FOR THE ARTS

Introduction

The study reported in this chapter responds to several specific objectives that have had wide recognition in the arts community: to broaden the audience for the performing arts; to determine the applicability of sophisticated tools of marketing to the problem of generating demand for the arts; to find the best predictors of arts attendance; and to develop strategies that will appeal to those who, by these predictors, are potential attenders. Such a study was needed because little has been known up to the present about why some persons become arts attenders and others do not, and about how the arts can attract greater patronage from nonattenders or infrequent attenders.

The two strategies that appear most promising for broadening both theater and symphony audiences because of their high impact on nonattenders are offering ticket buyers a second ticket at half price and including well-known performers in the arts events. Symphony attenders also responded well to the offers of half-price tickets on the day of the concert and an introductory talk that would inform them about the program to follow. Theatergoers responded more positively to changes in type of program, specifically to being offered more musical comedies.

Some arts managers will gain fresh insights from these findings and others will find scientific confirmation of their practical experience. All should note, however, that the study also suggests that many other commonly used audience development techniques may be substantially less effective. The methodology of this study introduces several new elements and techniques. To the traditional approach of examining the relationships between arts attend-ance and standard demographic and sociometric measures (Marder, 1974; National Research Center of the Arts, 1976; Winston-Salem/Forsyth County, 1974), the present study adds complex life-style and attitudinal measurements and simultaneously analyzes the relationships between planned arts attend-ance and all the predictor variables. Eric Marder's pioneering work reported probable aggregate gains or losses in arts attendance in response to certain offerings, but did not indicate whose attendance patterns would change.

Through the use of recent advances in attitude measurement, life-style analysis, market segmentation, and multivariate statistics, the study yields better predictors of future attendance, better explanations of responses to particular changes proposed for arts offerings, and more information about who responds to these changes—in sum, more specific and better ways to develop audiences.

Examination of the sample by life style revealed two groups disposed to attend arts events, three not so disposed, and one neutral. Analysis of the sample's responses to over a dozen proposed alterations in arts offerings clearly showed some strategies to be potentially much more effective than others in increasing attendance, and one strategy that promised to broaden attendance, especially for symphony. That strategy is the offer of second tickets at half price, which leads to what is probably the most important conclusion of this study for arts managers. This offer is particularly effective with members of the Socially Active group, to whom the second ticket represents a social opportunity. The second-ticket-half-off offering should be accompanied by a concentrated media campaign stressing the desirability of regular attenders bringing nonattenders with them on the half-price ticket.

Methodology

In order to achieve its objectives, this study develops basic attitudinal, life-style, and socioeconomic data on marginal and regular attenders of two of the performing arts, theater and symphony concerts. The study was carried out in four southern cities chosen from among several dozen with both a symphony and regular theater presentations: Atlanta, Georgia; Baton Rouge, Louisiana; Columbia, South Carolina; and Memphis, Tennessee.

The Sample

Data for the analysis were gathered by means of telephone interviews conducted with randomly selected respondents fourteen years of age or older from households with telephones in the four cities. At the outset, it was decided that a study aimed at broadening the audience should focus mainly on marginal attenders—those who do not now go frequently to theater or symphony but who might be induced to do so. For this reason, those judged to have virtually zero probability of attending theater or symphony were screened out; for the same reason, those who are already frequent attenders were intentionally undersampled.

Screening questions defined as potential attenders those who had done one of the following in the last twelve months: went to live popular or rock concerts; listened at least ten times to classical music on radio, television, records, or tapes; visited an art gallery or museum; went to a live classical music performance other than a symphony concert; saw a ballet either live or on television; saw one or two plays; went to a symphony orchestra concert once or twice. Also included were those who met one of the following qualifications: play a musical instrument; ever worked for a theater, music, or dance production; attended three or more live plays sometime in their lives but not in the past year; attended three or more symphony orchestra concerts sometime in their lives but not in the past year.

In all, 3,956 residential telephone numbers were selected for screening. Further screening left 1,733 households designated for complete interviews. In each of these households a random selection procedure was used to pick one individual to be interviewed from among all household members fourteen years of age or older. Of these, 14 percent were unavailable or refused to participate in the main interview, yielding a final sample of 1,491, divided by city as follows: Atlanta (357, 23.9%); Baton Rouge (358, 24.0%); Columbia (385, 25.8%); Memphis (391, 26.2%).

Comparisons with available census data suggest that the sample population is younger, better educated, from a higher income level, and substantially more often female than the general population of the four cities.

The Questionnaire

Respondents in the study were asked extensive questions about their attitudes and behavior toward theater and symphony, aspects of their leisure and general life styles, and their socioeconomic characteristics. Because of the length of the questionnaire, only one-third of the main sample in each city was asked about their attitudes toward attending the theater, another third was asked about their attitudes toward attending symphony concerts, and the final third was not asked either set of attitude questions.

The Approaches: Associational and Manipulations

To find the best predictors of anticipated future attendance, the associational approach used stepwise regression analysis using a battery of individual traits including demographic characteristics, prior experience with theater or symphony, a specially developed leisure life-style characterization, general life-style traits, attitudes toward theater or symphony, and stage in the family life cycle. The best predictors of anticipated future attendance for both theater and symphony were found to be attitudes toward attending these events, prior experiences with the arts (including childhood interests), and belonging to a leisure life-style group called Culture Patrons in this report. For theater the absence of two general life-style traits referred to here as Traditionalism and Self-Confidence/Opinion Leadership increased the level of anticipated future attendance beyond that suggested by the predictor variables shared with symphony.

The manipulations approach examined reported changes in the likelihood of future theater and symphony attendance if certain alterations were made in these offerings or in the controllable conditions surrounding them. Over a dozen different modifications commonly used by arts managers were considered in four basic areas: the event (type of performance, quality of performance, formality, and extent of learning opportunities); the event's price; the event's location; and the event, its price, and its location in various combinations.

Past and Future Attendance

Past Attendance

About 42 percent of all respondents in the study claimed that they had attended the theater in the past twelve months, and an additional 46 percent said they had not attended theater in the past year but had attended at least three times in their lives. By contrast, only 14 percent said they had attended a symphony concert in the past twelve months, and 19 percent said they had attended at some previous time. About 10 percent of the respondents said they had attended both symphony and theater, and 54 percent said they had attended neither in the past twelve months. Clearly, those who are concert-goers only are a small, exceptional group; concert attendance is more likely to be combined with theater attendance. Quite the opposite is true of theater attendance.

Future Attendance

Even though only individuals judged to be potential attenders based on their answers to questions about past attendance and other behaviors were included in this study, it was not expected that they would all be likely to attend in the next year or two. Clearly, if a respondent was not very likely to attend, questions about attending more or less often if certain changes were made in theater and symphony offerings were not likely to yield meaningful results. Therefore, respondents were further screened on their anticipated likelihood of attending theater or symphony concerts "in the next year or two." The proportion saying they were very likely or somewhat likely to attend was 21.2 percent for theater only, 22.8 percent for theater and symphony, and 6.0 percent for symphony only. Fifty percent said they were not very or not at all likely to attend either theater or symphony.

Associational Approach to Future Attendance

Does the arts audience come from a single group or from many groups? How important is early experience in arts-audience participation? Why do individuals attend or not attend arts offerings? This study seeks to answer these questions by dividing the population into life-style groupings according to use of leisure time; by developing a broad array of data on respondents' general life-style tendencies; by expanding the area of socioeconomic variables with new questions; by taking into account respondents' stages in the family life cycle; and by probing their attitudes toward and expectations of arts performances. To all these data the study applies advanced analytic techniques, such as analysis of variance, factor analysis, and multiple regression.

Life-Style as Predictor

In the field of marketing, the study of consumer life-styles, or psychographic profiles, has emerged in the past decade as a major part of an effort to provide detailed insight into consumer decision patterns. A description of a consumer's life-style typically notes the activities in which the consumer commonly participates (going to church, camping), the consumer's interests (liking to eat, liking to travel), and the consumer's opinions (everything is changing too fast these days; children are the most important thing in a marriage). Because of the fields of investigation, life-style data are often called activity/interest/opinion (AIO) data. By constructing a broad-based life-style profile, the market researcher's intent is to show how the consumption of a particular product or service fits into the context of the consumer's way of life.

To the marketing practitioner, analysis of consumer life-styles offers a means for probing into reasons for consumer choice more deeply than that provided by standard demographic variables such as age, income, and family size. In the present study, consumer life-style is measured at two different levels; the individual's use of leisure time, or what may be called "going-out behavior," and the individual's more general activities, interests, and opinions in which the leisure activities are imbedded.

Leisure Life-Style Characteristics

The first life-style analyzed was based on responses to a set of fifty questions about leisure-time activities, interests, and opinions.... Names for each group and the distribution of respondents across the groups are given in Table 13. The six leisure life-style groups are characterized in the next few paragraphs.

Passive Homebody. This group prefers family- and home-oriented activities. Its members watch a great deal of television, do not care for parties, have essentially negative attitudes toward cultural organizations and activities, and, in fact, tend to avoid nearly any such activity outside the home. These people recognize that they are homebodies, and that their days are routine and filled with unused leisure time.

Active Sports Enthusiast. In many ways this group is the antithesis of the previous group. Members take part in many active sports, such as tennis and bowling, and engage in other activities away from home, such as movies, parties, and spectator sports. They strongly deny that they are homebodies or like to spend a quiet evening at home. However, they are like the Passive Homebodies, but more extreme, in their negative attitudes toward theater, symphony, and other cultural activities.

Table 13. Distribution of Respondents, by Leisure Life-Style Group

Passive Homebody	295	19.8%
Active Sports Enthusiast	285	19.1%
Inner-Directed, Self-Sufficient	216	14.5%
Culture Patron	295	19.8%
Active Homebody	190	12.7%
Socially Active	210	14.1%
Total	1,491	100.0%

Inner-Directed, Self-Sufficient. Members of this group are best characterized by their participation in a number of home-oriented activities such as gardeniing, reading, and craft projects. They are family-oriented and prone to undertake outdoor activities such as hikes and picnics. They are inactive concerning cultural activities, although they are not negative toward these activities as are the Passive Homebody and Active Sports Enthusiast groups. They are not overburdened with leisure time as is the Passive Homebody. Instead, it appears that their leisure interests keep their leisure time occupied, either alone or with their families.

Culture Patron. Members of this group would be expected to be the best market for theater and symphony, since they report that they are now involved with these activities. This is a reflection of their general cultural orientation, with favorable attitudes toward and patronage of the arts in general. They lack the orientation toward home and family of the Passive Homebody and the Inner-Directed, Self-Sufficient, and the sports orientation of the Active Sports Enthusiast. They rely very little on television for entertainment or relaxation.

Active Homebody. Members of this group resemble the Passive Homebody group in their family- and home-orientation, but replace that group's nonactive television-watching with such activities as golf, working on the car, and gardening. They have a generally negative attitude toward the arts and do little reading, partying, or radio listening. They are not very socially active or media-oriented, but fill their time with what might be called productive "tinkering" activities.

Socially Active. This last group is also active, but in a more social vein. They give and attend parties, eat out often, and participate in clubs and other meetings. They are aware of theater and symphony offerings and have friends who are interested in these activities. Nevertheless, their patronage is not great at present. They are busy and they do not like leisurely pursuits such as reading or spending a quiet evening at home, nor do they participate in sports such as golf or tennis.

In the present context, then, the Culture Patron and Socially Active groups have leisure life-styles that appear conducive to attending the performing arts. On the other hand, the Passive Homebody, Active Homebody, and Active Sports Enthusiast groups appear negatively disposed toward attendance. Finally, the Inner-Directed, Self-Sufficient group appears generally uninformed, and possibly neutral, about the arts. These differences will prove instructive in the analyses of future behavior response to the manipulations to be explained later.

The six general life-style dimensions developed in this study were factor-analyzed and appear in Table 14.[1]

Table 14. Life-Style Factors, by Leisure Life-Style Group

General Life-Style Factor	Leisure Life-Style Group					
	Passive Home-body	Active Sports Enthusiast	Inner-Directed, Self-Sufficient	Culture Patron	Active Home-body	Socially Active
Traditionalism	Very high	Average	Average	Very low	Average	Average
Hedonism/Optimism	Very low	Average	Average	Very high	Average	Average
Defeatism	Low	Very high	Low	Average	Average	Average
Self-Confidence/ Opinion Leadership	Very high	Average	Low	Very low	Very low	Average
Cosmopolitanism	Very low	Average	Average	Very high	Average	Average
Outdoor Interest	Very low	Average	Average	Average	Average	High

Attitudes toward Theater and Symphony as Predictors

The life-style approach to explaining arts behavior is a general one; it examines how different kinds of arts behavior fit into more general life patterns. Attitude researchers, however, focus on predicting behavior by understanding the nature and value of various outcomes that an individual expects from engaging in a behavior, for example, attending theater or symphony.

Respondents gave highest importance, when attending theater, to play and performing characteristics, and to understanding what is going on. Finding friends there, having the occasion informal, and having the theater nearby appear to be the least important.

Stage in Family Life Cycle as Predictor

Social demographers offer a major alternative to the life-style and attitude theorists' approach. Social demographers argue that behaviors can be predicted by socioeconomic characteristics (such as education), which predispose one to engage in the behavior, or which (as with income) remove constraints that bar the carrying out of predispositions. These socioeconomic characteristics can be seen, then, as potential determinants of life-styles and attitudes which may determine behavior.

The present study includes a wide range of socioeconomic measures. One combined index developed from several of these measures is a family life cycle (FLC) index, based on behavioral patterns that are affected by the chronological stage a person occupies in the life cycle. Age in years only appproximates this chronology; a better measure is one that takes into account the significant points of change in a traditional life cycle that radically alter values (Lansing and Kish, 1957; Wells and Gubar, 1966). These stages, by groups, are seen in Table 15.

Predicting by Regression Analysis

The question this study now considers is whether these new variables are important predictors in multiple regression analyses of likely future symphony and theater attendance. (The deficiencies in this approach will be taken up later, particularly emphasizing that the correlations do not necessarily mean causation.) In these analyses, fifty-six variables were used to predict the likelihood of theater and symphony attendance.

Regarding a total prediction from these correlations between the variables and the likelihood of art attendance, one problem is that many of the variables are related. For example, as income increases, so does the likelihood that the spouse is employed and so do the number of cars in the family. The problem, then, is to conduct an analysis that makes it possible to assess the

Table 15.   Family Life-Cycle Stages, by Leisure Life-Style Group

Life-Cycle Stage	Sample	Passive Home-body	Active Sports Enthusi-ast	Inner-Directed, Self-Sufficient	Culture Patron	Active Home-body	Socially Active
Young Single	8%	Average	High	Average	High	Average	Average
Young Married	10%	Average	High	High	Average	Average	Average
Young Parent	22%	Average	Average	High	Average	Average	Average
Parent of School Children	27%	High	Average	High	Average	Average	High
Empty Nest	11%	High	Average	Average	Average	High	High
Widowhood	8%	High	Average	Average	Average	Average	Average

importance of several variables in explaining the likelihood of attendance while taking account of these variables' interrelationships. One useful technique for doing this is stepwise regression. In this technique, predictors are selected one at a time, starting with the single best predictor and adding at each "step" the one variable that most increases predictive accuracy. The examination process continues until, finally, the best remaining predictor that could be added produces no significant improvement in total predictive accuracy.

Theater.   Of the fifty-six variables examined, six were found to add to the prediction of theater attendance likelihood at the .05 level of significance. . . . . The variables that aided this prediction are, in descending order of usefulness: attitude toward attending theater; Culture Patron; interest in live theater when growing up; theater attendance during past year; Traditionalism; Self-Confidence/Opinion Leadership.

Attitude toward going to the theater is, by a substantial margin, the best predictor of anticipated future attendance. Not surprisingly, the more favorable one thinks the outcomes of attendance will be, the more important these outcomes are, and the more that significant others are seen as favoring attendance, the more one will report likely future attendance.

Symphony.   The five variables that explain about 29 percent of the variance in likely attendance at symphony concerts are: Culture Patron leisure life-style group membership; symphony attendance during past year; interest in classical music when growing up; and Socially Active leisure life-style group membership.

The single new variable in this equation is membership in the Socially Active leisure life-style group. It will be recalled that this was the second group with a life-style positively predisposed toward the arts. This finding may lend force to the conjecture that symphony attendance for some patrons serves social needs beyond any cultural needs it may fulfill.

Nonuseful predictors.   First, none of the standard socioeconomic variables—education, sex, income, occupation, and so forth—turns out to be a significant predictor of likely attendance when attitudes and life-style factors are considered.

Manipulating the Product

Respondents were asked to state their likely reaction to each of the following variables relating to the product: (1) the type of performance; (2) the quality of performance; (3) the formality of atmosphere; (4) the extent of learning opportunities; and also to variables relating to the price: (1) second ticket, one-half off; and (2) telephone/credit purchasing; as well as to variables relating to location.

Findings

The resulting indices, broken down separately for those who did and did not attend in the past year, are in Tables 16 and 17. The indices presented for nonattenders show two obviously superior strategies for drawing more members of this group to the theater and symphony: introducing more "star" performers, and offering second tickets for half price. Equally potent for theater nonattenders is the presentation of more musical comedies. Of somewhat lesser effect for concert nonattenders are the offer of tickets at half off

Table 16.   Effectiveness Index of Symphony Strategies

Strategies	Attenders	Non-attenders	All Respondents
Product			
Type of Performance			
More classical music	102	107	105
More romantic music	107	90	97
More contemporary music	53	54	54
More concertos	56	57	57
More choral music	31	49	43
Quality of Performance			
More famous performers	150	166	161
Formality of Atmosphere			
Dressing more informally	61	100	87
Extent of Learning Opportunities			
Short talk/discussion	101	121	114
Price			
Second ticket, one-half off	199	180	186
Telephone/credit purchasing	77	81	80
Combination			
One-half off day of performance, poorer seats	106	121	116
Nearer location, 20 percent discount	76	112	100

Table 17.   Effectiveness Index of Theater Strategies

Strategies	Attenders	Non-attenders	All Respondents
Product			
Type of Performance			
More musical comedies	142	150	145
More classical plays	32	15	25
More American drama	112	115	113
More modern comedies	124	104	116
More original plays	47	30	40
Quality of Performance			
More famous performers	160	160	160
Formality of Atmosphere			
Dressing more informally	65	83	72
Extent of Learning Opportunities			
Short talk/discussion	65	63	64
Price			
Second ticket one-half off	173	157	166
Telephone/credit purchasing	72	60	67
Combination			
One-half off day of performance, poorer seats	176	95	144
Nearer location, 20 percent discount	87	81	85

on the day of the performance, and the presentation of a short discussion of the work before the performance.[2]

Of critical interest to the issue of broadening the audience is whether there are also differential effects on attenders and nonattenders within each life-style group. To investigate this question, a series of cross tabulations was constructed comparing the responses of recent attenders and recent nonattenders within each life-style group. In four cases for symphony and two for theater, manipulations yielded different effects for attenders than for nonattenders within specific life-style groups. The preferred strategy for bringing in more past nonattenders is clearly to offer alternatives, such as second tickets at half price, that have a high impact on past nonattenders and also attract more patronage from recent attenders.

Notes

1. *Traditionalism.* As noted, this characteristic is associated with church-going, old-fashioned tastes, a feeling that things are moving too fast, and a wish for the good old days. It is also related to preferences for a traditional child- and family-centered home, where the man is in charge and the woman is home-oriented. Finally, it includes a preference for security and a reluctance to take chances.

Hedonism/Optimism. This characteristic encompasses wanting to look attractive and perhaps a little different, wishing to travel around the world or live in London or Paris for a year, and liking to eat. It is associated with the positive view that one's greatest achievements lie ahead.

Defeatism. This characteristic is marked by a depressed outlook due to a belief that things have not turned out well. One's present life is thought undesirable; if given the chance, one would do things differently. It is also associated with wishing for the good old days, thinking things are changing too fast, spending for today, and dreading the future.

Self-Confidence/Opinion Leadership. Two characteristics seem best to describe this dimension; a feeling of self-confidence and liking to be considered a leader.

Cosmopolitanism. This factor includes a preference for big cities and an acceptance of modern liberal ideas, such as women's liberation.

Outdoor interest. This dimension involves going on picnics and hiking.

2. *Type of performance.* It has been argued that a major vehicle for broadening audiences is to offer programs that would better meet the needs of infrequent attenders or nonattenders. Thus, in this study, respondents were asked whether they would go "much more often," "somewhat more often," "as often," or "less often" if more of the following were offered.

Symphony: Symphonies by classical composers such as Mozart and Beethoven; symphonies by romantic composers such as Brahms and Tchaikovsky; music by contemporary composers such as Stravinsky; concertos with soloists; choral music.

Theater: Musical comedies such as *South Pacific* or *Showboat*; classical plays such as *Hamlet* or *Macbeth*; well-known American dramas such as *Death of a Salesman* or *A Streetcar Named Desire*; modern comedies such as *The Sunshine Boys*; original plays that have never been done before.

Quality of performance. Again, it has been argued that new audiences can be attracted by the appearance of well-known performers. Respondents were asked if they would change their frequency of attendance in the following cases.

Symphony: If guest conductors and famous soloists appeared with the orchestra more frequently.

Theater: If famous actors and actresses appeared with the company more frequently.

Formality of atmosphere. Many nonattenders seem intimidated by what they think is the formality of arts performances, particularly at symphony concerts; respondents were asked whether they would go more or less often "if you knew that people were dressing more informally."

Extent of learning opportunities. Many of those who rarely or never go to arts events say they don't attend because they "would not understand what was going on."

Respondents therefore were asked whether they would attend more often in the following cases.

Symphony: If there was a short introductory talk about the music by the conductor before the performance.

Theater: If there was a short discussion of the play by the director after the performance.

Manipulating price.   Economists argue strongly that the demand for most goods and services is determined largely by price. A series of questions was asked to test this proposition by finding out if infrequent attenders and nonattenders might be responsive to price manipulations.

References

Hollis, Susan M. 1974. "The Arts and Center-City Revitalization: A Case Study of Winston-Salem, North Carolina." Paper presented at the Economic Impact on the Arts Conference, Ithaca, N.Y., Cornell University.

Lansing, John B., and Leslie Kish. 1957. "Family Life Cycle as an Independent Variable," *American Sociological Review*, 22 (October):512–19.

Eric Marder Associates, Inc. 1974. *The Finances of the Performing Arts.* New York: Ford Foundation.

National Research Center of the Arts, Inc. 1976. *Americans and the Arts.* New York: National Committee for Cultural Resources.

15

Interview: Clive Barnes

Criticism as a Kind of Work

J.K. *What aspects of your work do you like?*

C.B. *I like being in contact with really good minds. Very often people say, "How on earth can you do this job? You know, you go to the theater eight to ten times a week. . . That must be terribly boring." And then you find out that they're orthodontists who are looking down people's throats all the day, and they say my job is boring.*

It takes a certain talent to write a bad play. It takes an enormous talent to write a good play. But whichever way, you're dealing with some of the most talented people that you're going to find. I find that an enormous privilege.

J.K. *What aspects of your work do you like least?*

C.B. *Getting to the theater on time [in New York City]. Occasionally being bored by the work because, as everyone knows, not all theater is good. But even the bad work has some element of interest in it.*

I think I dislike the publicity associated with critics in this country, which is rather different from the European approach. I do find that the European approach of the critic as a noncelebrity is more beneficial to the art than the American approach, which offers the critic as a celebrity. I think this is absolutely nonsense. I can't see how a parasite, even a symbiotic parasite, can really be a celebrity. I think that the American idea of the critic is a little bit dangerous, dangerous to the critic, dangerous to the art, and makes the criticism almost more important than the thing being criticized.

Clive Barnes is the theater and dance critic of the *New York Post*. He was interviewed by Jack Kamerman at his home in New York City in July 1981.   241

The Power and Responsibility of Critics

J.K. *There's an old bromide that critics can close a show after one performance. What responsibility does a critic have and to whom?*

C.B. *I think the critic only has responsibility to him or herself.*

The power, much less than you think. I mean, for example, **Grease,** *which is the longest running musical ever on Broadway, got very bad notices, including my own. First, let's take a show closing on its first night. When a show closes on its first night, the closing notices have been placed a week before. Ask [Actors'] Equity. You cannot just close a show; well, you can, but you have to pay everyone [one week's salary]. So, in fact, the closing notices have been up a week before. It's an interesting myth, because producers don't put money in shows, or very few do. And therefore, they are responsible to "angels." These investors, angels, cannot be told, "Look, I absolutely goofed. I made quite a lot of money out of this show, but you have lost everything." Because, in fact, a producer never loses; a producer has a producer's fee every week the thing is on the road, every week the thing is in rehearsal. Very often you'll find that shows that run a considerable time, even a year, don't pay anything back to their investors. But he can't go to his angels, because he wants them to invest in another show, and say, "Look, I goofed. I couldn't get a good property. I took this rotten property, I did my best with it, but it was really no good." What he has to say to his angel is, "Well, I'm not saying it was a great show, I'm not saying it was* **King Lear;** *I'm not even saying it was* **The Sound of Music.** *But I am saying it was a family show and that if those goddamn critics hadn't killed it, it would still be on the boards." Well, of course, that's all so much bullshit. Critics do not in fact kill shows.*

Nowadays, shows are not so bad as they were. We have lost what used to be called the "vanity show," because it costs so much. You'd look at your playbill when you went in and realize with a spark of horror that the play has been written by Miss X and produced by her husband and that her brother is doing the designs and her son is actively involved. That did at one time happen. Nowadays, with the cost of everything, it's changed a bit.

Preparation for Criticism
and the Function of the Critic

J.K. *What kind of training do you think a critic should have?*

C.B. *Very little. One difficulty is that very often critics are frustrated actors, frustrated directors, or most likely—because they're in that kind of verbal area—frustrated playwrights. I'm not a frustrated anything. I'm a terribly fulfilled critic.*

I have never had an acting lesson in my life. I've never been guilty of taking a creative-writing course or doing anything like that. I have been guilty of teaching critical writing, but I've always started my course by saying that it was an impossible course. It always has been, and I gave it up.

I think the best background is wearing out pants on seats, going to performances night after night after night. I started to go to performances in 1937 when I was ten. There were periods during the war when I was evacuated to the country, and then I would go back to London for vacations. Apart from that period, I've been to the theater, I suppose, virtually every night of my life. It keeps you off the street and stops you from going to dinner parties. It's a good way of living.

I think the critic is a bridge between the audience and the artist. But it's a bridge that starts with the audience, not a bridge that starts with the artist. I'm not out to give lessons in playwriting. I'm not out to give lessons in choreography or dancing. . .I did take dance lessons incidentally. Don't know why I did, but I did for about two years with very good teachers. But I never intended to be a dancer. That's the limit of it from that side of the proscenium arch. From my side of the proscenium arch, by the time you reach fifty-four, you've certainly seen a great deal and that does establish some kind of standard. These standards are not objective; they're purely subjective, but the opinions are informed.

J.K. *You've probably heard performing artists claim that critics have no right to write criticism unless they've performed themselves.*

C.B. *I can understand that. But usually performing artists make very bad critics of the performing arts. They're either mean or jealous or just plain stupid or all three put together. You've also got to remember that as a critic I am incredibly criticized all the time. Certainly my fellow critics say the most terrible things about me. So I do know what it is to take criticism.*

We have this curious concept of criticism that criticism is adverse, it's an opponent situation, which it really isn't. We say in common usage, "Don't criticize me." It really annoys me because I don't think that criticism is a negative operation. I think that criticism is much more a positive contribution, making this bridge between the audience and the artist.

J.K.   *A number of people who might read your remarks about your major preparation for your career being attendance at more performances than anyone sitting in the audience might take exception to that. They might ask again, "What is your actual 'training'?" this being a world of professionals and licenses.*

C.B.   *The actual training. . .Art is synthesis, criticism is analysis. An artist takes his experiences, his genetic constitution, his inspiration, and puts them all together. The critic analyzes that product for the benefit of the audience. There have been exceptions. Hector Berlioz, for example, was a wonderful critic, and so was Schumann. Curiously, the exceptions are usually in music. I thought that Bernard Shaw was tolerably the best critic of the twentieth century. On the other hand, he was an absolutely awful playwright. He remained, of course, a very good writer. I would say you have to be a good writer, otherwise no one's going to read you.*

    People become critics in very obscure ways. One's reminded of the social worker who asks a whore on the corner, "What's a nice girl like you doing in a place like this?" And she replies, "Just lucky, I guess." And I suppose with every critic, there is this element of luck.

SECTION SIX

SUPPORT SYSTEMS

In order to survive, the artist must become a non-profit, tax-exempt institution with a board of directors, fund raisers, office space, and 75 percent of his time spent in the administration of his art.

Alwin Nikolais

The arts have always had to depend on some form of patronage in order to facilitate artistic production from its creation to its dissemination. In keeping with our theme of relating the arts to their sociocultural milieu, and thereby seeing the influence of such factors as patronage on the arts, this section will focus on the social groups and structures that have provided the arts with various forms of subsidies. Although the private individual or patron remains the single most significant source of contribution to the nonprofit performing arts, other sources of income continue to expand and are represented by government, foundation, and corporate funds.

It is unfortunate that neither the individuals who support the arts nor their motives for doing so have been analyzed in depth. Although census figures, tax exemptions, and other statistical data have accumulated and are available, little has been done to explain the annual contributions of "culture barons" as well as millions of individuals. Arts centers and individual performing arts groups are well aware of who their patrons are, but there has never been an integrated effort to study these sources. The few studies or special interest articles that appear in magazines and newspapers are, in general, haphazard, inconsistent, and unscientific. Fortunately, foundation, government, and corporate support of the arts has been well documented, as the chapters in this section evidence.

The growth of corporate support of the arts has been stunning, climbing from $22 million in 1967 to $436 million in 1979. This is especially surprising when one realizes that the relationship between business and the arts has only been taken seriously since 1965. However, the recent budget cuts, which have drastically reduced aid to state and local arts councils, will stimulate greater competition among individual artists, performing companies, and arts centers for the shrinking revenues.

It would seem, from the nature and structure of public and private support systems, that any change in the source of funding must have an impact on both the recipients and the nature of their art. Foundations and government are more formal in structure, have clearly established objectives for obtaining grants, and are sensitive to the source of their revenues, the public. Corporations, on the other hand, remain informal, with the power of decision invested in a few top-management executives. Different procedural requirements in obtaining subsidies have led to the willingness of corporations to sponsor individual artists and programs of esoteric or avant-garde nature. Foundations and government, however, share the requirement that a work of art or a performance should appeal to the general public.

At present, the arts are the fastest-growing area of corporate support, with symphony orchestras and museums the most favored recipients. Public television and public radio have also received a considerable proportion of corporate support since the late 1970s. The popularity of the arts as recipients of corporate support has been enhanced by the fact that the arts have been shown to improve both the profits and image of business. The legitimating and status-granting function of the arts has proven valid beyond a doubt, and in identifying with the arts, corporations enjoy both visibility and prestige.

Vera Zolberg analyzes the different types of social groups involved in disseminating art. Following a brief historical overview of the emergence of these groups, she addresses the degree of influence patrons have had on creators and performers. She stresses the fact that patronage offers status to those who engage in it, and concludes by raising issues with regard to the limitations on artists within a given support system.

The 1960s saw an enormous growth in audience attendance, concomitant with the building of arts centers and the renovation of decaying theaters and music halls in inner-city urban-renewal areas. This period was a time of rebirth and of an optimistic belief that the arts would flourish in all corners of the United States. This artistic expansion was supported by a generation of post-war babies, and a growing college-educated white middle class. In many cases, business and government collaborated and responded equally and in unison to the needs of downtown areas to revitalize their commercial centers, which included the arts centers. As these areas underwent renewal, and the arts attracted a clientele, business retail figures benefited from the change as well. The revitalization of the arts in the center city of Winston-Salem, North Carolina, is a case in point.

Government financing, which facilitated this development, also brought to light the lack of expertise in sophisticated accounting procedures in many of these organizations. However, recipients of government funds were obliged to accept government scrutiny, and to develop the techniques of audience composition analysis and cost-efficiency accounting. Financial analysis of nonprofit organizations also revealed their inability to reach economies of scale. Unlike business enterprises, arts organizations could not effect income gains by increasing output, nor could they efficiently control input resources. This feature of the nonprofit structure inevitably results in economic constraint, aggravated by inflation and expansion in the arts. Sam Schwarz reports on a major national study funded by the National Endowment for the Arts, which attempted an economic analysis of the nonprofit performing arts. A great deal of effort went to assessing the vocabularies used by the diverse performing arts in their respective budgets. Consequently, a uniform data base has been established, the most comprehensive and national effort made to date.

The final chapter in this section, "Art and Public Policy: Ideologies for Aesthetic Welfare," explores the effect of public support on the arts in America. Rosanne Martorella describes the developments that led to increasing government involvement, and devotes special attention to the consequences of certain policies and legislation on the arts and on artistic careers. Sociologists have emphasized the social organization of the artistic milieus of painting, music, film, and the like. There has been little attention to the role of government as the new patron of the arts. Although a few political scientists have studied the economic and political structure of the arts, focusing on their administrative structure, they have stopped short of evaluating the consequences of such developments. Both historical and theoretical circumstances can account for the lack of critical analysis in this area.

This brief introduction has raised some areas for consideration, in the hope of revealing how particular support structures may influence artistic activity in specific relation to both the careers of artists and stylistic developments.

16

Changing Patterns of Patronage in the Arts

—————•◦•—————

VERA L. ZOLBERG

Introduction

Patronage is only one of the many institutions that foster creation, reward artists, and permit or promote performance and display of their works. It has been and remains the most prestigious of the support structures, so prestigious, in fact, that its name is applied to forms of cultural support having little in common with what it connotes. In this chapter I will explore patronage, its relationship to other support systems, and their probable impact, separately and together, on the encouragement—as well as the limitation—of the arts.

Support systems, and their effects on the kinds of art produced, recognized as art, rewarded, and disseminated, have been documented by scholars working in a variety of disciplines (Hauser, 1951; Gombrich, 1972; Meiss, 1951; Trevor-Roper, 1976),[1] providing a basis for sociological analysis. Particularly within the field of the production of culture, research on the processes by which culture is created, creators rewarded, their output selected, by what gatekeepers, and how their works are diffused and received by publics, has resulted in clarification of and insight into culture–society relationships (Peterson, 1976). Following their lead, this chapter surveys change from individual patronage to newer patterns and sources of subsidy and financing of the arts, with particular, though not exclusive, attention to the United States.

A brief analytical overview will focus on three types of support: patronage, market, government. These sources will be analyzed as to whether they are personal, collective, or institutional: they may be organized either on a one- 251 to-one basis, in which patrons and artists interact directly; via intermediaries, such as impresarios; or bureaucratically, with administrative structures following regularized procedures to transmit or withhold support. The quality of the relationships in each of these role structures will be examined.

Exploring the meanings, functioning, and effects within the societal contexts in which each support structure predominates will be the second task. The characteristics of the environments in which artists exist, and the relative degree of dominance or equality they experience in relation to their supporters will be shown to influence the amount of freedom permitted them. Whereas in pre-modern societies the expection of loyalty of creators to their patrons and their desires was taken for granted, in more recent times, especially as a heritage of the romantic movement, artists are expected to reject external control over their creative processes. In this tradition artists must stand aloof from societal demands at whatever personal cost and follow the command of their inner genius. Concurrently, however, another set of ideas, also deriving in part from romanticism, demands that artists be responsive not to their muse alone, but to broader societal demands. In this view, they must direct their creative efforts to goals of social utility, reform, or uplift.

The contradiction inherent in these two views was not long in becoming evident. Under liberal regimes they have been openly debated, but in authoritarian regimes debate is trammeled by the foregone conclusion that the arts must serve regime goals. Support or patronage is forthcoming to artists who remain well behaved, but artists who deviate suffer rejection or persecution. The theme of opposition between autonomy and conformity underlies the present analysis, and will be discussed in relation to trends in contemporary support patterns.

Patronage and Market: Interpenetrations

In order to clarify the probable effects of their support sources on creators and their works, it is useful to examine the meanings of the terms employed: patronage and market. The forms of behavior to which they refer are institutions patterned in particular ways, but varying in relation to the societal conditions in which they occur. Patronage in the late Middle Ages differs significantly from that of the late nineteenth century, and even more from patronage today. The same may be said for markets. Furthermore, although patronage and markets coexist, their varying proportion to one another, and in relation to other support structures, means that each combination composes a unique opportunity structure from the artist's standpoint.[2]

A cursory examination of standard lexicographical sources (e.g., *Oxford English Dictionary*) reveals that usage of the term "patronage" has undergone profound change over time. Although an etymological analysis in and of itself does not provide irrefutable proof of a shift in socially significant meanings, this one strongly reflects the decline in patrimonialism, hierarchy, and diffuseness, and the concurrent growth of markets in utilitarian commodities, along with changing contractual relationships associated with them. Related to these, it may also denote a decline in the functions of the traditional patron as legal protector once civil liberties became established. With the rise of capitalism, increasing industrial production, and a corresponding growth in the prevalence of contractual relationships, the democratization of patronage (which, paradoxically, became synonymous with "clientage") indicates the weakening, or making problematic, of the relationship of superordinate and subordinate, and suggests the growth of egalitarianism in business relationships, in which hierarchy is based on material power and shrewdness rather than on ascribed condition. Whether this trend can appropriately be applied to relationships in the arts, however, remains to be determined.

Whereas patronage is fundamentally pervaded by patrimonialism, in which the relationship of patron and client is based on the assumption of personal loyalty, diffuse mutual obligations, and hierarchical dominance, a market relationship is typically structured in opposed terms: impersonality, specificity of obligations, and equality among role players. The ideal–typical nature of these attributes, however, obscures the overlapping of patronage and market. In its actual functioning, patronage was not as free from market elements as conventionally supposed, but has coexisted with them within varying political, economic, and social structural parameters (E. H. Miller, 1959; Shils, 1972).

Traditional patrons were expected to be magnanimous toward their artist–clients, permitting their admiration for the artists' achievements to outweigh the fundamental dependence of their clients on their goodwill. While gracious patrons existed, in fact, relatively few were totally magnanimous; most maintained haughtiness vis-à-vis fawning artists, musicians, and writers, who competed for a place in their entourage, only to complain once admitted of their patrons' neglect or exploitation. Haggling over fees of commissioned works between artists and patrons or municipal or church officials suggests that even as early as the late Middle Ages market matters intruded into this purportedly genteel domain (Antal, 1970:292). Although not denying the cases of mutual respect and warm personal attachment, we must recognize that traditional patronage was not necessarily paradise (Morgenstern, 1956:305–6). As Edward Shils has observed:

> We often hear the old system of patronage praised by those who bemoan its passing and contrast it with the vulgar insensitivity of the rich of the present century. It is well to remember, however, what misery and humiliation the older individual patronage often imposed on its beneficiaries, how capricious and irregular it was, and how few were affected by it during the period of its greatest prevalence. [Shils, 1972:111.]

The Maecenases, or patrons of the past, whose only goal was to support art for its own sake, are, therefore, largely a myth of nineteenth-century artists, facing the harsh realities of the market, a myth equally embraced by their parvenu supporters, anxious to link themselves to an idealized aristocracy of taste (Boime, 1976:140).

Just as patronage was not all that we may imagine, neither are market relationships. In practice, even in many purely economic transactions there remain precontractuaal understandings that subvert the total rationality implied by this structure. The presence of these understandings tends to have a braking effect on the total objectification of individuals, their work, and the pure profit motive itself. Commonly, this occurs when nationalistic aims outweigh goals of unfettered rationality, or when racial prejudice subverts achievement criteria. With respect to the fine arts in particular, symbolic elements with quasireligious significance may be retained or imputed to what has come to be defined as "serious" or "academic" art (Peterson, 1976:13). Thus, although capitalism is often berated for turning even fine art into commodity, not to speak of frankly commercial art (Adorno, 1976:12; Hadjinicolaou, 1978), total commodification is actually limited by the aura of disinterestedness that has come to surround the fine arts, an aura that enhances the value of art works both symbolically and materially (Benjamin, 1969:221), and may come to surround and thereby redefine even *non*-fine art, elevating it above its origins—the case, notably, of American jazz.

A social concomitant of the cultural tradition imbuing the arts with aura is the persistence of quasipersonalism even in commercial transactions involving artist and collector, writer and publisher, musician and impresario. Even where market considerations predominate, the injection of their components to the exclusion of traditional elements (*noblesse oblige*, with its deferential connotations) arouses dismay and disgust: commercialism *cheapens* fine art, the artists, and their supporters. It is in the interest of those involved in such transactions, therefore, to maintain at least the semblance of a patrimonial style (Gibbons, 1981).

Further complicating these relationships is yet a third source of support, beyond individual patronage by rulers or nobility, churchmen or magnates on the one hand, and the anonymous public of the market on the other. Government, representing the state, plays an active role in cultural production, sometimes substituting itself for other types of support, sometimes enhancing existing sources. Cutting across support sources are mediating techniques whereby support is channeled to artists. The direct relationship between patron and artist may be increasingly replaced, especially in the case of state support, by bureaucratic structures with rules of procedure. Bureaucracy is intended to deal efficiently with numerous cases in a neutral manner. Created to achieve purposes as various as tax collection, enforcement of

religious dogma, military training and warfare, the most prominent bureaucracies came to structure the academies that determined the selection of
candidates, training, and rewarding of certain kinds of artists, often in competition with church and guilds, aiming instead to create and enhance the
symbolic representation of the state (Trevor-Roper, 1976; Corvisier, 1978).
Bureaucracy has come to pervade even nongovernmental and nonacademic
support structures in recent times, with consequences for artists and their
work to be examined next.

Artist and Public: Changing Patterns of Dominance

An understanding of the shifting pattern of dominance between artists and
those who support them must take into account that dominance depends
directly on the extent to which artists must count on a single or limited source
of support, or may choose among a diversity. For this reason it is necessary
to consider changes in societal and cultural environments, which permitted
the growth in numbers of potential sources of support:[3] the autonomy of the
arts from crafts; the restratification of art forms; the growth of potential publics;
the emergence of intermediaries to organize arts distribution on a large scale;
and a context of political and religious tolerance, if not liberty. A historical
overview suggests important consequences of these changes in relation to the
arts, and points to the new support institutions that challenged the relative
monopoly of individual patronage and the church and the constricting influence of guilds.

Among these, official academies, created by kings—e.g., in France, where
the absolutist state first reached its developed form—formulated, established,
and maintained new standards for the arts, legitimated on the bases of ra-
tionales provided by humanistic, classical scholarship. By screening and carefully overseeing talent, they fostered and controlled creation and performance,
developing a *national* art, officially recognized as the "high" or "great" culture. In the process, unofficial art forms, whether representing the parochi-
alism of local cultural traditions, or the sacred universalism of a weakened
church, were relegated to the marginal status of "little" cultures (Corvisier,
1978).

Limited as they were initially, academies provided new avenues of career
advancement and encouraged the development of different kinds of art, independent both of restrictive guild regulations and churchly approval, but
with new restrictions and canons in line with the new ideology (Pelles, 1963;
White and White, 1965). The proper content and style of painting and music
were taught to aspirants, and the forms of these arts were hierarchically
ordered. Although fairly personalized at first, academies became more bur-

eaucratized as they grew. Although continuing to serve as clients until their demise, academies also promoted competition, specialization, and professionalization of artists in particular media by offering stipends and prizes only for established official categories of the arts, with some attention to quality, defined according to academic canons. Despite efforts of academies to control to the maximum all forms of fine art production, however, they were always being challenged. Their power, as well as that of other traditional patronage institutions, waned, supplanted by a largely nonaristocratic market.

Market processes emerged in response to the rigidity of academic canons, as a response to inadequate support structures for artists, and to meet the desires of new publics. For example, printed literature, formerly patronized by the nobility, paid for by political figures, commissioned by churchmen, became organized by the publishing business in England (E. H. Miller, 1959); painters in Holland, facing diminished church support because of Calvinist distaste for imagery, were driven to seek commissions from individuals, secular associations, or municipalities, or, more commonly, sell completed works to the public. The content of their work reflects this shift, with religious subjects giving way to genre and maritime scenes and portraits. With little regularized support, and in the face of large numbers of competitors, it is not surprising, as Nicolaus Pevsner has suggested, that artists were often obliged to engage in other sorts of trade, among which their creations became only one more commodity (1970: 364–66). Gradually, bourgeois (or burgher) patronage, either from individuals or from publics composed of more or less wealthy commoners, increased to such an extent that traditional patronage structures were swamped, or simply used as "feeders" of art to emerging institutions, such as concert societies or art collections (William Weber, 1975).

Concurrent with these developments, the political revolutions of the late-eighteenth and nineteenth centuries resulted in the weakening or superseding of *anciens régimes* by national states whose governmental bureaucracies became the successors to earlier official support structures of culture. Meanwhile, public demand for both visual and other forms of art increased rapidly, though not rapidly enough to provide for increasing numbers of artists, musicians, and writers (Dorian, 1964; Clark, 1973; Minihan, 1977). Even the French Academy, an efficient institution in the early nineteenth century, was unable to handle the growing number of aspiring artists whose output eventually created an overload on the system. In response, a new marketing institution, composed of dealers, channeled and promoted competition, specialization of artists, and professionalization of new, art-related roles, creating a support structure parallel to the official one, and in opposition to its canons (White and White, 1965; Paret, 1980).

While these changes in support structures were taking place in Europe,

the United States was developing along related, though different, lines. Although the recipient of many European institutions and ideas, America did
not acquire the three European support systems. The church in Europe most
closely associated with art patronage was the Catholic church, but in America
Catholicism was not only *not* the dominant religion, but throughout the
nineteenth century was considered dangerous by many groups. In addition,
certain Protestant denominations looked upon many of the arts (with the
exception of sacred music) with distaste or distrust (Sabloski, 1969). A pre-
and post-revolutionary intelligentsia of professionals was, in certain regions,
little substitute for a European aristocracy in providing regular private patronage (Harris, 1966). Except during periods of national emergency, government throughout most of the nineteenth century was kept at a fairly low
level. Thus, whereas European capitals were typically intended to be metropolitan centers, attracting all kinds of artists, capitals in the United States,
both national and state, were typically remote by design, and did not become
art centers. Aside from official commissions for government buildings and
decorations (monopolized to an overwhelming degree by artists' associations
known as academies), only toward the end of the nineteenth century, with
the success of popular education movements, was a moral justification for
government support of cultural dissemination provided, permitting local governments to grant subsidies to certain cultural institutions, such as museums
(Zolberg, 1980a). Hence, by default, for most of its history, American aesthetic culture has been dependent upon some pseudoaristocratic merchant
institution builders (L. B. Miller, 1966:218), occasional and atypical governmental funding and, as in the case of Europe as well, commercial markets
(DiMaggio and Hirsch, 1976).

The market caused a virtual revolution in artist–patron relationships. Instead of being dependent on the whim of an individual who could effectively
close the limited opportunity structure by refusing patronage, artists and
performers found themselves dealing with middlemen gatekeepers on a contractual basis, and dependent upon the whims of large, anonymous publics.
Nineteenth-century publics were heterogeneous, composed not only of nobles, churchmen, and magnates, but also of larger numbers of middle-class
people aspiring to cultural achievement, pleasure, and prestigious consum-
erism to which most had been neither born nor educated. They provided a
new outlet for artists who failed to gain entry into academies because they
resisted the latters' canons, did not qualify for their standards, or lacked the
social graces necessary to attract private patrons who might be influential in
obtaining their admission. Indeed, even magnates needed or wanted cultural
education, which was provided by cultural leaders—such as conductors, impresarios, and art and music critics—and cultural entrepreneurs of all kinds.

Typical of some of the outstanding actors in the transformation of patronage in America was the conductor Theodore Thomas. Through most of his career he combined many roles: player, impresario, travel agent, conductor, usher, ticket and program vender, and general factotum for his own orchestra. He was finally to achieve a stable position as full-time director of his orchestra; shortly after it was transformed to the Chicago Symphony Orchestra he married the daughter of a board officer. Because of his powerful connections, fame, and recognized ability, he was able to "educate" his collective patrons' musical taste, persuading them to accept music which they considered too advanced and difficult (Otis, 1924:22–97). His success in carving out a public for symphonic music among emerging elites in search of status was paralleled by others in major American cities.

For some artists, especially writers and virtuosi, these publics provided a market through which they achieved success and avoided servility. In rare cases artistic stardom might actually produce a reversal of the dominance relationship, with artists sought after by their public. The cases of Jenny Lind, Adelina Patti, Franz Liszt, and many others in the music world illustrate this pattern for performers, while writers such as Dickens in England and Eugène Sue in France made their fame through the new medium of serialized publication of their novels in widely disseminated, low-cost newspapers. Although artists strove to cumulate access to all available support structures, including private patrons, academies, and widespread public adulation, only relatively few attained their aim. For some, success at the cost of pandering to the public was unacceptable; for many, even pandering led to failure. As we examine the relationships of artists to the sources of their support in the twentieth century, we shall be confronted with the intensification of trends signaled above.

Monopolistic versus Pluralistic Patronage

Many of the institutional arrangements developed in the nineteenth century and earlier have survived in modified form to the present. Among the most striking of the modifications has been the growing bureaucratization in art-related institutions and activities. Governmental bureaucracies, such as ministries of culture and other agencies, exercise control over large sectors of artistic production by providing support for chosen aspirants or their works; individual patrons establish foundations run by staffs (Letwin, 1973); cultural institutions, including museums and performing arts companies, develop into heavily administered organizations (Martorella, 1977); impresarios and advisers become associated with corporations or absorbed by them. The pervasiveness of bureaucratic structures, both in liberal and authoritarian states, however, does not produce the same effects in terms of artistic outcomes.

European nations, as has been shown, have a long tradition of governmental support for artists. Unfortunately for artists in America—though not surprisingly, given its religious background, anti-elitism, occasional anti-European outlook, and characteristic reluctance to expand the public sector—the United States, in contrast with most other liberal democracies, has not until recently taken support for the arts to be a public obligation. The legacy of the New Deal is ambiguous because many of the programs initiated in that period were of an emergency nature, by the way of public works programs for destitute artists. Once the economic emergency was past, the programs vanished, leaving no permanently institutionalized foundation (O'Connor, 1969; McDonald, 1969). The second major government intervention in the arts was launched after World War II, coinciding with American cold-war goals, which made cultural exchanges an arm of U.S. State Department policy. Not surprisingly, choices of works and performers were likely to be made in terms of their ideological correctness or innocuousness. It is therefore understandable that the unprecedented growth of governmental patronage since the 1960s has raised discussion of policy in this sphere to a high level of intensity. Beyond current debates over whether subsidies should be given to popular as well as fine art, to innovative as well as to established institutions, to amateurs as well as to professionals, to participatory as well as to spectator-oriented activities, lie broader issues, of which the principal one concerns the extent to which, by providing subsidies, government will also come to dictate to recipients the content and form of the art product (Useem, 1976).

In modern authoritarian states, governments monopolize cultural support, often either discouraging the existence of parallel institutions (such as churches and the commercial market), or regulating them with bureaucratic efficiency in order to harness all cultural production to the ideological purposes on which their states are founded. Yet even under effective systems, unofficial art forms manage haltingly to survive, either through subversion of the regime's goals by its own officials (Goering's private "collection" included French impressionists, postimpressionists, and other "degenerate" works); by going underground with some support of sympathizers (Brenner, 1980:334; Badischen Kunstverein, 1980); or with the help of small nuclei of patrons of, for example, abstract art or unofficial literary works, as in the Soviet Union (Johnson, 1965:7). Furthermore, despite their enormous success in closing borders to external influences, these states have rarely maintained total impermeability. Complex systems, even when intentionally totalitarian, are composed of too many institutions and groupings with unofficial goals of their own. Changes in the relative strength of factions, external forces, pressure from allies, leadership succession, and sheer greed make it likely that art styles devalued at one point may be rehabilitated at another, or at least not be utterly destroyed.[4]

By comparison, liberal democracies with multiple sources of support provide material benefits and aesthetic liberty that make them attractive to exiles from authoritarian regimes. A free market for art in almost every medium and form competes with governmentally funded programs, philanthropic foundations, educational institutions, and private patronage. Yet artists face obstacles to the possibilities these sources contain: bureaucratic procedures to obtain funds so time consuming as to stifle spontaneity; financial shortfalls that make certain art forms, such as film making or video, available only to a small proportion of the many more-or-less talented aspirants; publics in communities who resist works whose themes they find abrasive, or lacking "fit" with conventional definitions of what constitutes art. In modern educational and cultural institutions, at a time when there is little consensus on aesthetic canons, artists working as creators and teachers are likely to become involved in conflict with administrators who, though often sharing the "conception of artists as a natural aristocracy," must put up with their "laxity" in practical matters (Adler, 1979:114).

If the endemic conflicts in bureaucratic iron cages are familiar matters, so are the problems presented artists by the free market. For, as romantic ideology dictates, artists, like aristocrats, must not sell themselves or their work. Since most artists at least pay lip-service to this notion, they must be pervaded by a sense of alienation. Inevitably, even if they do not work at commercial design or music, they lose control over their works as soon as they sell them. Moreover, art collecters or buyers of properties become alienated from the objects they collect, reducing their involvement into pure commerce as well. To the extent that art collecting becomes more akin to an investment and less like the primitive accumulation of the past, when the works served as status symbol, disinterested obsession—reflecting earnest conviction, not to speak of affection for particular works or artists—aesthetic values become increasingly remote. While primitive accumulation depended upon owning objects, collecting now evokes trading in stocks, or even in "puts" and "calls." Betting on the right moment for disposing of works, either for high profit or for tax deduction—which produces the same result (Netzer, 1978:33–35)— is coming to be what counts. In the future the individual collector or patron may become a rara avis, increasingly replaced by corporations as patrons and dealers, using art either as institutional advertising or as speculators dealing in options (Glueck, 1975), employing the services of art counselors just as they use brokers for other investments (Rosenbaum, 1979). Collecting resembles entrepreneurial activities on a large scale, with multinational firms increasingly dominant (Moulin, 1967).

Thus far, corporations seem to be accumulating rather than selling, and many choose work with less relationship to art-historical or museum fashion, and more to the corporate image they wish to present. The bulk of corporate collecting is of works by American artists, and is just as likely to include folk and regional art as contemporary fine art. Most reject abstract art, though a few, such as the Chase Manhattan Bank under David Rockefeller, have specialized in it until recently (Sloane, 1979). In general, however, the type of art collected and supported appears to constitute the elements of what can be called a corporate style: "decorative, flashy, safe, easy to live with and easy to sell—cosy landscapes and well-organized colorful abstractions," excluding the erotic, morbid, minimal, and conceptual (Rosenbaum, 1979:54).

Whether for their own, symbolic, or material benefit, purely altruistic aims, or as a public relations device, corporations have increased their expenditures for the arts at a phenomenal rate. Although constituting only around 12 percent of their total philanthropic spending, art accounted for about $22 million in 1963 and rose to $250 million by 1978, amounts said to be more than double those provided by the National Endowment for the Arts during the same period (Metz, 1979:43–44).[5] Although these figures and their probable impact may be inflated, although many corporations have no involvement in the arts at all, and although those that do rarely take full advantage of the tax incentives available to them, corporations' presence as "art patrons" is becoming highly visible (Teltsch, 1981:1).

In light of the increased corporate presence—added to governmental agencies, dealers, collectors, foundations, and universities, not to speak of performing arts organizations, for both live and reproduced arts, with their own goals—we may now ask how artists behave in pursuit of their own goals. We should not assume, however, that all artists share the same aims. As Howard Becker (1976) has perceptively suggested, artists are defined in the context of diverse art worlds, each of which is composed of different canons, peer groups, and publics. They include the "integrated professional," the "maverick," the "naive artist" and the "folk artist." While the first two types work either altogether within the canons or conventions of art forms and styles or in open opposition to them, the latter two use art as a means of personal expression, or only secondarily with an aesthetic purpose.

To be sure, given the emergence of an "anything goes" aesthetic, the works produced by any of these types have some potential for being incorporated into collections, providing material for established musical organizations, and being recognized, though not all to the same degree or with pecuniary rewards for the original artists. The naive artist and the folk artist, however, work outside the accepted networks and channels of communications of art and music, and may, therefore, only be discovered by chance. Our attention will be directed, rather, to the professional artists, especially those considered "fine" rather than "commercial," who actively seek recognition, even if, as in the latter case, they reject conventions and perhaps even existing support systems.[6]

As the case of Theodore Thomas illustrated, professional artists often find it necessary to act as entrepreneurs, seeking access to sources of subsidy, using success in one support structure to break into others. Either by themselves or by manipulating broker networks of agents, social elites, political influence, better-known peers, or specialists in grantsmanship, they raise their personal worth by obtaining fellowships and grants from foundations and government agencies, teaching positions in universities, commissions from business firms, exhibition space in commercial galleries and museums, and regular dealers with access to an appropriate clientele (Shils, 1972: 97–134; Kadushin, 1976). In the course of the juggling these activities require, artists must also achieve legitimacy by currying favor with art critics, journalists, and academics who explicate their work to the public (Wolfe, 1976). With slight variations, this pattern characterizes musicians and writers as well as plastic artists. As Dennison Nash suggested in his study of American composers, given the limited opportunities in proportion to aspirants, individual success is strongly dependent upon a capacity for "role versatility," itself derived from experiences of interaction and diverse contacts within related networks (1970: 262).

Serious artists' goal is to be able to live entirely from their chosen professional work rather than depend upon routine, commercialized forms of art, such as advertising and commercial music, journalism, commissioned portrait painting, or ghostwriting, since such activities remove artists from the realm of pure art and place them directly into the world of commerce (Rosenberg and Fliegl, 1965). Although integrated professionals are successful in these commercial endeavors, many continue to dream of freedom from market demands, considering only nonroutine forms of commercial activities as legitimate. When established artists, such as Calder or Magritte, supply designs for commercial airplanes or television logos, it is their names that provide symbolic enhancement of the organization obtaining their services, not the other way around. But fine artists who depend upon a purely monetary bread-and-butter wage violate the quasi-aristocratic character of art. Beside devaluing commercial or functional purposes in favor of higher goals, innate prowess, independent of mere craftsmanship, is crucial. Not only is art to be for the sake of art, but for the artist's sake, with full control over the content and style of his own work.

Understood in these terms, the Bohemian artist, or maverick, is potentially the most autonomous, at least if he can prove a modicum of reliability—for example, by meeting deadlines—to the gatekeepers of established and emerging institutions, both in private bureaucracies (museums, orchestras, publishing houses) and public bureaucracies. The maverick has an additional appeal for gatekeepers who act as investment counselors, trying to pick good speculative risks as candidates for stipends and advances for editors, impresarios, dealer, foundation officials and corporate advisers who play "futures" in the form of resale of works, percentages, and copyrights (or in the form of symbolic rewards for having recognized talent early). Given the inherent difficulty of successfully maneuvering through such a maze, it is not surprising that only a few artists, musicians, and writers are able to attain renown. Yet the diversity of sources of support is so great that by developing a degree of role versatility, at least some artistic hopefuls are likely to survive, on the peripheries of an art world if not at its center.

The state of affairs described is found in most Western, advanced-industrial, liberal democracies in which to varying degrees a large, heterogeneous market is supplemented by governmental support, both direct and indirect, much of it emerging in response to growing public demand, and argued for by lobbyists for cultural institutions, dealers, collectors, artists, and performers. Together lobbyists help to account for the salient characteristics of the contemporary art world and of art works: (1) growing differentiation and coexistence of art styles in response to varied "consumer" demand; (2) increasing technical proficiency, especially in the performed arts, both because of competition among performers and because of increasing sophistication of a large part of their public; (3) far more complex sets of role relationships between artists and diverse gatekeepers with whom they must interact; and (4) increasing opportunities for intermediaries to function, with the consequence of growth in art-related occupations, including especially administrative and bureaucratic positions.

As members of society, artists are subject to constraints that affect their life-style, career opportunities, and, to a certain extent, the aesthetic choices they make as to media, genres, and styles. In surveying the variations in support structures on which artists depend for a living, I have suggested that although monocentric authoritarian societies limit artistic creativity without necessarily producing "high quality" works, the polycentrism of modern liberal societies presents different but no less real constraints. No doubt from certain viewpoints the stresses on innovativeness and untrammeled creativity, which become the goals of many artists, collectors, and audiences, produce a certain faddishness and ridiculous excess. Yet it is difficult to imagine how a priori limitations on innovation can be justified. In fact, it has come to be considered valid to break down the over-solemnity that surrounds the fine arts, thereby rendering them more accessible to excluded groups. The coexistence of market and patronage permits artists to accomplish their purposes, while the numerous publics coexisting in contemporary, complex societies are able to find art forms compatible with their desires (Gans, 1974). That these publics also function indirectly or directly to maintain status barriers is another issue, which should continue to be studied (Bourdieu, 1966).

Conclusions

The sociological question that is the focus of this chapter has to do with the effect of different forms of support on creators and performers, on the works they produce, and on the amount of freedom they enjoy. But as I have suggested, patronage and clientage are a two-way street. Next to the exercise of creative genius itself, few activities offer the kind of symbolic rewards and prestige afforded by arts patronage to those who engage in it.

Contemporary forms of cultural support have little in common with the personalized, hierarchically structured, disinterested patronage of a largely mythical past, though to the extent that they approximate its attributes—for example, by avoiding the reduction of art to pure monetary transactions—they partake of traditional honor. Market forces, on the other hand, have become the bête noire of artistic freedom, since they may impel artists to deviate from their inspiration, in spite of the fact that to a great extent they have supported the development of the conditions for creative autonomy.

More worrisome is the threat to freedom of government support. This specter is raised by the well-known experience of authoritarian regimes, under which the arts have often been rendered sterile by being turned into hand-maidens of political policy, and consigned to the function of social utility according to rigidly defined criteria. It is unlikely that this will occur in an extreme form in liberal democracies, since such policies conflict with an equally pervasive modern tradition of artistic freedom, autonomy for indi-vidual creators, and art for the sake of art. However, given the impact of governmental support to science and education, the consequences of gov-ernmental support to the arts are likely to be far-reaching.

Most discussions fail to take into account that it is not so much a matter of whether the arts are free or constrained, but rather what the forms of constraint will be. I have tried to identify types of support systems to ascertain whether government patronage is more or less inhibiting than alternatives to it, including the absence of public support altogether. As I have tried to suggest, when public support is only one of a number of support structures, it can raise patronage (and perhaps the arts) to a higher plane than in the past.

Notes

1. A variety of scholars, both Marxist and non-Marxist, have addressed themselves to analyses of the relationship of the arts and society. To mention only a few: Lalo, 1921: Hauser, 1951; Kavolis, 1972; Sorokin, 1937; Max Weber, 1958.

2. The term "artists" is used here for all categories of cultural creators, whether in the plastic or visual arts, music, literature, or dance. Distinctions between those involved particularly in fine art, as opposed to commercial or folk arts, will be made when appropriate.

3. It is necessary to limit these ideas to relatively recent time and a fairly narrow space. Primitive societies, in which art is relatively undifferentiated from religion and artisanship (even though some occupational specialization exists) will not be considered, nor will Eastern or classical civilizations, such as Greece and Rome, whose civic patronage is analyzed by Paul Veyne (1976).

4. The history of Nazi art policy reveals conflicts between groups favoring a folkish art and others promoting Expressionism; concessions to Italian Futurism for foreign policy reasons; re-sale of "degenerate" art works on the world market, rather than their summary destruction. In the Soviet Union, works long suppressed (Constructivism and Suprematism) were permitted to represent the nation at the renowned Paris-Moscow Exhibit held at the Centre Pompidou in Paris in 1980. Virtually the same works were shown in the Soviet Union in 1981 as part of the exchange agreement with France.

5. It is extremely difficult to ascertain the amount of money devoted to patronage or support by corporations, or to evaluate the amount of NEA funding which reaches artists (Netzer, 1978, Chapter 1).

6. Diana Crane has pointed out that the "anomic conditions of contemporary art, where variety is stressed at the expense of continuity, have led to withdrawal from that system by some groups of innovators." She has in mind Minimalist artists who broke with existing art establishments by crossing and re-crossing the boundary "between art and non-art" (1976:69). It should be pointed out, however, that some of them are surely being somewhat disingenuous, since a number of "uncollectible" works have become collectors' items, and some have even been incorporated into museums in some form or other. A number of artists who play the game of rejecting the system manage to use the spectacular nature of their "refusal" as a public relations device to attract buyers of their less extreme work, and do not hesitate to apply for governmental or foundation funding (Zolberg, 1980 b).

References

Adler, Judith E. 1979. *Artists in Offices: An Ethnography of an Academic Art Scene.* New Brunswick, N.J.: Transaction Books.

Adorno, Theodor. 1976. *An Introduction to the Sociology of Music.* New York: Seabury Press.

Antal, Frederick. 1970. "Social Position of the Artists: Contemporary Views on Art." In *The Sociology of Art and Literature: A Reader,* ed. M. C. Albrecht et al., New York: Praeger (orig. ed. 1948), pp. 288–92.

Badischen Kunstverein. 1980. *Widerstand Statt Anpassung: Deutsche Kunst in Widerstand gegen der Faschismus 1933–1946*. Berlin: Elefanten Press.

Becker, Howard S. 1976. "Art Worlds and Social Types." In *The Production of Culture*, ed. R. A. Peterson. Beverly Hills: Sage, pp. 41–56.

Benjamin, Walter. 1969. "The Work of Art in the Age of Mechanical Reproduction." In *Illuminations*, ed. Hannah Arendt. New York: Schocken Books (orig. ed. 1936), pp. 217–52.

Boime, Albert. 1976. "Entrepreneurial Patronage in Nineteenth Century France." In *Enterprise and Entrepreneurs in Nineteenth and Twentieth Century France*, ed. E.C. Carter, III, et al. Baltimore: Johns Hopkins Univ. Press, pp. 137–86.

Bourdieu, Pierre. 1966. *L'Amour de L'art: Les musées d'art européens et leur public*. Paris: Editions de Minuit.

Brenner, Hildegard. 1980. *La politique artistique du national-socialisme*. Paris: François Maspero.

Brooks, John. 1976. "Fueling the Arts, or Exxon as a Medici." *New York Times*, Jan. 26, sec. 2, p. 1.

Clack, George. 1981. "Congress Scrutinizes 1982 Budget." *Cultural Post*, July/August, pp. 19–22.

Clark, T. J. 1973. *The Absolute Bourgeois: Artists and Politics in France 1848–1851*. London: Thames and Hudson.

Corvisier, André. 1978. *Arts et sociétés dans l'Europe du XVIIIᵉ Siècle*. Paris: Presses Universitaires de France.

Crane, Diana. 1976. "Reward Systems in Art, Science, and Religion." In *The Production of Culture*, ed. R. A. Peterson. Beverly Hills: Sage, pp. 57–72.

DiMaggio, Paul, and Paul M. Hirsch. 1976. "Production Organizations in the Arts." In *The Production of Culture*, ed. R. A. Peterson. Beverly Hills: Sage, pp. 73–90.

Dorian, Frederick. 1964. *Commitment to Culture*. Pittsburgh: Univ. of Pittsburgh Press.

Gans, Herbert J. 1974. *Popular Culture and High Culture: An Analysis and Evaluation of Taste*. New York: Basic Books.

Gibbons, Jacqueline. 1981. "The Social and the Symbolic in the Occupation of Art Dealing." Paper presented at the American Sociological Association Meeting, Toronto.

Glueck, Grace. 1975. "These Investors Are Bullish on the Art Market." *New York Times*, Jan. 12, p. 23.

Gombrich, E.H. 1972. "Aims and Limits of Iconology." In *Symbolic Images: Studies in the Art of the Renaissance*. New York: Phaidon Press, pp. 1–25.

Hadjinicolaou, Nicos. 1978. *Art History and Class Struggle*. London: Pluto Press (orig. ed. 1973).

Harris, Neil. 1966. *The Artist in American Society: The Formative Years, 1790–1860*. New York: George Braziller.

Haskell, Francis. 1976. *Rediscoveries in Art: Some Aspects of Taste, Fashion and Collecting in England and France*. London: Phaidon.

Hauser, Arnold. 1951. *The Social History of Art*. 4 vols. New York: Vintage Books.

Henning, Edward B. 1960. "Patronage and Style in the Arts: A Suggestion Concerning Their Relations." *Journal of Aesthetics and Art Criticism*, 17:464–71.

Johnson, Priscilla. 1965. *Khrushchev and the Arts: The Politics of Soviet Culture, 1962–1964*. Cambridge, Mass.: MIT Press.

Kadushin, Charles. 1976. "Networks and Circles in the Production of Culture." In *The Production of Culture*, ed. R. A. Peterson. Beverly Hills: Sage, pp. 107–220.

Kavolis, Vytautas. 1972. *History on Art's Side: Social Dynamics in Artistic Efflorescences*. Ithaca, N.Y.: Cornell Univ. Press.

Lalo, Charles. 1921. *L'Art et la vie sociale*. Paris: Doin.

Letwin, William. 1973. "The American Foundations: Fairy Godmothers or Avenging Angels?" *Encounter*, 41:53–56.

Martorella, Rosanne. 1977. "The Relationship between Box Office and Repertoire: A Case Study of Opera." *Sociological Quarterly*, 18: 354–66.

McDonald, William F. 1969. *Federal Relief Administration and the Arts*. Columbus: Ohio State Univ. Press.

Meiss, Millard. 1951. *Painting in .Florence and Sienna after the Black Death: The Arts, Religion and Society in Mid-Fourteenth Century*. New York: Harper & Row.

Metz, Robert. 1979. "The Corporation as Art Patron: A Growth Stock." *Artnews*, 78:40–46.

Miller, Edwin H. 1959. *The Professional Writer in Elizabethan England: A Study of Nondramatic Literature*. Cambridge, Mass.: Harvard Univ. Press.

Miller, Lillian B. 1966. *Patrons and Patriotism: The Encouragement of the Fine Arts in the United States, 1790–1860*. Chicago: Univ. of Chicago Press.

Minihan, Janet. 1977. *The Nationalization of Culture: The Development of State Subsidies to the Arts in Great Britain*. New York: New York Univ. Press.

Morgenstern, Sam, ed. 1956. *Composers on Music: An Anthology of Composers' Writings from Palestrina to Copland*. New York: Random House.

Moulin, Raymonde. 1967. *Le marché de la peinture en France*. Paris: Editions de Minuit.

Nash, Dennison. 1970. "Challenge and Response in the American Composer's Career." In *The Sociology of Art and Literature: A Reader*, ed. M. C. Albrecht et al. New York: Praeger (orig. ed. 1955), pp. 256–65.

Netzer, Dick. 1978. *The Subsidized Muse: Public Support for the Arts in the United States*. New York: Cambridge Univ. Press.

O'Connor, Francis V. 1969. *Federal Support for the Visual Arts: The New Deal and Now*. New York: Graphic Society.

Otis, Philo Adams. 1924. *The Chicago Symphony Orchestra: Its Organization, Growth and Development, 1891–1924*. Chicago: Clayton F. Summy.

Oxford English Dictionary (compact ed.). 1971. 2 vols. Oxford: Clarendon Press.

Paret, Peter. 1980. *The Berlin Secession: Modernism and Its Enemies in Imperial Germany*. Cambridge, Mass.: Harvard Univ. Press, Belknap Press.

Pelles, Geraldine. 1963. *Art, Artists and Society: Origins of a Modern Dilemma*. Englewood Cliffs, N.J.: Prentice–Hall.

Peterson, Richard A. 1976. *The Production of Culture*. Beverly Hills: Sage.

Pevsner, Nicolaus. 1970. "French and Dutch Artists in the Seventeenth Century." In *The Sociology of Art and Literature: A Reader*, ed. M. C. Albrecht et al. New York: Praeger (orig. ed. 1940), pp. 363–69.

Robert, Paul. 1978. *Dictionnaire Alphabétique et Analogique de la langue française*. Paris: Société du Nouveau Littré.

Rosenbaum, Lee. 1979. "How To Choose the Chooser." *Artnews*, 78:52–59.

Rosenberg, Bernard, and Fliegl, Norris. 1965. *The Vanguard Artist: Portrait and Self-Portrait*. Chicago: Quadrangle Books.

Sabloski, Irving L. 1969. *American Music*. Chicago: Univ. of Chicago Press.

Shils, Edward. 1972. *The Intellectuals and the Powers and Other Essays*. Chicago: Univ. of Chicago Press.

Sloane, Leonard. 1979. "Collecting at the Chase: Fine Arts Stands for Good Business." *Artnews*, 78:47–51.

Sorokin, Pitirim A. 1937. *Social and Cultural Dynamics*, vol. 1. New York: American Book Company.

Trevor–Roper, Hugh. 1976. *Princes and Artists: Patronage and Ideology at Four Habsbourg Courts, 1517–1633*. New York: Harper & Row.

Teltsch, Kathleen. 1981. "Minnesota a Model of Corporate Aid to Cities." *New York Times*, July 27, p. 1.

Useem, Michael. 1976. "Government Patronage of Science and Art in America." In *The Production of Culture*, ed. R. A. Peterson. Beverly Hills: Sage, pp. 123–42.

Veyne, Paul. 1976. *Le pain et le cirque: Sociologie historique d'un pluralisme politique*. Paris: Editions du Seuil.

Weber, Max. 1958. *The Rational and Social Foundations of Music*, trans. Don Martindale et al. Carbondale: Southern Illinois Univ. Press.

Weber, William. 1975. *Music and the Middle Class: The Social Structure of Concert Life in London, Paris and Vienna*. New York: Holmes & Meier.

White, Harrison C., and Cynthia A. White. *Canvases and Careers: Institutional Change in the French Painting World*. New York: John Wiley.

Wolfe, Tom. 1976. *The Painted Word*. New York: Bantam Books.

Zolberg, Vera L. 1980a. "Autonomy for the Arts: The Dilemma of Public Funding." In *Studies in the Sociology of the Arts: Selected Lectures Held at the 9th World Congress of Sociology (Uppsala, Sweden, 1978)*, vol. 1, ed. Ivan Vitanyi. Budapest: Hungarian Institute for Culture, pp. 379–402.

1980b "Displayed Art and Performed Music: Selective Innovation and the Structure of Artistic Media." *Sociological Quarterly*, 21: 219–231.

17

The Economics
of the Performing Arts:
A Case Study
of the Major Orchestras

SAMUEL SCHWARZ

Introduction

The performing arts: how do they survive?

In this chapter, I will analyze the economic behavior of nonprofit performing arts organizations. In the first part a mode of analysis for such organizations is introduced; next the focal point of the analysis, the well-known earnings gap, is discussed. Third, the analysis is applied to the behavior of a set of seventeen major orchestras over a period of three decades. In the final part, some conclusions are offered.

The Behavior of Performing Arts Organizations

Performing arts organizations are generally in the not-for-profit sector.[1] As such, their goal is not profit maximization but the dissemination of their services to the widest audiences, subject to (1) their individual budget constraints and (2) maintaining, or increasing, the present quality of their productions. For example, a symphony orchestra is not likely to switch to popular music, even though it could increase its audience immensely.

Performing arts organizations derive "earned income" from ticket sales and   269 other direct receipts from performances. The amount of earned income is limited by the number of performances live performers can give during a given time period and the seating capacity of the halls in which the performances are given. Hence, the organization can increase its earned income only by increasing ticket prices or fees for its performances. If expenditures were to be covered solely by earned income, performances would be priced out of reach of most consumers and attendance would be limited to a select group. Since their goal is to attract large audiences, performing arts organizations hesitate to raise prices even when it is profitable. This sentiment is expressed in the following excerpts from a letter to subscribers by the general director of the New York City Opera, Beverly Sills:

> . . . I've always believed that the arts are for everyone and that opera is not just for the elite. I knew I had to do something. So, as of today, I am cutting the cost of all City Opera subscriptions by 20% across the board.
>
> In the Spring of 1981, we raised our prices. We made money but lost people. This season we will finish $600,000 ahead at the box office, but our audiences who come to see our terrific young artists are down each night by 7 to 8%. I know what it feels like to look out on an audience and see empty seats and this spring we want all of our opera lovers back in them. . . . We're cutting back our prices so that everybody can afford to enjoy our performances. [*New York Times*, 1981:C27.]

Since earned income is insufficient to cover costs, another source must be found. As members of the nonprofit sector, performing arts organizations also have unearned, or contributed, income. Contributed income can come from both the private and government sectors and takes several forms. Part comes from contributions to be used during the period of its donation; part is in the form of earnings derived from long-term contributions, or endowments; and part is from principal that is transferred to operations, i.e., invasion of endowment capital. Although endowment earnings are sometimes treated as earned income, conceptually they are simply a long-term stream of contributions. For when donors contribute capital for endowment funds, they are really setting up mechanisms whereby contributions are made annually to the organization, in the form of earnings on the endowments, irrespective of whether they personally own the funds and make the contributions annually, or make all the annual contributions in advance by donating the funds to the organization. Hence, such earnings should be considered contributions to the organization. Regarding transfer of corpus principal, it should be treated separately from other earned income, even though it is derived from long-term contributions. For such use was not intended by the donor, and, furthermore, it indicates the lack of ability by the organization to balance the budget through earned income and contributions. Indeed, performing arts organizations make such transfers only exceptionally.

Returning to our overall budget constraint, each performing arts organization must balance its expenditures, earned income, and contributions—not necessarily on a year-by-year basis, but on a long-term basis, i.e., it cannot allow its deficit to accumulate indefinitely. It should be noted that this long term may span several decades, especially when the organization has an endowment corpus. For example, we shall see later that, in the past fifteen years, the major orchestras have been closing their deficits by dipping into their accumulated endowments. We have a system, then, where earned income, unearned income, and expenditures—as well as their components—are simultaneously determined, subject to the nonprofit budget constraint. Consequently, a change in any component is not an isolated event, but must also affect other components in order to bring the system back into balance. Our mode of analysis allows us to analyze the system as a whole, as well as the behavior and determinants of every component of the system. But the focal point of our analysis is the gap between expenditures and earned income, which we discuss more fully in the next section.

The Earnings Gap as the Center of Analysis[2]

In their economic analysis of the performing arts, Baumol and Bowen (1966) introduced the concept of an ever-increasing need for support of performing arts organizations. Ever since, analysis of the performing arts has focused on the *earnings gap*,[3] the difference between expenditures and earned income. It has been taken as a

> . . . fact, well-known to professionals in the field, that the labor-intensive performing arts, whose productivity cannot keep pace with the ever-increasing productivity of the industrial economy in which they exist, are faced with an ever-increasing gap between their operating costs and their earned income. The costs, principally wages, are set by the cost level of the economy; the earned income is limited by the inherent limit on the number of performances live performers can give and the number of seats in the halls [Ford Foundation, 1974:7].

The central proposition of the Baumol–Bowen study—the natural tendency of the earnings gap to widen as the "inescapable result of the technology of live performance" (1966:162)—is certainly correct, but it covers only a part of the story. For we must also take account of a widening of the gap due to an increase in output.

A simple example will illustrate. Suppose an arts organization has ten performances annually with expenditures of $50,000, earned income of $40,000, and a gap of $10,000. It now doubles its season to twenty performances and, for the sake of simplicity, its expenditures increase to $100,000, earned income to $80,000, and gap to $20,000. We have, then, a doubling of the gap without any increase in player wages.

If we now take the Baumol–Bowen thesis to its logical conclusion, it should be restated as follows: at the *same level of output*, there is a natural tendency for the earnings gap to widen as a result of the technology of live performance, allowing only for limited increases in productivity, which we shall call its "natural growth"; in addition, any increase in output will increase the earnings gap. This implies, then, that any measure of the growth rate of the earnings gap contains two elements: its natural growth and its growth based on an increase in output, which we shall call its "output growth." Hence, in order to measure the "natural growth" of the earnings gap, we must maintain output constant. Indeed, this is the true measure of the underlying growth rate dictated by the logical structure of the Baumol–Bowen thesis.

It should be noted that "output" in the arts consists not only of the number of performances, but also has a "quality" dimension as well; for a Beethoven symphony played by the Chicago Symphony Orchestra is not the same as when played by a high school band. Some determinants of quality are the number of players, the quality of players, and even the physical setting of the performance. Given a constant level of earned income, an increase in "output" will increase the earnings gap even in the absence of "natural growth." This, then, is the second segment of the growth of the earnings gap.

Our analysis leads us to a new interpretation of the earnings gap. Researchers have usually looked at only one side of the coin—growth of costs—forgetting that the other side consists of *contributions*. For without contributions there is no earnings gap. Thus, if, for example, a donor contributes $1 million to an arts organization, its earnings gap can be increased by $1 million. On the other hand, when contributions slacken, the organization is forced to contract and decrease the gap. This, then, points to a new interpretation of the earnings gap.

Traditionally, the total national earnings gap has been interpreted as "the amount which, at the present time, society must be prepared to contribute, by some means, if the nation's existing performing arts organizations are to be kept solvent" (Baumol and Bowen, 1966:150). Thus, projections of large growth rates of the earnings gap have served as the rationale for more support for the arts especially from government (cf. Ford Foundation, 1974: 104). This would imply that projection of a smaller growth rate indicates less need for support of the arts.

Our previous analysis indicates that precisely the contrary is usually true. Growth rates of the earnings gap *above* the natural growth rate indicate an expansion of the arts and are a sign of good health, and those *below* the natural growth rate are an indication of contraction and poor health for the arts.

This expansion and contraction can take the form of changes in both quantity and quality. For example, let us look at what has happened in the live professional theater: "smaller casts, smaller orchestras, . . . fuller houses, larger houses, lower-salaried casts, sparser sets" (Anderson and Maltezou, 1977:64). Although Anderson and Maltezou called these changes "economizing" and stated that they have "no way to judge the extent to which the economic condition of the theatre has been maintained and/or improved at the expense of artistry" (1977:64), the changes were, in great part, a decrease in "output." Of course, if we leave the vegetables out of the soup, we have "economized." Only now we have hot water and not soup.

Empirical Application: A Case Study of the Major Orchestras[4]

In this section, we want to subject our analysis to empirical application. In order to get meaningful results for behavior over time, one needs continuous data over an extended period. Since no such data base was available, we set out to create one. We therefore went to the only long-time series of raw data on the arts, gathered by the American Symphony Orchestra League (ASOL). We used the data on major symphony orchestras for the period 1949–1950 through 1978–1979 (except for the 1959–1960 season, for which there is no known existing data). Twenty-three major orchestras reported throughout this period, the rest entering the ranks of the majors during this period. However, some of these did not report for all the years, and we had to omit six orchestras.

The remaining seventeen are as follows: Baltimore, Buffalo, Chicago, Cincinnati, Cleveland, Dallas, Houston, Indianapolis, Los Angeles, Minnesota (formerly Minneapolis), National (formerly Washington), New Orleans, New York, Philadelphia, Pittsburgh, St. Louis, and San Francisco. These seventeen constitute a good cross-section of major orchestras, in terms of both expenditure levels and geographic locations. In terms of size, the depleted group contains one of the top orchestras, three of the smallest, and two of the middle range. The seventeen included either reported all the years, or missed a year or two, which we estimated so as not to bias the total amounts.

Figures 1 and 2 show, respectively, the total earnings gap and deficit for our seventeen orchestras over the entire period. In order to understand their

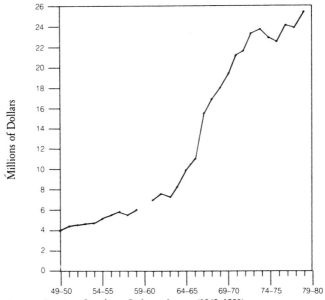

SOURCE: American Symphony Orchestra League (1949–1980).
NOTE: Figures have been deflated by the Consumer Price Index (1967 = 1.0).

Fig. 1. Total Earnings Gap (1967 Dollars)

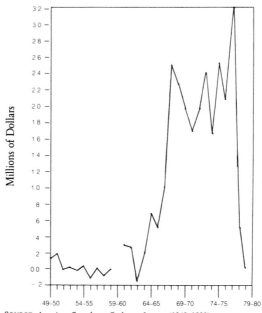

SOURCE: American Symphony Orchestra League (1949–1980).
NOTE: Figures have been deflated by the Consumer Price Index (1967 = 1.0).

Fig. 2. Total Deficit (1967 Dollars)

patterns as well as the finances of the orchestras in general, let us look more closely at the behavior of our system during these thirty years.

Total expenditures are determined by the amount of output and the prices of the factors used in producing that output. Since the performing arts are very labor-intensive, labor has a direct role in determining total expenditures through its key role in the determination of both the number of pay periods (which, in turn, determines output) and the wage rate per period. Thus, in order to determine total expenditures, we must look at the determination of the two dimensions of artistic wages, the rate per period and the number of periods. Whereas the prices of other factors of production are primarily exogenously determined (save for the wages of nonartistic personnel), artistic wages are endogenously determined, viz., they are affected by financial conditions in the orchestras. Hence, in order to analyze the determination of wages we must also look at the other side of the coin: income to the orchestras.

This immediately brings us to the long-standing question whether labor presses its demands even in the absence of an expected increase in income. This question arose with regard to the relationship between the tremendous wage increases of the 1960s and the huge symphony program instituted by the Ford Foundation in 1966.[5] Because the two events occurred almost simultaneously, some argue that the Ford Foundation grants set off the huge increases in wages. On the other hand, some argue that although the grants further stimulated player demands, these rising demands existed even in the absence of the Ford grants. We could point to the increases before 1966 to support this point. To obtain a fuller understanding, we must know the exact timing of the events and also look at what happened before and after the immediate period.

Although the Ford Symphony Program was not announced until 6 July 1966, there was a long planning stage—according to one reliable informant, at least three years—during which period it became known to the orchestras and players that such a program was in the planning. Hence, the salary increases in the preceding two years were arranged with the expectation of funding. In addition, a period of high expectations was brought on in the early 1960s by the Kennedy Administration, and a belief in a cultural boom.

Because of budget constraints, player demands will not be met no matter how strong unless there is an equal increase in the supply of funds. A recent case in point is that of New York City. Even the most powerful unions had to cut back their demands when the city was on the verge of bankruptcy. So long as the unions are aware of a supply—or an expected supply—of funds, they will press their demands. The expected supply need not be a definite source of funds, simply the expectation that somehow the unions' demands will always be met, as was the behavior in New York City. However, once the supply of funds dries up, unions will necessarily taper their demands rather than force the orchestra to close down, which is precisely what has happened in recent years. After the Ford Foundation program started, labor further pressed its demands, driving the ratio of player wages to manufacturing wages higher and higher. Yet, after driving it to a level that could not be maintained, the ratio dropped. During the 1970s, player wages just kept pace with the general price level.

If increases in expenditures can maintain themselves only if there is an increase in income, how can income be increased? Given the nature of demand for regular series tickets, ticket revenue can be increased by increasing ticket prices. However, because ticket income is only a part—and an increasingly smaller part—of total income, and because arts organizations hesitate to raise prices so as not to decrease admissions, increases in ticket income alone can only support a small increase in expenditures. This, then, brings us to contributions: specifically, can the orchestras influence contributions and thus have another "instrument" in balancing the budget, or are contributions determined elsewhere and treated by the orchestras as a "given" variable, which is outside their influence?

It is clear from the data that before 1960 the orchestras as a whole did not attempt to increase the level of orchestra contributions relative to total philanthropy. Rather, they treated contributions more or less as a deus ex machina: whatever came, they took, even though they were able to increase them as they later proved, especially after 1966. How, then, did they balance their budgets?

For the first decade, the finances of the major orchestras followed a very passive path: (1) output was relatively constant, while the players' real weekly salaries went up only slightly—the relative position of orchestra players declining—and expenditures grew slowly; (2) ticket price increases kept up roughly with those of the general price level, but the last half of the decade showed an increase in admissions and, therefore—because of the inelasticity of demand for regular subscription series tickets with respect to their real price—ticket income increased more than the general price level; (3) real per capita contributions increased somewhat, mainly because of increased income from endowments and grants, as those from the Regular Maintenance Fund (the yearly fundraising campaign) remained about constant. The goal was a zero-deficit budget, and indeed, this was more or less attained. Note the fluctuations of surpluses and deficits around the zero-level in Figure 2. The behavior of the period closely resembled that of a "natural growth" of the earnings gap at a constant level of output.

Then came the 1960s: grant income increased, union power increased, and expectations rose. Wage rates and length of season began increasing. But it was not until even greater expectations and their realization—the Ford program—that wages began skyrocketing. The program affected the orchestras in several ways. During this decade: (1) the average length of season increased by more than 50 percent; (2) the relative weekly wage rate increased to a new high level; (3) the fundraising mechanism was further developed so that not only endowment income was increased (as a result of the growing endowment corpus) but also the regular maintenance fund contributions increased greatly relative to total philanthropy;* and (4) a new goal was set for the level of the total deficit: about $2 million (Fig. 2). Rather than striving for a zero-deficit level, with an increased endowment corpus orchestras now sought to balance their budgets over the very long run.

The orchestras had now reached a new level of operation and, as a result, a much larger earnings gap and a continuous annual deficit. Because the ASOL data do not contain any information on how the orchestras funded the deficit, we turned to data gathered by the Ford Foundation for the years 1965–1966 through 1973–1974. The latter provided data on *corpus principal transferred to operations* for sixteen of our seventeen orchestras.

It is apparent from the data that the major orchestras dipped heavily into their endowment corpus to meet the deficit. Having set the deficit level at about $2 million, how did they balance their budgets up to this deficit?

Ticket prices increased at a quicker rate than during the 1950s, following a steady trend, but because of inflation, real prices, after first increasing, leveled off. As a result of this and of a steady increase in admissions, real ticket income first increased and then leveled off at the end of the decade. Because of the relatively small increase in real ticket income and the unprecedented rise in the orchestras' level of operation, player wage rates, and, hence, expenditures, the now immensely increased earnings gap was funded by an equally unprecedented rise in contributions, not only in income from grants and endowments but also from regular contributions and special projects. The behavior of the 1960s produced an increased earnings gap as a result not only of orchestras' "natural growth," but also of increases in output and wage rates immensely greater than those in the general economy.

After the dynamic growth of the 1960s, the 1970s were a period of settling down. With many of our orchestras at or close to seasons of fifty-two weeks, the average length of season increased only slightly. At the same time, real player wage rates remained constant over the decade, and hence real expenditures grew at a slower pace. Total real contributed income grew at a much slower rate than during the 1960s, and real ticket income increased somewhat.

It appears that the huge wage increases could no longer go on, and a period

---

*This was triggered by the Ford Foundation's requiring matching endowment funds during the first five years of the program. For this reason, it was not until 1969–1970 that relative contributions increased, since for the first three years much of the increase in contributions went to the endowment corpus rather than to meeting operating expenditures. Even after the matching funds period was over, the machinery was in place, with new sources of contributions opened.

of relatively natural growth of the earnings gap again ensued. Now, however, it was of a different and greater gap at a much higher level of output than that of the 1950s, and hence it required a greater growth of contributions. Part of the increase in contributions came from a continued steady depletion of their endowment capital, a policy that seemed firmly implanted. However, as is obvious from Figure 2, during the last two years the orchestras reduced their deficit level significantly, as their endowments became progressively smaller. This trend was continued in 1979–1980 and may continue through the next decade.

Conclusion

In this chapter, we have restated the accepted analysis of performing arts organizations and have expanded on it. We have dissected the growth of the earnings gap into two components: "natural" and "output" growth. Furthermore, we have introduced the concept of a unified system under an overall nonprofit budget constraint. This concept was then applied to a set of seventeen major orchestras over three decades. Our historical analysis showed these orchestras going from passive growth of the earnings gap in the 1950s to unusually dynamic growth in the 1960s, and then back again to slower growth in the 1970s; and all varied with the rate of contributed income. With the expected cuts in government aid in the 1980s, one can expect a continued slowdown in the next decade.

Notes

1. For a broader development of the economic behavior of arts organizations, see Schwarz and Greenfield (1977:18–31).

2. This section is excerpted from a larger article currently being prepared for journal publication.

3. This term was coined later, in the Ford Foundation study (1974). Baumol and Bowen (1966) referred to it as the "income gap."

4. This section is based on our work in an earlier study; see Schwarz and Greenfield (1977). The reader may consult that study for more detail.

5. The foundation committed over $39 million to the seventeen major U.S. orchestras: about $30 million to be held as endowment trusts until 1976 and to be released to the orchestra if it raised an agreed-upon sum by 1971

to be held in an endowment trust until 1976; and about $9 million in expendable grants and development grants over the period 1966–1971.

References

American Symphony Orchestra League. 1949–1980. *Annual Report*. Vienna, Va.: American Symphony Orchestra League.

Anderson, Robert J., Jr., and Sonia P. Maltezou. 1977. "The Economic Condition of the Live Professional Theatre in America." In *Research in the Arts: Proceedings of the Conference on Policy-Related Studies of the National Endowment for the Arts*. Washington, D.C.: The National Endowment for the Arts, the Walters Art Gallery, Baltimore, pp. 63–66.

Baumol, William J., and William G. Bowen. 1966. *Performing Arts: The Economic Dilemma*. New York: The Twentieth Century Fund.

Ford Foundation. 1974. *The Finances of the Performing Arts*, vol. 1. New York: The Ford Foundation.

Schwarz, Samuel, and Harry I. Greenfield. 1977. *A Model for the Analysis of the Performing Arts: A Case Study of the Major Orchestras*. New York: Center for Policy Research.

18

Art and Public Policy: Ideologies for Aesthetic Welfare

ROSANNE MARTORELLA

Economic Ideology: Nonprofit Art

Indirect subsidization of the arts has existed for over fifty years, and has included tax exemptions, land grants, urban renewal programs, park and recreation subsidies, and Title II, which provided funds through state education programs. The National Endowment for the Arts was formed in 1965, under President Johnson, with a $2.5 million budget. By 1976, its budget had risen to $126 million. In 1976, NEA awarded block grants of $205,000 to every state and encouraged the development of state arts councils. As a result, twelve hundred community arts agencies presently exist (DiMaggio and Useem, 1978). Netzer outlines government support to the arts in *The Subsidized Muse* (1978). Table 18 compares government grants with other income sources, including private contributions (unearned income). During the periods covered by the table, government was not the largest income source, but it has subsequently increased. In his analysis, Netzer concludes that government support, although minimal, has kept ticket prices down and has not discouraged other private contributions (pp. 101–2). By 1980, National Endowment for the Arts appropriations totaled $155 million, but this sum was quickly cut in half under the Reagan administration.

The establishment of the National Endowment for the Arts precipitated a need for a political lobby for the arts. Performing arts organizations found   281

Table 18. Percent Distribution of Total Operating Income, by Source, for Performing Arts Organizations

Source of Income	Theater Companies		Metropolitan Opera		Other Operas		Symphonies		Dance Companies		All, except Metropolitan Opera	
	1965–66	1973–74	1965–66	1973–74	1965–66	1973–74	1965–66	1973–74	1965–66	1973–74	1965–66	1973–74
Government Sources*	4	13	†	5	2	10	5	15	11	11	5	13
Ticket Income	68	52	52	44	50	40	38	30	42	27	44	35
Services Income, Nongovt.	1	2	11	11	3	5	9	9	8	19	7	9
Recordings, Radio, TV, Films	—	†	3	2	—	†	3	2	†	2	2	2
Nonperformance Earned Income‡	6	7	5	10	5	3	11	5	5	6	9	5
Other Unearned Income§	21	26	28	28	39	41	33	40	34	34	33	37
Total	100	100	100	100	100	100	100	100	100	100	100	100
Number of Organizations Covered	27	31	1	1	30	28	91	78	17	15	165	152

SOURCE: Netzer (1978:101).

NOTE: Because of rounding, detail may not add to 100 percent.

*Includes services income from government sources and government grants.

†Less than 1/2 of 1 percent.

‡ Income from performance of other groups, school income, and receipts from concessions, program advertising, facilities rentals, etc.

§Unearned income other than government grants, that is, individual, business, and foundation contributions and grants and endowment earnings.

that they had to coordinate their lobbying activities with their "competitors," and they looked increasingly to businessmen and financiers with political connections to integrate such efforts.

In the late 1960s and early 1970s, arts companies began for the first time to scrutinize their budgets, study their audiences (by conducting surveys), and employ top labor negotiators. In an attempt to legitimate their public funding requests, the organizations set out to prove that the arts were serious business enterprises, whose nonprofit bases had profound consequences both on the job market and life-style of a civilized culture, and on the economic survival and vitality of the already decaying inner cities of the major metropolitan centers (Baumol and Bowen, 1966; Martorella, 1975; Nelson, 1976; New York State Council on the Arts, 1973).

The desperate economic situation was made visible with the publication of *The Performing Arts: The Economic Dilemma* (Baumol and Bowen, 1966) and the Rockefeller Foundation report, *The Performing Arts: Problems and Prospects* (1965). The economic impasse caused by a constantly enlarging gap between income and expenses has integrated the fragmented and diverse interests of each of the performing arts into a common cause. Individual attempts at fund raising and competitive attitudes had to take a secondary position. Each organization came to realize that in numbers there was strength. Out of the uncontrollable economic burdens of the early 1970s, a coalition emerged. Board members, aided by lawyers, corporate executives, and volunteers, applied legal and organizational skills to the arts. Numerous committees, forums, and conventions were formed. The obvious place to begin was by coordinating the various fund-raising committees and councils of individual companies. Next came the integration of arts centers, regions, and councils under the Partnership for the Arts, Washington, D.C. The various state councils and their regional organizations incorporated under the Associated Councils of the Arts. This insured a liaison with politicians in state legislatures and the federal government. Other committees, like the Business Committee for the Arts and the Lincoln Center Consolidated Corporate Fund Drive, both in New York City, acted to spur corporate interest in and consciousness of the arts. Individual guilds, committees, and devotees have lobbied for the appropriations bills in the Senate and Congress.

Management began to say, "This is it! We've done our job and the arts just can't survive unless the government steps in to help." This was no half-hearted approach. The campaign was direct, concisely verbalized, and loud.

The music critic of the *New York Times* joined in the plea. Applying the economic-legitimacy argument, Harold Schonberg stated:

> . . . that the arts in America are authentically Big Business, as fully worthy of Federal help as Lockheed or Grumman (the arts employ more, spend more, take in more); that the leaders of symphony orchestras, opera houses,

museums, and drama companies throughout the country are solid businessmen, not radicals or egg-heads, anxious to throw away money in a great
cultural boon-doggle [1973a].

Later, he wrote:

The National Endowment, advised by the various arts councils and Partnership for the Arts, is not going to scatter money around promiscuously.
Partnership for the Arts, for one, has worked up a very severe set of criteria
for organizations seeking aid, and has also suggested that the total of state
and federal help for any organization should not exceed the amount of
private support that organizations can raise. The people running American
cultural organizations are not radicals; they are bankers, brokers, philan-
thropists, and businessmen who are as much exponents of private enterprise
as anybody in the inner circles of the present Government [1973b].

When the federal government came in strongly in the mid-1970s with
subsidies of over $100 million, arts people dreamed of greater support for
individual artists and freedom from the constraints of the market. Museum
administrators hoped for more possibilities to commission artists, while performing arts directors longed for innovation in repertoire. Unfortunately,
economic constraints continued to prevail, given the conservative position
lobbyists themselves took, as well as the government's desire to allocate monies
nationally to insure an egalitarian and nonelitest distribution of public funds.
Small towns and folk art, therefore, benefited from this policy.

Political Ideology: The Democratization of Art

Arts people thought that, in asking the biggest business in America for help,
a particular definition and role of the arts had to be "legitimated" with a style
and vocabulary politicians, lawyers, and bankers could understand. To this
end, state arts councils, regional committees, board members, and corporations sought to "organize" by forming coalitions on a national level under
the ideological umbrella "art for the community."

To provide information on the arts to the public and politicians, arts
councils, performing arts companies, and museums undertook studies: councils commissioned consultant firms, formed volunteer committees, or engaged
the services of societies like Opera America, the American Symphony Orchestra League, and the National Research Center on the Arts. What is
significant is the part played by the data thus accumulated in providing a
justificatory and ideological definition of the arts: "the arts reflect the needs
and interests of the community." Arts proponents pointed to the enormous
attendance at concerts, the ethnic programs supported by arts centers, and

the economy's inflationary effect on the arts. Government appropriations, it was argued, represented a meager 10 percent of the $2 billion spent by the American people on the nonprofit arts. All of these statistics pointed to the ubiquitousness of the arts and their nationwide financial need. Art as a reflection of, and insofar as supported by, the public, became the rationale and legitimation for government subsidies.

> Non-profit cultural organizations employ 33,000 people—as many persons as the State steel industry! The operating expenditures of non-profit cultural institutions, $350-million, are more than half the operating expenditures of the State's agricultural business. . . Arts and cultural institutions in New York State have a total estimated value of more than $6-million assets, properties, and holdings, equivalent to the national holdings of General Motors Corporation. . . .The arts swell the tourist industry, which is a $3.5 billion activity in the State. The salaries of those working in the arts are taxed and all those buildings and activities are customers of the local trades. [New York Council on the Arts, 1973.]

And so the statistics continued to be accumulated and disseminated to legitimate art, but not on a philosophical level or for their own sake. The final step of such lobbying was to rid art of its elitist image and align it with cross-cultural, cross-class, and cross-geographic aims. The study *Arts and the People* did much to stress the importance to the arts of individuals from all classes, interest groups, and neighborhoods. Its authors viewed the arts as representative of the "ethnics," and pointed to the relation of the arts to social problems. Thus, the report commented, "And this is true in the city and country and regardless of social background or age. In New York City schools where absenteeism in public high schools rises about 28% in some cases, it drops to 5% for arts activities" (National Council of the Arts, 1973a).

In 1966, at the Central Opera Service Convention in Washington, D.C., Charles Young, chairman of the executive committee of the National Council of the Arts, defined the role of the arts in a democratic setting:

> I think the reason the public subsidy is necessary is because we are moving as a democracy to the place where the arts are no longer the province of the elite; where we must increasingly take care of both quality and quantity. . .and stress. . . the importance of always keeping the artist—the performer, as well as the creative artist—as the focal point, whether the discussion revolve[s]. . . around artistic administration or budgets.

The ideological basis of such developments is easily exposed. The history of art, the proliferation of various schools and styles of art, and the present arts consumer (DiMaggio and Useem, 1978) all suggest that historically only upper-class patrons have had the status and power to influence art content and style. Fox (1976:6) specifically reveals the interlocking relationships of decision makers affecting the arts from both the government and corporate worlds. He writes:

> The *taste culture*, to use Gans' term, most catered to by government arts agencies is the upper-middle one. Public subsidies, for the most part, are not spent on either mass culture or high culture (creator-oriented) products. Secondly, those upper-middle taste institutions which get the bulk of the government subsidies are either controlled or heavily influenced by the very wealthy.

Opera, perhaps more than any other of the performing arts, has had to work toward stripping itself of its patrician roots and its image as an elitist institution. The "big business" approach to securing subsidies for the arts did much to point to the desperate need for government support and to legitimate ideologically the arts in American society. People in the arts are redefining themselves as "practical, democratic, egalitarian, expedient, and middle class," in order to continue receiving government subsidization.

Public Accountability: Art as Service

Government has had profound consequences on the arts, despite its naively accepted claim that it provides financial aid independent of artistic decision making: increased bureaucratization of the arts, support to conservative institutions, the proliferation of standard repertoire according to criteria established by NEA, and formalization of artistic careers. The role of the arts is being redefined as public policy is being formed.

The publication of Herbert Gans's book *Popular Culture and High Culture* (1974) did much for the support of popular culture. Gans asserted that high culture is ideological, without acknowledging the manipulative and political implications of mass culture. His relativistic position on art led him to accept all culture equally. Unfortunately, such liberalism led him to view art as a "service." After government intervention, art is no longer analyzed in terms of its primary productive function (creater-orientation), but is seen in terms of who and what purposes are served by art (Bensman, 1973). "Art as service" has affected the growth of the arts in the United States. In the beginning, the cities and prestigious music companies claimed larger percentages of government monies, but more recently, government has aided the arts' extension into isolated and rural areas of the United States. This trend has occurred on both national and state levels. For example, up-state legislators in New York have criticized the dominant role of urban regions, especially New York City, in utilizing government revenue.

Analogies of art to other nonprofit, government-sponsored services, however, neglect to address the unique nature and dilemma of the arts in American society today. It is no wonder, therefore, that government funding has come to support extra-aesthetic goals and ancillary occupations (for example, managers and administrators). In so doing, government claims artistic autonomy. Yet, the future seems to indicate a leveling off of funding, and competition for scarce revenue (Netzer, 1978).

Government intervention came when arts companies and museums threatened bankruptcy and curtailed new productions. The economic justification continued to be legitimate. Given the nature of the "product" and its minority support, however, the arts will always have economic problems. Idealized notions about the importance of "culture" in a democratic society had to emerge to re-inforce the economic arguments. In typically American fashion, the synthesis of economic justification with the democratization of the classical arts has resulted in a specific resolution on the issue of "accountability": public funds must serve public interests.

References

Arts Management News Service. 1976. "State Programs Reach Out to Reach New Audiences." No. 98 (November–December):1.

Associated Council of the Arts. 1975. *Americans and the Arts (A Survey of Attitudes Toward and Participation in the Arts and Cultures of the U.S. Public)*. New York: National Research Center of the Arts, Inc. (570 Seventh Avenue, New York, N.Y. 10018).

Bensman, Joseph. 1973. "The Future of Cultural Services." *Journal of Aesthetic Education*, 7 (October):81–96.

Burgard, Ralph. 1976. *The Creative Community: Report of a Creative Plan That Outlines the Potential Role of Future Community Arts Councils or Their Alternatives*. New York: Association of Council of the Arts.

Cornwell, Terri. 1982. "Democracy and the Arts." Mimeographed. Dept of Political Science, University of Maryland.

DiMaggio, Paul, and Michael Useem. 1978. "Cultural Property and Public Policy: Emerging Tensions in Government Support for the Arts." *Social Research*, 45:356–89.

Donner, William H. 1975. *A Survey of Art Administration Training in the U.S. and Canada*. New York: Donner Foundation.

Eddy, Junius. 1970. *A Review of Federal Programs Supporting the Arts in Education*. New York: Ford Foundation.

Ford Foundation. 1974. *The Finances of the Performing Arts*. New York: Ford Foundation.

Fox, Douglas M. 1976. "Government Support of the Arts." *Public Administration Review*, 36:451–54.

Franz, Peter. 1973. *Cultural Policy in the Federal Republic of Germany*. Paris: UNESCO.

Gans, Herbert J. 1974. *Popular Culture and High Culture*. New York: Basic Books.

Greyser, Stephen A. (ed.). 1973. *Cultural Policy and Arts Administration*. Cambridge, Mass.: Harvard Univ. Press.

Harris, John. 1970. *Government Support of the Arts in Great Britain*. University: Univ. of Alabama Press.

Jones, Charles O., and Robert D. Thomas. 1976. *Public Policy Making in a Federal System V.III*. New York: Russell Sage.

Kavolis, Vytautas. 1973. "The Institutional Structure of Cultural Services." *Journal of Aesthetic Education*, 7:63–80.

Levi, Albert William. 1973. "Art and the General Welfare." *Journal of Aesthetic Education*, 7:39–48.

Metropolitan Opera. 1974. *White Paper*. New York: Metropolitan Opera Association.

Mulcahy, Kevin V. 1975. "The Administration of Cultural Affairs: The Case of New York City." Paper presented at the 71st Annual Meeting of the American Political Science Association, San Francisco, September.

National Committee for Cultural Resources. 1975. *National Report on the Arts*. New York: NCFCR.

National Council of the Arts. 1973a. *Arts and the People*. New York: Cranford Wood Co.

   1973b A *Study of the Non-Profit Arts and Cultural Industry in New York State*. New York: Cranford Wood Co.

National Endowment for the Arts. 1974. *Museums: USA*. Washington, D.C.:NEA.

   1975–76 *NEA Guide to Programs*. Washington, D.C.: U.S. Government Printing Office.

Nelson, Charles A., and Federick J. Turk. 1976. *Financial Management for the Arts: A Guidebook for Arts Organizations*. New York: American Council for the Arts.

Netzer, Dick. 1978. *The Subsidized Muse: Public Support for the Arts in the United States*. New York: Cambridge Univ. Press.

New York State Council on the Arts. 1973. A *Study of the Arts and Cultural Non-Profit Industry in New York State*. New York: Cranford Wood Co.

Nielsen, Waldemar A. 1972. *The Big Foundations*. New York: Columbia Univ. Press.

Reiss, Alvin H. 1974. *The Arts Management Handbook*, rev. 2d ed. New York: Law–Arts.

Rockefeller Foundation. 1965. *The Performing Arts: Problems and Prospects*. New York: McGraw–Hill.

19

Interview: Daniel Fallon

Corporate Support for the Arts

R.M.   *What is the role of the corporation in supporting the arts?*
D.F.   *This depends entirely on the corporation. There are as many reasons for this as there are corporations . . . No one reason exists. One can generalize with two basic motives: first, philosphical. It's a good thing for the corporation to be doing! They are located in communities, with customers, suppliers, employees, and shareholders. There are a number of different publics that corporations have to be accountable to. In answer to pressures from these various publics, it is good sound business to support the arts. This has been enhanced by the fact that the arts have become much more popular. Both management and employees on the assembly line, are among the people interested in the arts. Companies are seen to be good neighbors in those communities that do support the arts. Second, pragmatic. It's just good business, and has to do with corporate image. While one cannot measure "corporate image" everybody knows that corporate image is important. Pragmatically, by their very nature, the arts are visible in our society. For example, a chemical company may be spending millions of dollars on research; this fact doesn't reach the public unless a major discovery is made. No one sees what they do. The arts rely on visibility, and if corporations associate with the arts, which symbolize quality, the corporations get a quality image too. Some companies even go so far as*

Daniel Fallon is Director of Communications at the Business Committee for the Arts in New York City. He received his Ph.D. from Yale University in Music. He was interviewed by Rosanne Martorella in his office in New York City in February 1982.   289 to say that supporting the arts is very inexpensive public relations. The arts provide a lot of mention for companies to get listed in society and art review columns as well. Their names appear on programs, dinner announcements, reception committee bulletins, etc. If the right people are at the opening, it puts them [the corporations] in good company. It's really very inexpensive "PR". I don't find anything bad about this. The arts aren't used for promotion or sales; all the companies want is a "thank you."

R.M.   Can you give me some examples of corporate support?

D.F.   SCM is a good example of a company that was growing, and wanted their company name to be known. It's a good way to get a lot of good press, and to promote the company.

Another company wants to be invisible, to avoid criticism about having any ulterior motive for their support to the arts; they feel that the right people will find out anyway about their support. They do not want to be visible; they want to avoid any criticism that their motives are anything but honorable.

Exxon is a company that has gone out on a limb in their support for American composers, and American theater, including the avant-garde. They are involved in exposing American composers, getting them performing contracts. Of course, their corporate grants officer is a Ph.D. in English, and knows very well what is going on. At a recent conference, he showed us [the audience] two reviews on programs sponsored by Exxon, which were experimental. One [review] praised Exxon for underwriting something experimental, and for using their resources as a sort of risk or venture capital. On the other hand, the other review criticized the adventuresomeness of Exxon, and said how ridiculous they were for supporting such an esoteric piece!

Changes in Corporate Support

R.M.   Mr. Fallon, have there been any significant changes with regard to corporate support?

D.F.   When the Business Committee for the Arts was formed in 1967, our early mission was to get corporations interested in this idea. Back in the 60s, this idea for many CEOs was farfetched. It has changed because the nature of management has changed. Corporate managers not only see themselves as making a profit. They realize they have a lot of constituents that they are answerable to. The corporation is an entity in society. Corporate executives make speeches on everything, including the current administration; and one of these issues is their

Another change since 1967 has been the dollar increase, and the growing number of corporations involved. Our group [BCA] has served as a catalyst. Table 19 gives a picture of the dollar increase since 1967.

Issues in Corporate Support

R.M.: *What is the current relationship between corporate giving and government policy?*

D.F.: *Since the government is now looking to the corporation to offset its budget cuts, we feel we can now talk louder and faster. We have always existed to encourage corporate giving.*

There is some truth that NEA funding encourages corporate support, since a grant from NEA gives credibility to the recipient. But it distorts the picture that corporations wouldn't be doing it on their own. I think corporate support would have grown anyway. It's two separate issues. Corporations aren't going to get involved simply because the government gives a stamp of approval. On the other hand, some corporations do not have the internal mechanisms to evaluate art programs.

In the summer of 1981, the amount of pretax earnings that a corporation can give to philanthropy is up to 10 percent. Most corporations give around 1 percent. However, there are the "5 percent clubs." These clubs are hard to evolve in a highly diverse community. What works for Minneapolis may not work in New York. In Minneapolis, the government, community, and business leaders all know each other, they have lunch every week, belong to the same clubs, and it works there.

Table 19. Business Support of the Arts

Year	Amount
1967	$ 22 million
1970	68 million
1973	144 million
1976	221 million
1979	436 million

SOURCE: Business Committee for the Arts, *Triennial Survey of Business Support of the Arts*, 1979. New York: Business Committee for the Arts, 1501 Broadway, New York, N.Y. 10036.

R.M.: *How do corporate support programs resolve the dilemma between meeting the diverse interests of a general public, the community, or the clients they serve, the product it produces, and a board of trustees who may not want to see profits spent on social responsibility programs?*

D.F.: *It is a balance of these factors. Lindley Clark feels that the corporation is there to make a profit, pay its shareholders, and not give to charity itself, but to have individuals decide! BCA responds to this in the following manner: This is an unbalanced equation. Mr. Clark errs when he equates the shareholder with the corporation. Shareholders are part—one part—of the corporation, along with suppliers, employees, communities, and customers. . . . The corporation is an entity on its own, and it should have its own management and direction and decide its own course of action.*

R.M.: *Patrons, as a support system, determine artistic trends in a variety of ways, and sociologists have always addressed this relationship. Is there any direct influence upon artistic decisions made by corporate support programs?*

D.F.: *They leave the artistic director alone. They are in it for good public relations, and to tamper with artistic direction is the easiest way to get the worst press publicity, and the corporation is too smart and knows that. . . If I were a development manager of an arts organization, I would want to know what the demographics of the audience were. The manager of arts companies, to survive, wants to appeal to the audience. The artistic direction has as much, if not more, to do with programming and so forth as do corporate patrons.*

Selected Bibliography

Adorno, Theodor W. 1945. "A Social Critique of Radio Music." *Kenyon Review*, 7:208–217.
_____. 1973. *The Philosophy of Modern Music*, trans. Anne Mitchell and Wesley Blomster. New York: Seabury Press.
_____. 1976. *Introduction to the Sociology of Music*, trans. E. B. Ashton. New York: Seabury Press.
_____. 1978. "On the Fetish Character in Music and the Regression of Listening." In *The Essential Frankfort School Reader*, ed. Andrew Arato and Eike Bebhardt. New York: Horizon, pp. 270–99.
Albrecht, Milton, James H. Barnett, and Mason Griff, eds. 1970. *The Sociology of Art and Literature: A Reader*. New York: Praeger.
Allen, Warren Dwight. 1962. *Philosophies of Music History: A Study of General Histories of Music 1600–1960*. New York: Dover.
Alter, Judy, Diane Derman, and Frank Barron. 1972. "Dancers Write of Themselves and Dance Education." In Barron (1972), pp. 86–112.
American Association of Fund-Raising Councils. 1976. *Giving U.S.A.: A Compilation of Facts and Trends on American Philanthropy for the Year 1975*. New York: American Association of Fund-Raising Councils.
Arian, Edward. 1971. *Bach, Beethoven, and Bureaucracy: The Case of the Philadelphia Orchestra*. University: Univ. of Alabama Press.
Barron, Frank, ed. 1972. *Artists in the Making*. New York: Seminar Press.
Barron, Frank, and Diane Denman. 1972. "Students in the Theater Arts." In Barron (1972), pp. 75–83.
Barzun, Jacques. 1956. *Berlioz and His Century: An Introduction to the Age of Romanticism*. Cleveland: Meridian Books.
Batten, Joe. 1956. *Joe Batten's Book: The Story of Sound Recording*. London: Rockliff.
Baumol, William J., and William G. Bowen. 1966. *Performing Arts—The Economic Dilemma: A Study of Problems Common to Theater, Opera, Music, and Dance*. New York: Twentieth Century Fund.
Baumol, William J., and Hilda Baumol. 1974. *Last-Minute Discounts on Unsold Tickets: A Study of TKTS*. New York: Theater Development Fund.
Becker, Howard S. 1974. "Art as Collective Action." *American Sociological Review*, 39:767–76.
_____. 1982. *Art Worlds*. Los Angeles: Univ. of California Press.
Bensman, Joseph. 1967. "Classical Music and the Status Game." *Trans-Action*, 4:54–59.
_____. 1973. "The Future of Cultural Services." *Aesthetic Education*, 7:81–96.
Berg, Ivan, ed. 1968. *The Business of America*. New York: Harcourt, Brace.
Blackman, Clarence. 1964. *Behind the Baton*. New York: Claros Enterprises.
Bland, Alexander, and Michael Peto. 1963. *The Dancer's World*. New York: Reynal.
Bogue, Donald J. 1973. *The Radio Audience for Classical Music: The Case of Station WEFM*. Chicago: Communication Laboratory, Univ. of Chicago.
Bunzel, J. H. 1970. "The Theater as a Social Institution." *Indian Sociological Bulletin*, 7:107–12.
Burnham, Sophy. 1973. *The Art Crowd*. New York: David McKay.
Burns, Elizabeth. 1972. *Theatricality: A Study of Convention in the Theatre and in Social Life*. New York: Harper & Row.
_____, and Tom Burns. 1973. *Sociology of Literature and Drama*. Baltimore: Penguin.
Carberry, James. 1978. "The Corporation as Patron of Architecture." *Wall Street Journal*, 27 Oct.:23.
Carse, Adam. 1949. *The Orchestra from Beethoven to Berlioz*. New York: Broude Brothers.
_____. 1969. *The Orchestra in the 18th Century* (orig. ed. 1940). New York: Broude Brothers.
Chagy, G., ed. 1970. *Business in the Arts*. New York: Paul E. Erickson.

Chew, V. K. 1967. *Talking Machines 1877–1914: Some Aspects of the Early History of the Gramophone*. London: Her Majesty's Stationery Office.

Coro Foundation. 1980. *Programming for Corporate Community Support: A Study of Charitable Donations in the Southern California Business Community*. Los Angeles: Coro Foundation.

Craft, Mary Anne. 1979. "The Corporation as Art Collector." *Business Horizons*, June:20.

Dace, William. 1972. *Subsidies for the Theater: A Study of the Central European System of Financing Drama, Opera, and Ballet: 1968–1970*. Manhattan, Kan.: AG Press.

Daniels, Ellen. 1977. *A Survey of Arts Administration Training*. New York: American Council of the Arts.

DiMaggio, Paul, and Michael Useem. 1978. "Social Class and Arts Consumption: The Origins and Consequences of Class Differences in Exposure to the Arts in America." *Theory and Society*, 5:141–61.

DiMaggio, Paul, Michael Useem, and Paula Brown. 1978. *Audience Studies of the Performing Arts and Museums: A Critical Review*. Washington, D.C.: National Endowment for the Arts.

Dorian, Frederick. 1942. *The History of Music in Performance*. New York: W. W. Norton.

Eels, Richard. 1967. *The Corporation and the Arts*. New York: Macmillan.

Einstein, Alfred. 1947. *Music in the Romantic Era*. New York: W. W. Norton.

Elicker, Paul H. 1978. "Why Corporations Give Money to the Arts." *Wall Street Journal*, 31 March:15.

Etzkorn, K. Peter. 1964. "Georg Simmel and the Sociology of Music." *Social Forces*, 43:101–7.
_____. 1973. *Music and Society: The Later Writings of Paul Honigscheim*. New York: John Wiley.
_____. 1974. "On Music, Social Structure, and Sociology." *International Review of the Aesthetics and Sociology of Music*, 5:43–49.

Faine, Hyman. 1972. "Unions and the Arts." *American Economic Review*, 62:70–77.

Faulkner, Robert R. 1973. "Careers Concerns and Mobility Motivations of Orchestra Musicians." *Sociological Quarterly*, 14:334–49.
_____. 1982. *Music on Demand: Composers and Careers in the Hollywood Film Industry*. New Brunswick, N.J.: Transaction Books.

Federico, Ronald Charles. 1968. "Ballet as an Occupation." Ph.D. diss., Northwestern Univ. Evanston, Ill.
_____. 1974. "Recruitment, Training, and Performance: The Case of Ballet." In Stewart and Cantor (1974), pp. 249–61.

Ford Foundation. 1974. *The Finances of the Performing Arts. Part I: A Survey of 166 Professional Nonprofit Resident Theaters, Operas, Symphonies, Ballets, and Modern Dance Companies. Part II: A Survey of the Characteristics and Attitudes of Audiences for Theater, Opera, Symphony, and Ballet in 12 U.S. Cities*. New York: Ford Foundation.

Forsyth, Sondra, and Pauline M. Kolenda. 1966. "Competition, Cooperation and Group Cohesion in the Ballet Company." *Psychiatry*, 29:123–45.

Fremont-Smith, Marion R. 1972. *Philanthropy and the Business Corporation*. New York: Russell Sage Foundation.

Gaisberg, F. W. 1942. *The Music Goes Round*. New York: Macmillan.

Galaskiewicz, Joseph, et al. 1979. "Metropolitan Corporate-Cultural Linkages." Paper presented at the Sociology of the Arts Conference, William Paterson College, Wayne, N.J., 2 April.

Galkin, Elliott W. 1960. "The Theory and Practice of Orchestral Conducting since 1752." Ph.D. diss., Cornell Univ., Ithaca, N.Y.

Gans, Herbert. 1974. *Popular Culture and High Culture: An Analysis and Evaluation of Taste*. New York: Basic Books.

Gelatt, Roland. 1965. *The Fabulous Phonograph: From Edison to Stereo*, rev. ed. New York: Appleton–Century.

Gingrich, Arnold. 1969. "The Arts and the Corporation." *Board Record*, March:29.

_____. 1969. *Business and the Arts: An Answer to Tomorrow.* New York: Paul S. Eriksson.

Goldfarb, Jeffrey. 1976. "Theater behind the Iron Curtain." *Society*, 14:30–34.

Goldin, Milton. 1969. *The Music Merchants.* New York: Macmillan.

Goldman, Eric. 1969. *The Season.* New York: Harcourt, Brace, & Jovanovich.

Greyser, Stephen, ed. 1973. *Cultural Policy and the Arts.* Cambridge, Mass.: Harvard Univ. Press.

Grout, Donald. 1965. *A Brief History of Opera.* New York: Columbia Univ. Press.

Gruen, John. 1976. *The Private World of Ballet.* Baltimore: Penguin.

Hacker, Andrew. 1967. "When Big Business Makes Gifts (Tax-Deductible)." *New York Times*, 12 Nov.:sec. 6:34–35.

Hart, Philip. 1973. *Orpheus in the New World: The Symphony Orchestra as an American Cultural Institution.* New York: W. W. Norton.

Hearn, H. L., et al. 1968. "Identity and Institutional Imperatives: The Case of 'Professionalization' of the Student Actress." *Sociological Quarterly*, 9:47–63.

Henderson, William J. 1921. *Early History of Singing.* New York: Amsterdam Press.

Hendon, William S., and Alice J. MacDonald, eds. 1980. *Economic Policy for the Arts.* Cambridge, Mass.: Harvard Univ. Press.

Hennion, Antoine, and J. P. Vignolle. 1978. *Artisans et industriels du disque. Essai sur le mode de production de la musique.* Paris: École Nationale Supérieure des Mines.

Hollis, Susan Mooring. 1981. "The Arts and Center-City Revitalization: A Case Study of Winston-Salem, North Carolina." Paper presented at the Economic Impact of the Arts Conference, Cornell Univ. Ithaca, N.Y., 27 May.

Hughes, Charles W. 1948. *The Human Side of Music.* New York: Philosophical Library.

Kaplan, Max. 1951. "The Musician in America: A Study of His Social Roles. Introduction to a Sociology of Music." Ph.D. diss., Univ. of Illinois, Urbana.

_____. 1955. "Telepractice: A Symphony Orchestra as It Prepares for a Concert." *Social Forces*, 33: 352–55.

Kavolis, Vytautis. 1968. *Artistic Expression: A Sociological Analysis.* Ithaca, N.Y.: Cornell Univ. Press.

_____. 1973. "The Institutional Structure of Cultural Services." *Journal of Aesthetic Education*, 7:63–80.

_____. 1974. "Social and Economic Aspects of the Arts." In *Encyclopedia Britannica*, 15th ed. Chicago: Encyclopedia Press, pp. 102–22.

Keim, Gerald D. 1980. "On the Evaluation of Corporate Contributions." *Public Choice*, 35:129–36.

Kirstein, Lincoln. 1978. *Thirty Years: Lincoln Kirstein's The New York City Ballet.* New York: Alfred A. Knopf.

Kolodin, Irving. 1966. *The Metropolitan Opera 1883–1966: A Candid History.* New York: Alfred A. Knopf.

Leblond, Richard E., Jr. 1968. "Professionalization and Bureaucratization in the Performance of Serious Music in the United States." Ph.D. diss., Univ. of Michigan, Ann Arbor.

Lehrmann, Robert O. 1978. "Corporate Fine Arts Support: A Marketing Tool." *Advertising Age*, 6 Nov.:49–50.

Leiter, Robert D. 1953. *The Musician and Petrillo.* New York: Bookman Associates.

Loft, Abraham. 1950. "Musicians' Guild and Union: A Consideration of the Evolution of Protective Organizations among Musicians." Ph.D. diss., Columbia Univ., New York, N.Y.

Longstreth, Bevis, 1973. *Corporate Social Responsibility and the Institutional Investor.* New York: Praeger.

Lowery, W. McNeil, ed. 1978. *The Performing Arts and American Society.* Englewood Cliffs, N.J.: Prentice–Hall.

Lyle, Cynthia, ed. 1977. *Dancers on Dancing.* New York: Drake.

Lyon, Eleanor. 1974. "Work and Play—Resource Constraints in a Small Theater." *Urban Life and Culture,* 3:71–97.

_____. 1982. "Stages of Theatrical Rehearsal." *Journal of Popular Culture,* 16: 75–89.

Mackenzie, Compton. 1956. *My Record of Music.* New York: G. P. Putnam's Sons.

Mann, P. H. 1966. "Surveying a Theatre Audience: Methodological Problems." *British Journal of Sociology,* 17:380–87.

_____. 1967. "Surveying a Theatre Audience: Findings." *British Journal of Sociology,* 18:75–90.

_____. 1975. *The Audience for Orchestral Concerts.* London: Arts Council of Great Britain.

Martorella, Rosanne. 1977. "The Relationship between Box Office and Repertoire: A Case Study of Opera." *Sociological Quarterly,* 18:354–66.

_____. 1977. "The Structure of the Market and the Social Organization of Opera: Some Inquiries." *Revue International di Sociologia,* 5:12–16.

_____. 1979. "Occupational Specialization and Aesthetic Change in Opera: Some Historical Inquiries." *International Review of the Aesthetics and Sociology of Music,* 10:89–98.

_____. 1982. *The Sociology of Opera.* South Hadley, Mass.: J. F. Bergin.

Matson, Katinka. 1978. *The Working Actor: A Guide to the Profession.* Baltimore: Penguin.

McDonagh, Don. 1970. *The Rise and Fall and Rise of Modern Dance.* New York: Mentor.

McHugh, Peter. 1969. "Structured Uncertainty and Its Resolution: The Case of the Professional Actor." In *Changing Perspectives in Mental Illness,* ed. Stanley C. Plog and Robert D. Edgerton. New York: Holt, Rinehart & Winston, pp. 538–55.

Mendoza de Arce, Daniel. 1981. "On Some of the Sociocultural Factors Affecting the General Characteristics of the Western Musical Styles during the Low Middle Ages." *International Review of the Aesthetics and Sociology of Music,* 12: 51–63.

Metz, Robert. 1979. "The Corporation as Art Patron: A Growth Stock." *Art News,* May:40.

Miller, J. Irwin. 1969. "Business Has a War to Win (Thinking Ahead)." *Harvard Business Review,* March/April:122.

_____. 1978. "Business and the Arts—Why?" *Across the Board,* May:87.

Mitchell, Ronald E. 1970. *Opera: Dead or Alive Production: Performance and Enjoyment of Musical Theater.* Madison: Univ. of Wisconsin Press.

Moore, Jerrold Northrup. 1976. *A Voice in Time: The Gramophone of Fred Gaisberg 1873–1951.* London: Hamish Hamilton.

Moore, Thomas Gale. 1968. *The Economics of the American Theater.* Durham, N.C.: Duke Univ. Press.

Moskow, M. H. 1969. *Labor Relations in the Arts.* New York: Associated Council on the Arts.

Mueller, John H. 1951. *The American Symphony Orchestra: A Social History of Musical Taste.* Bloomington: Univ. of Indiana Press.

Nash, Dennison J. 1957. "The Socialization of an Artist: The American Composer." *Social Forces,* 35:307–13.

National Council of the Arts. 1973. *A Study of the Arts and Cultural Non-Profit Industry in New York State.* New York: Cranford Wood.

National Endowment for the Arts. 1975. *Cases in Arts Administration.* Washington, D.C.: Research Division, N.E.A.

_____. 1976. *Employment and Unemployment of Artists: 1970–1975.* Washington, D.C.: Research Division, N.E.A.

_____. 1977. *Arts and Cultural Programs on Radio and Television.* Washington, D.C.: Research Division, N.E.A.

_____. 1977. *Economic Impacts of Arts and Cultural Institutions: A Model for Assessment and Case Study in Baltimore.* Washington, D.C.: Research Division, N.E.A.

_____. 1977. *Understanding the Employment of Actors.* Washington, D.C.: Research Division, N.E.A.

_____. 1978. *A Second Look: The Nonprofit Arts and Cultural Industry of New York State.* Washington, D.C.: Research Division, N.E.A.

_____. 1978. *The State Arts Agencies.* Washington, D.C.: Research Division, N.E.A.

_____. 1980. *Artists Compared by Age, Sex, and Earnings in 1970 and 1976.* Washington, D.C.: Research Division, N.E.A.

_____. 1980. *Arts Management: An Annotated Bibliography.* Washington, D.C.: Research Division, N.E.A.

_____. 1980. *Public and Private Support for the Arts in New York City: A Review with Recommendations for Improvements in the 80s.* Washington, D.C.: Research Division, N.E.A.

_____. 1981. *Audience Development: An Examination of Selected Analysis and Prediction Techniques Applied to Symphony and Theater Attendance in Four Southern Cities.* Washington, D.C.: Research Division, N.E.A.

_____. 1981. *Conditions and Needs of the Professional American Theater.* Washington, D.C.: Research Division, N.E.A.

_____. 1981. *Economic Impact of Arts and Cultural Institutions.* Washington, D.C.: Research Division, N.E.A.

National Research Center for the Arts, Inc. 1973. *Arts and the People: A Survey of Public Attitudes and Participation in the Arts and Culture in New York State.* New York: Publishing Center for Cultural Resources.

_____. 1975. *Californians and the Arts: A Survey of Public Attitudes toward and Participation in the Arts and Culture in California.* Sacramento: State of California.

_____. 1976. *The New York Cultural Consumer.* New York: Publishing Center for Cultural Resources.

Nelson, Charles A., and Frederick J. Turk. 1976. *Financial Mangement for the Arts: A Guidebook for Arts Organizations.* New York: American Council for the Arts Publications.

Nelson, Ralph L. 1970. *Economic Factors in the Growth of Corporation Giving.* New York: Russell Sage Foundation.

Nettel, Reginald. 1948. *The Orchestra in England: A Social History.* London: Jonathan Cape.

Netzer, Dick. 1978. *The Subsidized Muse: Public Support for the Arts in the United States.* New York: Cambridge Univ. Press.

Nielsen, Waldemar A. 1972. *The Big Foundations.* New York: Columbia Univ. Press.

Peters, Anne K. 1974. "Aspiring Hollywood Actresses: A Sociological Perspective." In Stewart and Cantor (1974), pp. 39–48.

Poggi, Jack. 1968. *Theater in America: The Impact of Economic Forces 1870–1967.* Ithaca, N.Y.: Cornell Univ. Press.

Poggioli, Renato. 1968. *The Theory of the Avant-Garde.* Cambridge, Mass.: Harvard Univ. Press.

Read, Herbert. 1966. *Art and Society.* New York: Schocken.

Read, Oliver, and Walter L. Welch. 1976. *From Tin Foil to Stereo: Evolution of the Phonograph,* 2d ed. Indianapolis: Howard W. Sams.

Reiss, Alvin H. 1972. *Culture and Company.* New York: Twayne.

Rockefeller Foundation. 1965. *The Performing Arts: Problems and Prospects.* New York: McGraw–Hill.

Rosen, Charles. 1971. *The Classical Style: Haydn, Mozart, Beethoven.* New York: Viking Press.

Ross, Irwin. 1976. "Public Relations Isn't Kid-Glove Stuff at Mobil." *Fortune,* Sept.:106–11.

Roth, Ernst. 1969. *The Business of Music: Reflections of a Music Publisher.* New York: Oxford Univ. Press.

Ryser, Carol Pierson. 1964. "The Student Dancer." In *The Arts in Society,* ed. Robert N. Wilson. Englewood Cliffs, N.J.: Prentice–Hall, pp. 95–147.

Salem, Mahmoud. 1976. *Organizational Survival: The Case of the Seattle Opera Company.* New York: Praeger.

Schlesinger, Janet. 1971. *Challenge to the Urban Orchestra: The Case of the Pittsburgh Symphony*. Pittsburgh: J. Schlesinger.

Schonberg, Harold. 1967. *The Great Conductors*. New York: Simon & Schuster.

Scotese, Peter G. 1978. "Business and Art: A Creative, Practical Partnership." *Management Review*, Oct.:20–22.

Shakely, Jack. 1977. "Exploring the Elusive World of Corporate Giving." *Grantsmanship Center News* (Los Angeles), July/Sept.:35.

Siegel, Marcia. 1968. *At the Vanishing Point: A Critic Looks at Dance*. New York: Saturday Review Press.

Siegmeister, Elie. 1938. *Music and Society*. New York: Critics Group Press.

Silbermann, Alphons. 1963. *The Sociology of Music*. London: Routledge & Kegan Paul.

Sinclair, John, and Robert Levin. 1971. *Music and Politics*. New York: World.

Stebbins, Robert A. 1976. "Music among Friends: The Social Networks of Amateur Musicians." *International Review of Sociology*, 12:52–73.

Stevens, Franklin. 1976. *Dance as Life: A Season with the American Ballet Theatre*. New York: Harper & Row.

Stewart, Phyllis L., and Muriel G. Cantor, eds. 1974. *Varieties of Work Experience*. New York: John Wiley.

Sutherland, David Earl. 1976. "Ballet as a Career." *Society*, 14:40–45.

Teran, Jay R. S. 1974. "The New York Opera Audience: 1829–1974." Ph.D. diss., New York University, New York, N.Y.

Toffler, Alvin. 1964. *The Culture Consumers*. New York: St. Martin's Press.

Tovstonogov, G. 1975. *The Profession of the Stage Director*. Leningrad: Gorky Theater.

Wagner, Susan. 1978. *A Guide to Corporate Giving in the Arts*. New York: American Council for the Arts.

Weber, Max. 1958. *The Rational and Social Foundations of Music*, trans. and ed. Don Martindale et al. Carbondale: Southern Illinois Univ. Press.

Weber, William. 1975. *Music and the Middle Class: The Social Structure of Concert Life in London, Paris, and Vienna*. New York: Holmes & Meier.

Westby, David Leroy. 1957. "The Social Organization of a Symphony Orchestra, with Special Attention to the Informal Associations of Symphony Members." M.A. thesis, Univ. of Minnesota, Minneapolis.

————. 1960. "The Career Experience of the Symphony Musician." *Social Forces*, 38:223–30.

Westrup, Sir Jack. 1955. *An Introduction to Musical History*. London: Hutchinson Univ. Library.

Wolff, Janet. 1975. *Hermeneutic Philosophy and Sociology of Art: An Approach to Some of the Epistemological Problems of the Sociology of Knowledge and the Sociology of Art*. London: Routledge & Kegan Paul.

Young, Percy M. 1965. *The Concert Tradition from the Middle Ages to the Twentieth Century*. New York: Roy.

List of Contributors

Howard S. Becker, Department of Sociology, Northwestern University, Evanston, Ill.

Joseph Bensman, Department of Sociology, Graduate Center, City University of New York, New York, N.Y.

Stephen R. Couch, Department of Sociology, Pennsylvania State University, Schuylkill Campus, Schuylkill Haven

Paul DiMaggio, Departments of Sociology and Organization and Management, and Program on Non-Profit Organizations, Yale University, New Haven, Conn.

Robert R. Faulkner, Social and Demographic Research Institute, and Department of Sociology, University of Massachusetts, Amherst

Ronald Federico, School of Social Work, Iona College, New Rochelle, N.Y.

Karen Gaylord, Department of Sociology, Adelphi University, Garden City, N.Y.

June Riess Goldner, Department of Sociology, Queens College of the City University of New York, Flushing, N.Y.

Jack Kamerman, Department of Sociology and Social Work, Kean College of New Jersey, Union

Rosanne Martorella, Department of Sociology, and Policy Analysis Honors Program, William Paterson College of New Jersey, Wayne

Samuel Schwarz, Department of Economics, Queens College of the City University of New York, Flushing, N.Y.

Dmitri Shostakovich (1906–1975)

Michael Useem, Department of Sociology, Boston University, Boston, Mass.

Vera L. Zolberg, Department of Behavioral Sciences, Purdue University, Calumet, Hammond, Ind.

Acknowledgments

Chapter 2, by Ronald Federico, is a revised version of a paper presented at the Annual Meetings of the American Sociological Association, Chicago, September 1977.

Chapter 3, by Robert Faulkner, is reprinted with the permission of the *Sociological Quarterly*, where it appeared under the title, "Orchestra Interaction: Some Features of Communication."

Chapter 5, by Rosanne Martorella, was made possible by the Assigned Release Time of the Academic Development and Research Division of William Paterson College.

Chapter 6, by Stephen R. Couch, is a revised version of a paper presented at the Annual Conference on Social Theory and the Arts, Albany, N.Y., April 1976. An earlier revision appeared in *Society*, 14 (1976):24–29. Partial funding for research related to the present chapter was provided by a Chairman's Grant from the National Endowment for the Humanities (FT-10755-80-1625) and from the Faculty Scholarship Support Fund of Pennsylvania State University.

Chapter 9, by June Riess Goldner, is based on research supported in part by Grant No. 13500 from the PSC-CUNY Research Award Program of the City University of New York. For help on various drafts, the author would like to thank Fred H. Goldner and Jack B. Kamerman.

Chapter 10, by Jack B. Kamerman, is a revised version of a paper presented at the Sociology of the Arts Conference, State University of New York, Albany, April 1976.

Chapter 11, by Dmitri Shostakovich, is excerpted from Solomon Volkov, ed., *Testimony: The Memoirs of Dmitri Shostakovich* (copyright 1979 by Solomon Volkov; English translation copyright by Harper and Row), and is reprinted by permission of Harper and Row.

Chapter 13, by **Paul DiMaggio** and **Michael Useem,** is reprinted by permission of the Society for the Study of Social Problems. The authors are grateful to Paula Brown for research assistance, to Jane Gallup for typing, administrative assistance, and editorial suggestions, to the National Endowment for the Arts for financial support, and to the Center for the Study of Public Policy for institutional support. The authors also thank Richard A. Person and Richard Scotch for valuable comments on an earlier draft. This was a fully collaborative effort and the authors' names are in arbitrary order. The interpretations offered are the authors' and do not necessarily reflect the views of the individuals and organizations acknowledged.

Chapter 14, by the Research Division of the National Endowment for the Arts, is excerpted from Report No. 14, January 1981, of the National Endowment for the Arts, Washington, D.C. Report No. 14 may be obtained in full by writing to the NEA.

Chapter 17, by **Samuel Schwarz,** is based on research supported in large part under a contract from the National Endowment for the Arts to the Center for Policy Research (NEA C 164). The author is grateful to Harold Horowitz, Research Director at the NEA, for his patience and encouragement, and to Mary G. Peters of Informatics Inc. for her very helpful suggestion on the direction of this chapter.

Chapter 18, by **Rosanne Martorella,** was made possible by the Assigned Release Time of the Academic Development and Research Division of William Paterson College.

Index

301

Typography and binding design by Jeanne Ray Juster
Edited by Jenna Schulman
Set in VIP Electra by Trade Composition, Inc., Chicopee, Massachusetts
Printed and bound by Edwards Brothers, Inc., Ann Arbor, Michigan